The Cambridge Introduction to
Eighteenth-Century Poetry

For readers daunted by the formal structures and rhetorical
sophistication of eighteenth-century English poetry, this introduction
by John Sitter brings the techniques and the major poets of the period
1700–1785 triumphantly to life. Sitter begins by offering a guide
to poetic forms ranging from heroic couplets to blank verse, then
demonstrates how skillfully men and women poets of the period used
them as vehicles for imaginative experience, feelings and ideas. He
then provides detailed analyses of individual works by poets from
Finch, Swift and Pope to Gray, Cowper and Barbauld. An approachable
introduction to English poetry and major poets of the eighteenth
century, this book provides a grounding in poetic analysis useful to
students and general readers of literature.

John Sitter is Mary Lee Duda Professor of Literature at the University of
Notre Dame.

The Cambridge Introduction to
Eighteenth-Century Poetry

JOHN SITTER

CAMBRIDGE UNIVERSITY PRESS
Cambridge, New York, Melbourne, Madrid, Cape Town,
Singapore, São Paulo, Delhi, Tokyo, Mexico City

Cambridge University Press
The Edinburgh Building, Cambridge CB2 8RU, UK

Published in the United States of America by Cambridge University Press, New York

www.cambridge.org
Information on this title: www.cambridge.org/9780521612784

First published 2011

Printed in the United Kingdom at the University Press, Cambridge

A catalogue record for this publication is available from the British Library

Library of Congress Cataloguing in Publication data
Sitter, John E.
    The Cambridge introduction to eighteenth-century poetry / John Sitter.
        p.   cm. – (Cambridge introductions to literature)
    Includes bibliographical references and index.
    ISBN 978-0-521-84824-4 (hardback) – ISBN 978-0-521-61278-4 (paperback)
    1. English poetry – 18th century – History and criticism.   I. Title.   II. Series.
    PR553.S58   2011
    821′.509–dc23   2011028105

ISBN 978-0-521-84824-4 Hardback
ISBN 978-0-521-61278-4 Paperback

For Katrina fair

Contents

Acknowledgments   *page* x
Note on texts and titles   xii

Introduction   1

PART I VOICE   5

Chapter 1 Voice in eighteenth-century poetry   7

Poem as script   8
Poems on pages   13

Chapter 2 The heroic couplet continuum   16

Closing the sense   17
The example of Donne and eighteenth-century versification   20
Couplet wit and beyond   26
The verse paragraph   29

**Chapter 3 Vocal engagement: reading
              Pope's *An Essay on Criticism***   34

Chapter 4 Talking in tetrameter   46

Butler and burlesque   48
Familiarity breeds tetrameter   52
Marvell and the meditative line   56
Trochaic variations   59

Couplet "odes" and hymns   62

Reading Swift's tetrameter: the *Satirical Elegy on the Death
of a Late Famous General* and *Cadenus and Vanessa*   67

Chapter 5 Blank verse and stanzaic poetry   74

Blank verse   74

Stanzaic poems   81

PART II POETIC CONSCIOUSNESS   91

Chapter 6 Satiric poetry   93

Formal verse satire   95

Pope's *Epistle to Dr. Arbuthnot* and Swift's *Verses on the
Death of Dr. Swift*   100

Formal verse satire after Pope   107

Chapter 7 Pope as metapoet   114

Autobiography and self-reflexivity in Pope's early poetry   115

The Rape of the Lock as "tertiary epic"   119

The early *Dunciad* as epilogue and prologue   124

The metapoetics of Pope's later career   128

Chapter 8 Metapoetry beyond Pope   133

The vocation of invocation: melancholy, contemplation,
celebration   133

Collins, Gray, and modern ambition   139

Smart's *Song* and Cowper's *Task* as metapoems   143

PART III VISION   149

Chapter 9 Reading visions   151

Chapter 10 Personification   157

Recovering personification   157
Personification herself?   164
The knowledge of personification   169

Chapter 11 Prophecy and prospects of society   178

Personification and "society"   179
Elizabeth Tollet and William Wordsworth on Westminster
Bridge   181
Commerce, Liberty, Dulness, and other goddesses   184
Villages of the whole: Goldsmith, Gray, Crabbe   189
Social redemption and negative sociology   193

Chapter 12 Ecological prospects and
natural knowledge   198

"Was it for this?"   199
Nature's people, including humans   201
The ecology of eighteenth-century nature poetry   203
"Physicotheology" and nature poetry   206
The Task and social ecology   210
"Ecographic" poetry?   214

A concluding note: then and now   216

Notes   219
Further reading   236
Index   238

Acknowledgments

Several years ago the plan for this book began to take shape during research leave time supported by a fellowship at the Bill and Carole Fox Center for Humanistic Inquiry of Emory University. Later, I was able to complete some of the writing thanks to a sabbatical leave at my new professional home, the University of Notre Dame. I am very grateful to both universities for their assistance and to many colleagues for encouragement and advice. In recent years, my partners in eighteenth-century studies at Notre Dame, Margaret Doody and Chris Fox, have given good counsel and example. Steve Fallon took hours from labors Miltonian to read and help clarify several chapters, and Henry Weinfield turned from his large study of blank verse to correct my small discussion of it in Chapter 5. At Notre Dame I have also benefitted from conversations with and in some cases research assistance from former and current doctoral students: Samara Cahill, James Creech, Erin Drew, Ethan Guagliardo, Wes Hamrick, Patrick Mello, and John Traver. This book could not have been completed in its present form had not Laura Fuderer of Notre Dame's Hesburgh Library, Chris Fox, and the Office of the Provost expedited the purchase of *Eighteenth Century Collections Online* shortly after my arrival at Notre Dame.

Colleagues at other institutions have been generously helpful. David Fairer, J. Paul Hunter, and David Morris helped shape and refine the plan for this book. Jennifer Keith improved my understanding of the poetry of Anne Finch. John Richetti's invitation to write about poetry after Pope for the *Cambridge History of English Literature, 1660–1780* led me to think more clearly about the latter half of the century, and Pat Rogers's invitation to contribute to *The Cambridge Companion to Alexander Pope* helped me formulate some thoughts about Pope's voice and versification that figure in Chapter 2 of this book. Conversations with my son, Zak Sitter, whose Romantic studies extend backwards and forwards, have helped make my daily commutes to the eighteenth century even more pleasant, as has the cheerful encouragement of Amelia Sitter and Ben Sitter. Paula Backscheider and Catherine Ingrassia very kindly shared the manuscript of their important anthology, *British Women Poets of the Long*

Eighteenth Century, prior to its publication by Johns Hopkins University Press in 2009. A part of Chapter 12 appeared in different form in a special issue of the journal *Religion and Literature*, Spring, 2008. I am grateful to Kate Rigby, the issue editor, for the invitation to contribute, and to the journal editor, my colleague Susannah Monta, for permission to use some of that material here. The illustration on p. 14 of a page from the Alexander Pope's first collected *Works* of 1717 is provided by courtesy of the Special Collections division of the Hesburgh Library.

My greatest debt is to Kate Ravin, who inspired the whole and improved each page.

Note on texts and titles

Where possible I have used first or very early eighteenth-century editions of the poems quoted. References are noted on the first appearance with the publication date; the place of publication is London unless specified. Within the text I have followed the practice advocated by the *Chicago Manual of Style* to italicize titles of individual poems regardless of whether they were originally published separately.

Introduction

Esther Greenwood, the twenty-year-old narrator of Sylvia Plath's *The Bell Jar*, was studying literature in the 1950s, but her assumptions remain common in some quarters today:

> There were lots of requirements and I didn't have half of them. One of the requirements was a course in the eighteenth century. I hated the very idea of the eighteenth century, with all those smug men writing tight little couplets and being so dead keen on reason. So I skipped it.[1]

I hope this book will help readers overcome the barriers – ranging from Romantic and Modern myths to inexperience – that often dull our senses to eighteenth-century poetry. Early chapters aim to test and sharpen our hearing as readers; several of the later ones focus on vision. Along the way it should become clearer, to take the young Esther Greenwood's preconceptions individually, that the period's poets included many women as well as men, that they were no more smug on average than poets of other eras, that what complacency they harbored was not due to a confidence in reason (which they mostly distrusted), that they wrote blank verse, odes, and various other stanzaic forms as well as rhymed couplets, and that the couplets they did write were not automatically "little," often aspiring instead, like the late twentieth-century poet A. R. Ammons, toward a versification capable of the "sweet ingestion" of nearly anything, a poetry "multiple and embracing."[2]

An "introduction to eighteenth-century poetry" requires some explanation: an introduction for whom and on what terms? And what exactly is meant by the eighteenth century? The latter question may be answered briefly: for practical reasons this volume deals mostly with the "short" eighteenth century, from about 1700 to 1785. In introducing the poetry of this period I try to keep in mind readers who may have read little of it and who may not feel fully comfortable with poetry of any period. I have found the latter group quite large, including not only undergraduate students but also many pursuing advanced degrees in literature, many teachers, and even many academic critics. If this work helps guide some of those teaching as well as those reading eighteenth-century poetry for the first time, it will serve its purpose.

I have aimed less at coverage than at "uncoverage," hoping through select-ive commentary to remove some barriers to experiencing eighteenth-century poems as poems. The emphasis falls much more on *how* to read than on *what* to read. Many important poems and several interesting poets go unmentioned here, but perhaps by engaging fewer works more closely this book will leave the reader wanting to range abroad in the period and better prepared to do so. I begin by emphasizing poetic forms and voices. Indeed, the first third of the book might be thought of as a "*formal* introduction" to the subject. This approach seems the best way of seeing the poems as poems and not as some-thing else, quotable pieces of a "discourse" interchangeable with any other from which ideas are to be abstracted. Thematic approaches to poetry run the risk of the sort of criticism implied by the quip that "Wagner's music is better than it sounds."[3] The joke, of course, is that whatever idea we might have of music is inseparable from how it sounds. The same, I argue, should be true of our idea of poetry. No doubt with later poetry in mind, Wallace Stevens remarked that "above everything else, poetry is words; and … words, above everything else, are, in poetry, sounds."[4]

I emphasize form, then, not for the sake of categorizing techniques but in order to experience the insistent materiality of eighteenth-century poetry. Counting syllables or lines is pointless in itself, but modes of attention that help us hear a voice, or often voices, within a poem can enlarge our engage-ments with other minds and ways of being in the world. Perhaps because the referential pull of eighteenth-century poems can be so strong – for instance, their use of real names in satire – it is worth keeping in mind the rest of Ste-vens's proposition, that in a radical sense the "poet's words are of things that do not exist without the words." A contemporary poet and theorist of poetry, Allen Grossman, gives this claim a more cognitive emphasis: "What are poems for? A good poem gives rise to thinking. About what? About states of affairs that would not, except for the poems, come to mind, be seen as problems, or the solutions seen to be solutions."[5]

It hardly needs saying that this book is not a literary history of the period. Much is omitted, often including attention to movements or group affiliations. There is no discussion of the Scriblerian poets (Alexander Pope, Jonathan Swift, John Gay, Thomas Parnell) as a group, for instance, or of the "Johnson circle." I do not discuss women poets as a group but rather side by side with male writers.[6] Finally, this book is not a study of "backgrounds" – social or intellectual – to its subject. Instead, I focus on ideas as they become "fore-grounds," emerging in poetic performance itself. Thus, considerable space is given to quotation and practical criticism throughout and, in Chapters 7 and 8, to some of the period's "metapoetry" (self-reflexive poems about poetry).

Critics and scholars like to imagine that readers will read their books exactly in the order presented. This probably happens rarely, especially with a book meant to introduce a subject, to which some will come looking for guidance on this topic or that. I can only say that later chapters assume progressively more familiarity with the period's poetry than do the earlier ones. I hope the final three chapters in particular will have something to say to long-time students of the period as well as to newcomers. Chapters 10, 11, and 12 explore ways of seeing, often closely dependent on personification, especially as these tend toward theorizing about society and about the ecology of the natural world. "Society" is a word that gathers resonance as the century progresses; the word "ecology" would not come into use until the next century, but its perspectives are frequently anticipated in the providential orientation of the period's natural theology and nature poetry.

As these last examples suggest, I have tried to alert readers to continuities between eighteenth-century poetry and that of our own age but to stress differences as well. No doubt some sections will seem to emphasize too much the familiar or the unfamiliar, but the simple premise throughout is that if we can find nothing like ourselves in what we study, we are likely to stop studying it, while if we can find only ourselves we need not begin.

Part I

Voice

Chapter 1

Voice in eighteenth-century poetry

Poem as script   *8*
Poems on pages   *13*

> For the VOICE is from the body and the spirit—and it is a body and a spirit.
>
> —Christopher Smart, *Jubilate Agno*

"Voice" is the most elemental and elusive part of poetry. Hearing a poem's voice, or voices, is essential to experiencing it *as* a poem, but saying exactly what we mean by that is difficult. In one sense, "voice" is a metaphor, since black letters on a white page are literally silent. And yet the concept of voice in poetry seems far more than figurative because a poem that remains inaudible also remains inaccessible. Voice, as Christopher Smart's line suggests, is where the poem's mentality and physicality join.[1]

One of the most influential early readings of an eighteenth-century poem appears in Wordsworth's 1800 Preface to the second edition of *Lyrical Ballads*, and it shows the challenge of paying adequate attention to poetic voice. Hearing a poem fully is an act of sympathetic imagination, not simply intelligence. Wordsworth was an astute critic as well as a great poet, but his reading of Thomas Gray's *Sonnet on the Death of Richard West* is a misreading, the sort of partial portrait ambitious young poets often need to create of their predecessors. Wordsworth uses Gray's sonnet (1742, published 1775) to illustrate what he regarded as the lamentable "poetic diction" that had infected poetry over the past century. We will take up the question of diction elsewhere in this book. Pertinent here is Wordsworth's view of his and Coleridge's *Lyrical Ballads* as an experiment in liberating poetry from eighteenth-century phrasing. He quotes Gray's sonnet in full and insists that only five lines, which he put in italics, possess "any value," supposedly because they use the direct language of prose:

> In vain to me the smiling mornings shine,
> And reddening Phoebus lifts his golden fire:

The birds in vain their amorous descant join,
Or cheerful fields resume their green attire:
These ears, alas! for other notes repine,
A different object do these eyes require.
My lonely anguish melts no heart but mine;
And in my breast the imperfect joys expire.
    Yet morning smiles the busy race to cheer,
And new-born pleasure brings to happier men:
The fields to all their wonted tribute bear;
To warm their little loves the birds complain.
I fruitless mourn to him that cannot hear,
And weep the more because I weep in vain.[2]

In purportedly separating Gray's wheat from his chaff, Wordsworth seems to assume what countless critics since have assumed about Gray's poem, that direct personal statement is struggling to emerge from an encumbering artificiality. But the real difference runs deeper than the overt disagreement over diction.

Wordsworth keeps the autobiographical baldness that is the poem's most "Wordsworthian" feature, while he misses or disregards Gray's melancholy wit and self-mockery. Gray expresses a complex consciousness by beginning both the sonnet's octet (its first eight lines as a unit) and sestet (its final six) with the conventional language of pastoral and even epic poetry. In such language landscapes regularly "smile," the sun is Phoebus (Apollo), a river flowing seaward might "bear its wonted tribute" to the ocean, as one had not long before in Pope's translation of Homer, or birds might sing an "amorous descant," as they had in Milton's *Paradise Lost*. Gray then shifts abruptly to direct statement, in the lines Wordsworth italicized. The *contrast* between these two voices is essential, just as the poem's subject is the *disjunction* between natural fruition and human frustration, not merely the latter. We lose both the tone and meaning of the poem by favoring one voice over the other. Gray dramatizes a mood and moment in which the fertile "busy race" and the "fruitless" speaker make equal poetic claims.

Not all eighteenth-century poems are quite so richly dialogic as Gray's, but his exacting poise suggests the sort of alertness to voice that the period's poetry often demands. How does a reader learn to pay the right sorts of attention? In one sense, the answer can only be "one poem at a time." Different poems invite different kinds of attention. But we can begin with some general principles.

Poem as script

When we sit down to read a play, a piece of music, or a screenplay, we soon remember that we do not really have in hand the play, the musical composition, or the film. What we are holding instead is a script or score, a set of instructions for how to *produce* the work. Reading the text of a play, we have to think – if only vaguely and intermittently – about who's speaking to whom, in what possible tone of voice, with what other characters present and with what facial expressions. Many readers are not used to thinking of poems as scripts or scores, but it helps greatly to do so. Reading the lines on the page as instructions for performance then becomes a continuous experiment in *producing the poem*. How might these words be read aloud? How could they be performed to make sense, especially resonant and powerful sense? Not only our physical experience of the poem but our interpretation of it depends on such vocalization, even when only *sub*vocalized, and on such decisions even when less than fully conscious. In fact, we might say that the poem, as opposed to the text of the poem, comes into being as we produce it.

If this model of reader-as-producer applies to the engaged understanding of poetry in general, how does it apply to eighteenth-century poetry in particular? Any single answer oversimplifies since poets wrote so many kinds of poetry; but we can start with the fact that poets of the period were more likely than their Renaissance predecessors or their Romantic successors to think of poetry in terms of conversation. Pope referred to much of his mature poetry as "talking on paper," and countless other poets of the age wrote poems in the form of letters, dialogues, or both. Such a conversational norm differs greatly from some earlier ideas of poetry as inspired monologue (epic, for example), as song (odes and many smaller lyric forms), or as soliloquy. This last, essentially Romantic idea was articulated memorably in John Stuart Mill's insistence that "eloquence is *heard*, poetry *over*heard."[3] As we will see, that definition removes poetry further from a social world of give and take than many eighteenth-century poets would want.

Let us look at what might be involved in "producing" a passage from one of Pope's epistolary "conversations" with a friend, the *Epistle to Cobham* (1734). In these eight lines Pope opens an implied discussion with Lord Cobham "Of the Knowledge and Characters of Men" (the subtitle of the poem), a subject they seem to have taken up several times before:

> Yes, you despise the man to Books confin'd,
> Who from his Study rails at human kind;
> Tho' what he learns, he speaks and may advance
> Some gen'ral Maxims, or be right by Chance.
> The coxcomb Bird, so talkative and grave,
> That from his Cage cries Cuckold, Whore, and Knave,
> Tho' many a Passenger he rightly call,
> You hold him no Philosopher at all.

Readers new to the eighteenth-century are often struck by the novelty of coup-lets (about which more in the next section) and may tend to emphasize the iambic meter and the rhyme words more than the sense demands. (In iam-bic meter an unstressed syllable is followed by a stressed one, these two syl-lables together making an "iamb"; if a poem's lines contain five iambs we call the meter iambic pentameter.) A reader overly worried about the meter and rhyme might produce something like this version of the opening sentence, in which the (theoretically) stressed second syllable of each iamb is in **bold** type and the final syllable of each line (mistakenly given most emphasis) is **bold and underlined:**

> Yes, **you** des**pise** the **man** to **Books** con**<u>fin'd</u>**,
> Who **from** his **Study rails** at hu**man** **<u>kind</u>**;
> Tho' **what** he **learns**, he **speak**s and **may** ad**<u>vance</u>**
> Some **gen**'ral **Max**ims, **or** be **right** by **<u>Chance</u>**.

The result is stilted and mechanical. But we can easily get to a more mean-ingful reading by starting with two different assumptions. First, the meter need not be slavishly regular. Second, most lines of English poetry can be read as containing one syllable that we should stress most heavily, but it will often *not* be the rhyme.[4] I will call this the "strongstress." ("Hyperstress" or "overstress" might do as well, did they not sound like medical conditions.) Occasionally, two syllables might contend for this major emphasis. With these principles in mind we might more productively read these same lines thus:

> Yes, **you** des**pise** the **man** to **<u>Books</u>** con**fin'd**,
> **Who** from his **Study** <u>**rails**</u> at hu**man** kind;
> **Tho'** what he **learns**, he <u>**speaks**</u> and **may** ad**vance**
> Some **gen**'ral **Max**ims, or be **right** by **<u>Chance</u>**.

This hypothetical performance sounds more human and expresses the prose sense of the lines more richly: "You have no respect for the man limited to mere *book*-knowledge, who *rails* (instead of speaking discriminately) without leaving his *study* (perhaps punningly his specialization as well as his room), even though he *tells* us everything he *reads* and may offer a few generalizations or even fall into accuracy – by *accident*."

That is a lot to get into four lines, creating an effect somewhat dense for "conversation"; but the next four lines unpack them by way of humorous sim-ile, restatement, and implied quotation. The lines might be performed like so:

> The **cox**comb **Bird**, so <u>**talk**</u>ative and **grave**,
> That from his **<u>Cage</u>** cries "**Cuck**old!" "**Whore**!" and "**<u>Knave</u>**!"

Tho' **man**y a **Pass**enger he **right**ly **call**,
You hold him **no** Phi<u>los</u>opher at **all**.

In this reading only one of the four lines, the last, contains the five stresses supposedly required, and even that line is not exactly iambic. The important thing is to let ourselves hear an utterance that makes sense before wondering how the spoken sentence or sentences might play out metrically.

What sort of poem have we "produced" so far? First, we find ourselves in the middle of a conversation between friends that has apparently been going on for some time, whether conducted just before the "now" of the poem, or over several previous occasions, or perhaps by letter. The poem's first two words, "Yes, you," express both the familiarity of the topic and the familiar relationship between the two parties. The "you" is someone curious enough to be interested in assessing human character and worldly enough to distrust the cloistered scholar. By the time we get to the second set of four lines, it becomes clear that poet and addressee can converse playfully. The comparison of the bookish man to a parrot in a cage, the rapid shift from a word like "whore" to "philosopher," and the joke that someone shouting "knave" out the window at passersby will often be right on target all signal a shared sense of humor as well as shared values.

The reader will have noticed that we have come this far without speaking of poems' "themes," "underlying ideas," "background," or "historical context." We have begun instead with how the poems might sound, and for two reasons. The first is to emphasize that poems are fundamentally *experiences* rather than instances, examples, or symptoms of something else. Without attention to their voices they become merely rough paraphrases of themselves, interchangeable with any other documents, and they lose the particularity that makes reading them worth the trouble. Working from the sound up, so to speak, seems the best way to approach most poetry, regardless of period; but the second reason for beginning with vocalization is more historically specific. We need to hear the poems' voices because a crucial subject of much eighteenth-century poetry *is* voice.

As it happens, the poem we have been listening to, the *Epistle to Cobham*, actually begins before its first line, with an epigraph on the subject of voice. Pope quotes Horace (65–8 BCE), the Roman poet so influential for eighteenth-century writers, from *Satire* X.i, on the kind of style, or styles, best suited for a poetic "*sermo*," or conversation. Such a work should be sometimes grave (*modo tristi*), often playful (*saepe jocoso*), sometimes in the voice of the orator (*rhetoris*), sometimes that of the poet (*Poetae*), and sometimes that of the urbane man (*urbani*) who deliberately lessens the force of his words. If a good poem includes all of these manners then clearly Mill's distinction between poetry and rhetoric is much too restrictive for Pope or Horace. This is not to say that Mill's distinction is without value; it describes very keenly certain effects of lyric poetry, especially of the Romantic and post-Romantic periods, up to the present. The same might be said of Yeats's stirring pronouncement that "We make out of the quarrel with others, rhetoric, but of the quarrel with ourselves, poetry," which may help us respond to varieties of self-expression in Keats or to interior soliloquies in Wallace Stevens, or perhaps even to understand the difference between Yeats himself at his most and least compelling. But it will not alert us fully to the mixture of public and intimate voices in a large number of eighteenth-century poems.

Thinking of many of these works as about voice itself need not turn them wholesale and anachronistically into modernist or postmodernist metapoetry (poetry about poetry), although I will have more to say about eighteenth-century poems about poetry in later chapters. The truth is both simpler and more complex. Many of the period's poems are addressed to another person – not only the epistles that make up a large part of the century's work but odes and other forms as well. In such poems the act of finding the proper voice in which the poet can speak to the addressee inevitably models questions of friendship, social relationships, and ethical as well as decorous behavior. Reflecting on voice is a kind of self-consciousness, but one that opens rather than closes possibilities beyond self-referentiality. Moral issues are overwhelmingly interpersonal, and most interpersonal considerations surface one way or another in questions of how we might best speak and listen to each other.

The reader of eighteenth-century poetry encounters a range of voices rendered through various poetic forms. Most of these are rhymed, often in stanza patterns that had been popular since the Renaissance, but couplets become increasingly popular, partly for their *flexibility*. Stanza patterns, once chosen, commit the poet to building blocks of fixed and sometimes large size. To take an extreme example, a poem in Spenserian stanzas is necessarily in nine-line units with a complex interlocking rhyme scheme, while a poem in couplets can be of any length, as can the verse paragraphs within it. Unrhymed poetry, excluding drama, may represent only about one percent of the poems published in the eighteenth century. But this percentage (derived from searching the Chadwyck-Healey database, *English Poetry*) is significant because it marks a fourfold increase over the early seventeenth century, before the influence of Milton's *Paradise Lost* (1667).[5] Moreover, the blank verse poems of the eighteenth century include a number of long, very popular, and influential works, such as James Thomson's *The Seasons* (1726–30, revised and expanded until 1746), Edward Young's *Night Thoughts* (1742–5), Mark Akenside's *Pleasures of the Imagination* (1744), William Dyer's *The Fleece* (1757), and William Cowper's *The Task* (1785). We will consider several verse forms in this book, beginning with what Adam Smith in 1759 would look back on as the dominance in the early eighteenth-century of "long verses" and "short," that is, the pentameter and tetrameter couplet as refined by Pope and Swift.[6] The point of paying attention to poetic forms is not to catalogue kinds of verse but to resist the tendency to disembody poems that is a hazard of literary criticism. Before going any further in trying to imagine how poems sounded to eighteenth-century readers, and how they can most richly sound to us, however, we need to attend to how they *looked*. This means focusing first on a kind of "body" other than what Christopher Smart had in mind: the existence of poems in print and in books.

Poems on pages

Modern readers usually come to eighteenth-century poems in anthologies, where lines are crowded onto pages with small margins, the texts' spelling and punctuation silently normalized. These same poems appeared quite differently to their original readers. Figure 1 reproduces a page in facsimile of *Eloisa to Abelard* as it first appeared in Pope's collection of his *Works* in 1717.

We might note first some period typographic conventions conspicuously present in this early printing of lines 171–90. (One convention is absent: while many printers, especially in the early decades, routinely capitalize nouns and italicize proper nouns, this text already shows the simpler style that would later prevail.) Readers not yet familiar with older books will notice at once that the lowercase letter *s* often looks like a modern *f*. This "long" *s* had no difference in sound value; it was simply used anywhere it might join another letter, that is, anywhere but at the end of a word. But other typographic differences are significant. Apostrophes used in words other than possessives are generally guides to pronunciation. A contraction of "prayer" as "pray'r" means that the word is one syllable rather than two, as indeed it often remains in ordinary speech. The words "ev'n" and "heav'n" are a little harder to reduce to single syllables, but we might think of them as something between one and two syllables. The contracted form of a verb or participle, such as "confess'd" or "turn'd," distinguishes it from a form in which the "-ed" ending might be sounded (as in the modern difference between the verb "learned" and adjective "learn-ed"). Anthology editors naturally want to make texts accessible to modern readers, but it is useful to understand that editorial decisions go

426   *MISCELLANIES.*

Yet here for ever, ever muſt I ſtay;
Sad proof how well a lover can obey!
Death, only death, can break the laſting chain;
And here ev'n then, ſhall my cold duſt remain,
Here all its frailties, all its flames reſign,
And wait, till 'tis no ſin to mix with thine.
Ah wretch! believ'd the ſpouſe of God in vain,
Confeſs'd within the ſlave of love and man.
Aſſiſt me heav'n! but whence aroſe that pray'r?
Sprung it from piety, or from deſpair?
Ev'n here, where frozen chaſtity retires,
Love finds an altar for forbidden fires.
I ought to grieve, but cannot what I ought;
I mourn the lover, not lament the fault;
I view my crime, but kindle at the view,
Repent old pleaſures, and ſollicit new:
Now turn'd to heav'n, I weep my paſt offence,
Now think of thee, and curſe my innocence.
Of all, affliction taught a lover yet,
'Tis ſure the hardeſt ſcience to forget!

How

Photograph of lines 171–90 of Alexander Pope's *Eloisa to Abelard* from *The Works of Mr. Alexander Pope* (1717), p. 426, courtesy of Special Collections, Hesburgh Libraries, University of Notre Dame.

into producing the text we may be reading and that those decisions may affect interpretation.

More pervasive and perhaps more significant features of the text reproduced in Figure 1 are the larger size of the type and the greater spaciousness of the poem's layout, even more impressive in actual texts than in this illustration. The pages of a typical quarto book in the eighteenth century would have been roughly eight by eleven inches, closer to the size of a sheet of computer paper than to a page of this book, about six by nine inches. Instead of the twenty lines on Pope's page, today's reader will usually confront forty to fifty lines on a page. If we follow the arithmetic through, we realize that the modern edition allows about *one-third* the space per line that Pope's contemporaries would have seen. Now, what this meant to them is admittedly difficult to specify. But it seems likely that the relation of line to line and the various parallelisms of lines and half-lines would have been easier to see, literally.

While comparing the consciousnesses and experiences of a past period with our own must remain speculative, it also seems likely that roomier formats for the printing of poetry both reflected and encouraged more leisurely reading practices. Slowing down again will be an important part of our attempt to recover eighteenth-century poems, body and spirit, in the following chapters.

Chapter 2

The heroic couplet continuum

Closing the sense *17*
The example of Donne and eighteenth-century versification *20*
Couplet wit and beyond *26*
The verse paragraph *29*

Many readers firmly associate eighteenth-century poetry with couplets, as did Plath's Esther Greenwood, and especially with those pairs of iambic pentameter lines known as "*heroic* couplets." Even readers well aware of other verse forms in the period tend to think of the heroic couplet as the age's emblem. This tendency bears examination since the pentameter couplet has been one of the most common poetic forms in English, from Chaucer into the nineteenth century. It made several appearances in the twentieth century and not only, as we might assume, in witty epigrams or light verse. Here are the opening, wistful lines of Robert Frost's *The Tuft of Flowers*, from his first book, *A Boy's Will* (1915):

> I went to turn the grass once after one
> Who mowed it in the dew before the sun.
>
> The dew was gone that made his blade so keen
> Before I came to view the levelled scene.
>
> I looked for him behind an isle of trees;
> I listened for his whetstone on the breeze.
>
> But he had gone his way, the grass all mown,
> And I must be, as he had been,—alone ...

Frost's are not the sort of lines brought to mind by the phrase "The Age of Pope." Nor are these lines, from Browning:

> Will't please you sit and look at her? I said
> "Frà Pandolf" by design, for never read
> Strangers like you that pictured countenance,
> The depth and passion of its earnest glance,

> But to myself they turned (since none puts by
> The curtain I have drawn for you, but I)
> And seemed as they would ask me, if they durst,
> How such a glance came there; so, not the first …

This passage is from *My Last Duchess* (1842), a poem many readers do not realize is in couplets on first reading. Finally, the term "heroic couplet" does not put most readers in mind of lines that sound like these:

> I shal seye sooth; tho housbondes that I hadde,
> As thre of hem were goode and two were badde.
> The thre were goode men, and riche, and olde;
> Unnethe mighte they the statut holde
> In which that they were bounden unto me.
> Ye woot wel what I mene of this, pardee![1]

These examples from the twentieth, nineteenth, and fourteenth centuries illustrate the persistence and variability of the iambic pentameter couplet in English poetry but not its particular development in the late seventeenth and eighteenth centuries.

Closing the sense

Just what sort of lines *do* readers think of as "eighteenth-century" couplets? Here are some probable candidates:

1. All humane things are subject to decay,
   And, when Fate summons, Monarchs must obey:
   This *Fleckno* found, who, like *Augustus*, young
   Was called to Empire, and had govern'd long;
   In Prose and Verse was own'd, without dispute
   Through all the realms of *Non-sense*, absolute.

   —John Dryden (1682)

2. Know then thy self, presume not God to scan;
   The proper study of Mankind is *Man*.
   Plac'd on this Isthmus of a middle state,
   A Being darkly wise, and rudely great:
   With too much knowledge for the Sceptic side,
   With too much weakness for the Stoic's pride,
   He hangs between, in doubt to act or rest,
   In doubt to deem himself a God, or beast …

   — Alexander Pope (1733–4)

  3. Unnumber'd Suppliants croud Preferment's Gate,
      Athirst for Wealth, and burning to be great;
      Delusive Fortune hears th' incessant Call,
      They mount, they shine, evaporate, and fall.
      On ev'ry Stage the Foes of Peace attend,
      Hate dogs their Flight, and Insult mocks their End.

— Samuel Johnson (1749)[2]

What marks the couplets in these three passages and differentiates them from both the earlier and the later poems? Most conspicuously, the late seventeenth- and eighteenth-century lines are overwhelmingly end-stopped. Only the third line of Dryden's poem does not conclude a significant syntactic unit, such as a phrase, clause, or sentence. While Chaucer's lines sometimes end at the end of a phrase, the effect seems almost accidental; a line may just as readily end with a verb that pulls us forward to the next line for the completion of the meaning ("the statut holde / In which ..."). And Browning quite determinedly runs across line endings – and rhymes – by severing phrases that we naturally read together; thus a verb is separated from its subject ("never read / Strangers") or its object ("puts by / The curtain").

Alignment of syntax with the verse line became the ideal in the later seventeenth century. Looking back at this development from the next century, the satirist Charles Churchill (1731–64) would single out Edmund Waller (1606–87) for having created the heroic couplet as it would be used during most of the Restoration and eighteenth century:

  Waller, whose praise succeeding bards rehearse,
  Parent of harmony in English verse,
  Whose tuneful Muse in sweetest accents flows,
  In couplets first taught straggling sense to close.

(*The Apology*, 1761, lines 362–5)

The verb "close" seems to mean two things here: enclose and conclude. Waller's couplets confine what had otherwise been "straggling" meaning within the poetic line, and they end with the completion of a syntactic whole. John Dryden (1631–1700) had singled out Waller in similar terms a full century earlier. According to Dryden, Waller "first made" rhymed poetry "easily an art" because he "first showed us to conclude the sense, most commonly in distichs [two-line units], which, in the verse of those before him, runs on for so many lines together, that the reader is out of breath to overtake it." Pope shared this view of Waller as a refiner, although he saw Dryden's own contribution as greater: "Waller was smooth; but Dryden taught to join / The varying verse, the full resounding line, / The long majestic march, and energy divine."[3]

Most Restoration and eighteenth-century readers and writers, from Dryden to Churchill and beyond, tend to think that the "closing" of the couplet is an improvement, a move toward a more "natural" mode of expression. But what does natural expression mean when, as we have seen, clearly other ways of writing couplets could seem natural to other ears in other eras? In what sense can a form as demanding as the rhymed couplet be made to appear more natural by being made still more demanding? The answer seems to be that increasing the demands on the author eases some of those on the reader. This is not to say that eighteenth-century poetry is "easier" than earlier poetry. True, to speak of writing as "easy" in the period was usually to praise it, but we will see that ease turns out to be a difficult achievement. Pope demonstrates as much by way of simile:

> True ease in writing comes from Art, not Chance,
> As those move easiest who have learned to dance.[4]

The movement is easiest in the experience of the appreciative observer, not necessarily for the dancer, who has worked hard to achieve it. Similarly, poets who must now balance syntactic units as well as meter and rhyme may themselves have a more difficult task technically, but they simplify the reader's task of sense-making by speaking in smaller phrases and putting them in more predictable places.

Since modern readers do not always find reading eighteenth-century poetry a simple matter, some practical comparisons between late sixteenth- and early eighteenth-century poems will help illustrate both the relative simplicity and the possible subtlety of the latter period's closed heroic couplets. Before proceeding to that comparison, however, I should acknowledge that there are of course good closed couplets and bad ones. Readers new to the period sometimes assume that they are all pretty much alike, since the form is exotic for us. But it does not take much practice in reading couplets to hear and feel the difference between the passages above from Dryden, Pope, and Johnson and these inert lines by a well-meaning but prosaic clergyman, Daniel Hallows, versifying the angel Gabriel's annunciation to Mary:

> … Of all the Virgins which in *Israel* be,
> God hath been pleas'd to make his Choice of thee,
> To be the Mother of his only Son,
> By a mysterious Operation.[5]

The lines are tolerably regular, end-stopped, and easily understood, but they are intolerably plodding and devoid of the sort of ease Pope had in mind. (Some reasons: meter and sense do not co-exist very readily here, as the first line, for example, elevates the insignificant "which" to a position of heavy stress; even more awkward is the forced enlistment of the final syllable of "opera**tion**" to fill out a rhyme.)

The example of Donne and eighteenth-century versification

A good way to grasp what Pope and his age valued as poetic "ease" is to compare John Donne's manner of writing satire in the 1590s with Pope's modernizations of Donne in the 1730s. Pope revived two of Donne's satires for political as well as artistic reasons: he could invoke the memory of the respected Church of England clergyman while making potentially dangerous attacks on the government. But his versions of Donne's satires afford a quick comparison of versification and voice in the late sixteenth and early eighteenth centuries. Here is Donne describing various kinds of bad writers, including those who write for the stage:

> One, (like a wretch, which at Barre judg'd as dead,
> Yet prompts him which stands next, and cannot read,
> And saves his life) gives Ideot Actors means,
> (Starving himself) to live by his labour'd scenes.
> As in some Organ, Puppets dance above
> And bellows pant below, which them do move.[6]

The lines are difficult, even for Donne. They are so partly because we have no ready image in mind for the elaborate organ Donne refers to, complete with attached puppets, but more largely because Elizabethan writers believed that satire should be crabbed and rugged in language and pacing, speaking as they imagined an angry "satyr" would. Donne's parenthetical simile is somewhat obscure as well as sudden. It alludes to the old provision (originally "benefit of clergy") by which a defendant who could read might escape the death penalty; Donne imagines the dramatist as a doomed man prompting another to pass the literacy test. Then he just as quickly imagines him as the invisible bellows of the organ, imparting motion to its visible puppets.

All of this would have been difficult enough in the late sixteenth century; by the early eighteenth century it was growing hopelessly obscure. Pope attempts to make it clearer for an audience further removed from Donne's allusions and assumptions:

> Here a lean Bard whose wit could never give
> Himself a dinner, makes an Actor live:

The Thief condemn'd, in law already dead,
So prompts, and saves a rogue who cannot read.
Thus as the pipes of some carv'd Organ move,
The gilded puppets dance and mount above,
Heav'd by the breath th' inspiring bellows blow:
Th' inspiring bellows lie and pant below.

Pope initially avoids the abruptness of Donne's courtroom simile by delaying it until the reader at least has a chance to see what it refers to. Then he expands Donne's last two lines to paint a scene he knows the reader may never have viewed and uses repetition to enact the comical huffing and puffing of "Th' inspiring bellows."

A further comparison illustrates how changes in form may also be changes in voice and point of view. Donne's complaint about the several sorts of bad writers reaches a climax with his denunciation of the plagiarist:

But hee is worst, who (beggarly) doth chaw
Others wits fruits, and in his ravenous maw
Rankly digested, doth those things out-spue
As his owne things; and they are his owne, 'tis true,
For if one eat my meat, though it be knowne
The meate was mine, th' excrements his owne.

(25–30)

In Pope's version, Donne's breathless exasperation becomes cool detachment, more in keeping with the sense Pope and his age had of Horatian satire. Technically, the change depends on making all but the first of Donne's enjambed (run-on) lines end-stopped and syntactically self-sufficient (and even that exception bears a slight pause):

Wretched indeed! but far more wretched yet
Is he who makes his meal on others wit:
'Tis chang'd indeed from what it was before.
His rank digestion makes it wit no more:
Sense, past thro' him, no longer is the same,
For food digested takes another name.

(29–34)

While these differences in versification enable Pope's comic urbanity, they do not fully explain the different effect. The scatological simile remains: plagiarism is like stealing another's food and then defecating in public. By putting the last couplet in more polite diction Pope plays at being more fastidious: unlike Donne, he will not use the word "excrement," substituting for it the euphemistic phrase "another name." But this fastidiousness is of course only apparent and fleeting. The audience must now supply the unspoken "name," and it is the rare reader who will not fill in the blank with a term cruder than Donne's.

Once regularity has become the norm, small departures from it may resonate. In the passage from Donne above, five of the six lines are enjambed; when they occur frequently, run-on lines may contribute to a general impression of exasperation but will not call much attention to themselves individually. In Pope's poems, where enjambment is the exception, the absence of a decisive line break can bear more weight. Here is a couplet from another of Donne's poems, *Satire IV*, as Pope modernized it. The lines describe a character suspicious-looking enough to be considered a clerical spy during an outbreak of anti-Catholicism:

> One whom the mob, when next we find or make
> A Popish plot, shall for a Jesuit take …
>
> (*The Fourth Satire of Dr. Donne*, lines 34–5)

Normal speech patterns follow syntax and keep verb and direct object together (we find or make a plot), but the line break, especially given Pope's practice, suggests a pause. In the tension between sentence structure and lineation we are in fact likely to hesitate, performing the lines something like so:

> One whom the mob, when next we find—or **make**—
> A Popish plot …

Pope's lines strongly suggest that the original "plot" of 1678 was a fabrication, constructed rather than discovered, and that such fabrications will recur whenever fear "next" spreads. As part of the feared Roman Catholic minority, Pope needs to propound all of this indirectly. Here he does so by using the smallest details of versification to convey a large-scale view of history.

The closed heroic couplet tends toward parallelism not only between its two lines but within the lines as well. Another example from Donne's *Satire IV* will illustrate fairly typical differences. Here is Donne, describing a visit to court in which the poet is accosted by a persistent gossip. (Some explanations in advance: "stayes" or stays means "pauses"; a "sembriefe" or "semibreve" is a long musical note and here means a long pause; Hollingshed, Hall, and Stowe all wrote chronicles.)

> He takes my hand, and as a Still, which stayes
> A Sembriefe, 'twixt each drop, he niggardly,
> As loath to inrich me, so tells many a ly,
> More then ten *Hollensheads*, or *Halls*, or *Stowes*,
> Of trivial houshold trash …
>
> (94–8)

Here is Pope's version of these lines ("simples" are plants processed for use in medicines):

> He hears, and as a Still with simples in it,
> Between each Drop it gives, stays half a Minute:
> Loth to enrich me with too quick replies,
> By little, and by little, drops his Lies.
> Meer hous[hould] trash! of birth-nights, balls, and shows,
> More than ten *Hollingsheads*, or *Halls*, or *Stows*.

> (126–31)

Although Pope prized and regularly achieved concision, he frequently finds it necessary to expand Donne for intelligibility and balance. Here four and a half lines become six. Pope's first couplet adds some explanatory information to Donne's, eliminates the technical musical term, and frames the simile within a complete unit of verse. He also uses the second line to juxtapose two phrases, the adverbial "Between each drop it gives," and the verb + complement, "stays half a minute." The adverb ending Donne's second line, "niggardly," on the other hand, depends on the next line's verb, "tells," for its sense. Pope also elaborates Donne's simile through repetition and rhythm in the next couplet, explaining that the court bore hoards his answers and passes his falsehoods slowly: "By little, and by little, drops his Lies." He elaborates Donne's half-line and cryptic dismissal "Of trivial household trash" into a self-contained line in which the second half illustrates the first: "Meer houshould trash" – of what kind? – "of birth-nights, balls, and shows" (a "birth-night" is a royal birthday celebration).

In describing Pope's modernizations of Donne as achieving greater "ease" I do not mean to cast them as improvements. Literary history is usually better thought of as change rather than progress. In refinements something is lost and something is gained. Pope loses Donne's impetuous, sometimes breathless, and crabbed vigor, achieving in its stead a more conversational equipoise and equanimity. The change may seem a diminution for some readers, although perhaps not many. Modern readers, even most Renaissance students, seem largely to have given up on at least four of Donne's five satires, however high the regard for his other poetry remains. But let us try simply to understand rather than evaluate the differences between Donne's satires and Pope's versions of them.

Changes in the relation of poet to audience between Donne's day and Pope's help explain their stylistic differences. Not printed until after his death, Donne's satires were written for manuscript circulation among a small and homogeneous audience. Donne probably knew most of his first readers, fellow

Londoners and law students in their twenties. In contrast, by the time Pope remodeled Donne, he was writing for publication, like most of his contemporaries, and for an audience primarily of strangers. While the audience for even the best-known poet of the early eighteenth century was not as broad as that for prose writers, Pope's readership was considerably less culturally elite than Donne's.[7]

The only satire of Donne's that most modern readers encounter is *Satire III*, on religion, arguably the least satiric of the group. As it happens, this poem, too, was modernized in the early eighteenth century, by Thomas Parnell, a talented friend of Pope's. The fact that this poem of Donne's is more accessible to us today and that Parnell, while a very good poet, is not of Pope's genius may help us concentrate somewhat more on *typical* differences between Elizabethan and eighteenth-century couplet versification. Donne's poem, probably written shortly after he left the Roman Catholicism of his birth for the Church of England, ruminates on one's duty not to be complacent in the difficult search for the true religion. It opens with paradoxical phrases that acknowledge the speaker's ambivalence; he feels too much human compassion ("Kind pity") for simple anger, but too much indignation ("brave scorn") for tears:

> Kind pity checks my spleene; brave scorn forbids
> Those tears to issue, which swell my eye-lids,
> I must not laugh, nor weep sins, but be wise,
> Can railing then cure these worn maladies?

Parnell expands these lines into six:

> Compassion checks my spleen, yet Scorn denies
> The tears a passage thro' my swelling eyes;
> To *laugh* or *weep* at sins, might idly show,
> Unheedful passion, or unfruitful woe.
> *Satyr*! arise, and try thy sharper ways,
> If ever Satyr cur'd an old disease.[8]

The changes in both form and content are instructive.

Several of Parnell's changes move toward genteel explication. His "Compassion" and "Scorn" soften the oxymoronic abruptness at the start of "Kind pity" and "brave scorn" (an oxymoron is an apparent contradiction). Donne's third and fourth lines each become a couplet. The parallelism and antithesis of Donne's "not laugh, nor weep" prompts Parnell to a two-step explanation. The first line of his couplet sets up the binary contrast between laughing and weeping and the next splits right down the middle – the caesura or pause occurring after the fifth syllable – to deliver the pair of negative results: "Unheedful passion, or unfruitful woe."

Parnell's next couplet introduces a degree of literary self-consciousness barely implied in Donne's "Can railing then cure these worn maladies?" Parnell's expansion of "railing" into "Satyr" and its "sharper ways" raises explicitly the question of literary genre: is satire, which usually exposes topical issues, the right genre for curing "an old disease"? Such self-consciousness concerning genre reminds us that Donne and Parnell are separated by a century of literary theory and criticism. Much of that criticism concerned the art of satire itself, including questions about the relative importance of laughter and anger, tone and appropriate targets.

A final comparison of Donne and Parnell will add a few details to our analysis of voice to this point. The next five lines of Donne's *Satire III* become eight lines in Parnell. Here are the two passages:

> Is not our Mistress, fair Religion,
> As worthy of all our Souls devotion,
> As Virtue was in the first blinded Age?
> Are not heavens joyes more valiant to asswage
> Lusts, as earths honour was to them? Alas …

(Donne, 5–9)

> Is not *Religion* (Heav'n-descended dame)
> As worthy all our soul's devoutest flame,
> As Moral Virtue in her early sway,
> When the best Heathens saw by doubtful day?
> Are not the joys, the promis'd joys above,
> As great and strong to vanquish earthly love,
> As earthly glory, fame, respect and show,
> As all rewards their virtue found below?

(Parnell, 7–14)

If decorum prompts Parnell to elevate Donne's "mistress" Religion to the status of a chaste personification, it also allows him to pair her with a similarly personified Moral Virtue. We will come back to the prevalence of such heavenly "dames" later, but we can observe here that they are more than decorative, often providing, as in this case, shorthand means of explanation and generalization. In expanding Donne's opposition of "heavens joyes" and "earths honour" (8–9) into two complete couplets, Parnell gives the reader more breathing room. That phrase is usually metaphorical, but reading these passages aloud gives it literal force. In place of Donne's haste and the forced enjambment of "asswage / Lusts," Parnell scripts pauses both at the end of lines and within them, only some of which are punctuated: in addition to the marked pauses, unmarked pauses fall after "Virtue," "strong," and "rewards." These suggest the

polite pace of conversation, slight hesitations just conceivably allowing interruption and participation. Donne's rhetoric, in comparison, is that of monologue rather than dialogue.

Couplet wit and beyond

Thus far we have looked at the heroic couplet as used in satires and an epistle
with satiric elements. But the form was used in many other kinds of poems.
Indeed, its name derives from the perceived suitability of its long line for heroic
genres such as epic and tragedy. During the Restoration, rhymed heroic lines
(the heroic couplet) became common in tragedy and heroic drama, as well as
epic. (Milton's defense of his choice of blank verse for *Paradise Lost* in 1667
suggests the dominance of the heroic couplet in the late seventeenth century.)
Pope used it to translate Homer before using it for his first great satire.

A comparison of part of his first Homeric publication, the *Episode of Sarpedon* from Book XII of the *Iliad*, and the part of *The Rape of the Lock* that he
based on it, Clarissa's speech in Canto V, will let us see the heroic and satiric
side by side. The differences are especially subtle here because Pope is deliberately imitating his own epic translation in his mock-epic poem, but they
are also particularly suggestive. In the following speech, Sarpedon, leading the
Lycians in aid of Troy, persuades Glaucus to join in attacking the Greek forti-
fications by arguing that valor becomes their high rank:

> Why boast we, *Glaucus!* our extended Reign,
> Where *Xanthus'* Streams enrich the *Lycian* Plain,
> Our num'rous Herds that range the fruitful Field,
> And Hills where Vines their purple Harvest yield,
> Our foaming Bowls with purer Nectar crown'd,
> Our Feasts enhanc'd with Music's sprightly Sound?
> Why on those Shores are we with Joy survey'd,
> Admir'd as Heroes, and as Gods obey'd?
> Unless great Acts superior Merit prove,
> And vindicate the bount'ous Pow'rs above.
> 'Tis ours, the Dignity they give, to grace;
> The first in Valour, as the first in Place.[9]

> (*Iliad*, XII.371–82)

When he added Clarissa's speech to *The Rape of the Lock* in 1717, Pope called
attention to the parallel with a footnote. It follows closely indeed:

> Say why are Beauties prais'd and honour'd most,
> The wise man's passion, and the vain man's toast?

Why deck'd with all that land and sea afford,
Why Angels call'd, and Angel-like ador'd?
Why round our coaches croud the white-glov'd Beaus,
Why bows the side-box from its inmost rows?
How vain are all these glories, all our pains,
Unless good sense preserve what beauty gains:
That men may say, when we the front-box grace,
Behold the first in virtue, as in face!

(The Rape of the Lock, V.9–18)

Parallelism always suggests comparison, emphasizing likeness or unlikeness or frequently both. Here it operates on many levels. Beginning with the "macro" or top-down, we have first the parallel of the entire two poems, in which the protracted taking of Troy and the quick theft ("rape") of a lock of hair play side by side in the reader's imagination. Next, we have the large parallel of a speech by a warrior in the great epic of the Trojan War and a speech by a young woman in an eighteenth-century English drawing room. Finally, we have the more exacting parallels of particular phrases, such as Sarpedon's "first in Valour, as the first in Place" and Clarissa's "first in virtue, as in face!" One can understand why Pope added a footnote calling attention to Clarissa's lines as "a parody of the speech of Sarpedon to Glaucus in Homer," hoping that such echoes would not fall on deaf ears. Yet the point would seem to be more than wanting his cleverness appreciated. As many readers have noticed, this speech emphasizes a moral and satiric complexity in *The Rape of the Lock* that goes beyond laughter at the modern characters. Silly though they are in mistaking their trivial quarrel for something of epic importance, the poem's beautiful young people are not *merely* silly for not being warriors of a vanished age. They are thoroughly mortal – "frail beauty must decay," "painted, or not painted, all shall fade" – and, like the reader, thoroughly modern.

If we shift our attention from these epic and mock-epic themes to voice and versification, we see – or hear – differences in the use of parallelism *within* the passages, in fact within individual couplets. These differences are all the more important because the passages are so similar in being dramatic speeches by individual characters rather than parts of the epic or mock-epic omniscient narration. The stately march of Pope's Homer comes through in sequences of whole lines parallel to each other and without significant internal pauses: for example, eight of the twelve lines quoted from Sarpedon's speech, the second through seventh and the ninth and tenth, are unbroken phrases or clauses. Clarissa's speech, however, moves in smaller steps, characteristically paralleling half a line with the other, the lines themselves comprising two noun phrases or verbs:

The wise man's passion,	and the vain man's toast ...
Why Angels call'd,	and Angel-like ador'd ...
How vain are all these glories,	all our pains ...

Or, a few lines later in the same speech:

Oh! if to dance all Night,	and dress all Day,
Charmed the Small-pox,	or chas'd old Age away ...
Charms strike the Sight,	but Merit wins the soul.

This symmetry within symmetry, paralleling of smaller units, has two effects at once: it slows the performance of the line slightly but also quickens the play of ideas against each other. The effect is often witty rather than solemn, especially when the relation between the two half-lines includes contrast, with something of the feeling of a punch line, as in Pope's own definition of wit in *An Essay on Criticism*:

| True Wit is Nature   [but] | to advantage dress'd |
| What oft was thought | but ne'er so well express'd. |

But the "wit" of such versification can of course be philosophically serious. The internal division of the line is used famously by Pope to dramatize internal psychic division in *An Essay on Man*. The human animal (and near-angel) is "A being darkly wise, and rudely great," a conflicted creature:

Born but to die,	and reas'ning but to err;
Alike in ignorance,	his reason such,
Whether he thinks too little,	or too much:
Chaos of thought and passion,	all confus'd;
Still by himself abus'd,	or disabus'd;
Created half to rise,	and half to fall;
Great Lord of all things,	yet a prey to all ...

(Essay on Man, II.4, 10–16)

Internal parallelism plays a quieter but important role when the relation is less one of contrast than one of likeness, as in Samuel Johnson's catalogue of the hazards of old age:

| New Sorrow rises | as the Day returns, |
| A sister sickens, | or a Daughter mourns ... |

The effect is more muted still when divided lines alternate with undivided ones:

Year chases Year,   Decay pursues Decay,
Still drops some Joy from with'ring Life away;

New Forms arise,   and diff'rent Views engage,
Superfluous lags the Vet'ran on the Stage.

(*Vanity of Human Wishes*, 301–2, 305–8)

The particular kind of intensity created by balancing half-line against half-line tends to give way as the century progresses to a looser parallelism that crosses the couplet's line breaks. William Cowper, in the last major poems he wrote in couplets before turning to blank verse, often seems deliberately to avoid pointed epigram by balancing the second half of one line with part or all of the next. Here, in Cowper's *Retirement* (1782), a semi-repentant politician asks his native village to take him back as he leaves office:

Receive me now, [a1] not uncorrupt as then,
[a2] Nor guiltless of corrupting other men …

In the next couplet, enjambment forces the reader to cross the line to grasp one idea (the "staying" or supporting of a nation) that will then be contrasted with its counterpart (undermining a nation):

But vers'd in arts that, while they [b1] seem to stay
A falling empire, [b2] hasten its decay.[10]

Opposition and parallelism are as important in these lines for Cowper as they are in Pope, but Cowper mutes the effect, so that it almost seems accidental.

The many kinds of phrasing possible within the "heroic" pentameter line and especially within the heroic couplet as a unit provide great variety. But performing or producing couplets for the greatest effect requires attention as well to the larger units of which they are almost always a part. Context is all, and on a strictly formal level the context of a couplet, emphasized by the medium of print, is usually a paragraph, the open-ended construction to which we now turn.

The verse paragraph

Epigrams aside, we encounter heroic couplets as building blocks of larger units of assimilation – either whole poems or, usually more meaningfully, verse paragraphs. In this light, heroic couplets are not necessarily instruments of closure. We have thus far looked primarily at their self-contained syntax and conceptual independence to understand certain possibilities of voice. But "closed" couplets must also be understood, paradoxically, as instruments of *suspense*. That is, they allow for the suspension, elaboration, and variation of meaning. The simple fact that couplets are usually not parts of stanzas of predetermined length (typically four to nine lines in the Renaissance) or parts of poems of set size (such as sonnets) allows them instead to function as parts of verse paragraphs. These structures may range in size from a few lines to scores of lines. Logic and syntax give shape to verse paragraphs, rather than the poet's commitment to a recurrent pattern.

This freedom has not been emphasized often enough by literary historians and scholars, but the contemporary poet Hayden Carruth puts the matter sympathetically. He notes that the heroic couplet

> which seems to us the height of artifice, was just the opposite in the minds of those who used it. Dryden chose the couplet because he thought it the plainest mode available, the verse "nearest prose," and he chose it in conscious reaction against the artificial stanzaic modes that had dominated English poetry during most of the sixteenth and seventeenth centuries. In short, he and his followers thought they were liberating poetry, just as Coleridge and Wordsworth liberated it a hundred years later, or Pound and Williams a hundred years after that.[11]

The performative challenge, then, is to learn to read past – or, better, *read through* – the couplet to the paragraph. The individual units remain important, but their emotional force and meaning will emerge most richly as part of a larger utterance. If that does not happen, we are not alert readers or the poet has fallen into the temptation of facile exclamation. Even so precocious a reader as the youthful Coleridge tended to give the individual couplet more emphasis than it necessarily calls for. Reading Pope at school, he found that "still a point [i.e., always an exclamation point] was looked for at the end of each second line," so that the poems seemed to be sequences "of epigrams."[12] But that is a response Pope would have considered partial, a failure to acknowledge the power of the whole:

> In Wit, as Nature, what affects our Hearts
> Is not th' Exactness of peculiar Parts;
> 'Tis not a *Lip*, or *Eye*, we Beauty call,
> But the joint Force and full *Result* of *All*.
>
> (*An Essay on Criticism*, 243–6)

Some works make the demand of wholeness more insistently than others. Anne Finch's lovely *A Nocturnal Reverie*, a single sentence of some fifty lines, gives a reader little choice. Here are its first eight couplets:

> In such a *Night*, when every louder Wind
> Is to its distant Cavern safe confin'd;
> And only gentle *Zephyr* fans his Wings,

> And lonely *Philomel*, still waking, sings;
> Or from some Tree, fam'd for the *Owl's* delight,
> She, hollowing clear, directs the Wand'rer right:
> In such a *Night*, when passing Clouds give place,
> Or thinly vail the Heav'ns mysterious Face;
> When in some River, overhung with Green,
> The waving Moon and trembling Leaves are seen;
> When freshen'd Grass now bears it self upright,
> And makes cool Banks to pleasing Rest invite,
> Whence springs the *Woodbind*, and the *Bramble*-Rose,
> And where the sleepy *Cowslip* shelter'd grows;
> Whilst now a paler Hue the *Foxglove* takes,
> Yet checquers still with Red the dusky brakes …[13]

The poem will roll on to the end, as Finch suspends grammatical closure through a series of adverbial modifications (the successive "When" phrases). She finally releases the main verb ("let … remain") in the closing lines:

> In such a *Night* let Me abroad remain,
> Till Morning breaks, and All's confus'd again;
> Our Cares, our Toils, our Clamours are renew'd,
> Or Pleasures, seldom reach'd, again pursu'd.

In this instance, the effect of suspension is twofold: producing a voice of quietly breathless anticipation and building up a complex, layered present moment, in which all the things that must be represented successively, given the nature of language, are also represented as simultaneous.

Suspension is usually less syntactically extreme than Finch's tour de force, and eighteenth-century poems commonly do not give us a choice of reading for closure *or* suspense. We need to be open to both. The verse paragraph at the opening of the second epistle of *An Essay on Man* that we glanced at above offers not merely several parallelisms of half-line and line. An open-eared reading of the whole (II.1–18) discovers a growing *series* of such pairs, with the cumulative effect of making the human "isthmus of a middle state" an increasingly mysterious landscape. Something similar occurs in any number of Pope's more individualized human portraits, the character sketches in his epistolary satires that accumulate detail and deepen over twenty or thirty lines, or in the semi-tragic exempla that lend so much weight to Johnson's *Vanity of Human Wishes*. But we can also see the interplay of couplet closure and sequential movement in a somewhat more playful and less familiar example, the finely constructed verse paragraph that opens Mary Leapor's *Man the Monarch*.

This passage, our last long quotation, essentially consists of two complex statements and one ostensibly simple question. (This is a good place to note that eighteenth-century punctuation often has more to do with sound than with grammar. Typically, a semi-colon indicates a longer pause than does a comma, and a colon or period a more decisive one than a semi-colon.) I have spatially set off the major syntactic units to emphasize the logical movement:

> Amaz'd we read of Nature's early Throes
> How the fair Heav'ns and pond'rous Earth arose:
> How blooming Trees unplanted first began;
> And Beasts submissive to their Tyrant, Man:
> To Man, invested with despotic Sway,
> While his mute Brethren tremble and obey;
> Till Heav'n beheld him insolently vain,
> And checked the Limits of his haughty Reign.
>
> Then from their Lord, the rude Deserters fly,
> And, grinning back, his fruitless Rage defy;
> Pards, Tygers, Wolves, to gloomy Shades retire,
> And Mountain-Goats in purer Gales respire.
> To humble Valleys, where soft Flowers blow,
> And fatt'ning Streams in crystal Mazes flow,
> Full of new Life, the untam'd Coursers run,
> And roll, and wanton, in the chearful Sun;
> Round their gay Hearts the dancing Spirits rise,
> And rouse the Lightnings in their rolling Eyes:
> To cragged Rocks destructive Serpents glide,
> Whose mossy Crannies hide their speckled Pride;
> And monstrous Whales on foamy Billows ride.
> Then joyful Birds ascend their native Sky:
>
> But where! ah! where, shall helpless Woman fly?[14]

Leapor's first sentence retells, in brief and secular form, the Creation and Fall. Seven of its eight lines elaborate the first line's "Throes." The second part describes the effects of the Fall, cataloguing the variety of places – forests, mountains, valleys, rocks, seas, sky – to which the animals have fled as they seek refuge from Man. And the third part, dependent on the widening sweep of the first two units and the protracted triplet of lines 19–21, delivers the rueful payoff.

The joke is a complex one thanks to Leapor's mixture of comedy and pathos, and it derives from three complementary reversals at once as the paragraph ends. These reversals are temporal, syntactic, and, ultimately, conceptual: a) temporally, units of eight and fourteen lines yield to a one-line sentence; b) syntactically, statements yield to a question; and c) conceptually, the presumed meaning of *Man* shifts suddenly from *humans* to *men*. The wit of this passage at first seems to reside in the conceptual shift, but it is not the wit of epigram. The shift is arresting because of the ideas developed in the cumulative rhetoric of lines 1–8 and 9–22. The last line by itself, or even as part of a closed couplet –

> Then joyful Birds ascend their native Sky:
> But where! ah! where, shall helpless Woman fly?

would be nothing without the gathering momentum of the verse paragraph.

If couplets take on their fuller meanings within the larger unit of the verse paragraph, paragraphs ultimately function within whole poems. It is time we turned our more sustained attention to reading a major, complex poem. Pope's *An Essay on Criticism* will offer an ideal territory in which to observe the dynamic interplay of epigram, paragraph, and whole structure.

Chapter 3

Vocal engagement: reading Pope's *An Essay on Criticism*

A forced march through *An Essay on Criticism* (1711) probably has led far too many students to dislike both the poem and the poet. Pope's elegant and influential *Essay* is often included in hurried survey courses as a "two-for": a poem by a major author *and* a handy compendium of "critical ideas." One is likely to walk away from such an experience with the general idea that Pope thought it was important to know the Ancients, take writing seriously, and follow "Nature," which is "Order" and which will somehow teach the "Rules" all would-be writers need to know. A reader is also likely to get the impression of Pope as clever but dogmatic and perhaps arrogant: "right opinionated," Thomas Berger's hero in *Little Big Man* says after recalling how Pope was read aloud to him as a boy, "like that fellow had the last word on everything."[1]

This impression is not what Pope was after. One of his rules for good critics is that they must be amiable as well as accurate, speaking with "seeming Diffidence" even when sure of their views, and avoiding "positive" pronouncements:

> Men must be *taught* as if you taught them *not*;
>
> And Things *unknown* propos'd as Things *forgot*.[2]

Why this discrepancy between Pope's aim and a common effect? One reason is the modern reader's unfamiliarity with the "essay" in verse, a common kind of poem in the late seventeenth and eighteenth centuries, deriving largely from Horace's *Ars Poetica* (an "art of poetry" written in epistolary form probably between 20 and 8 BCE). A related reason is our sense that there is something odd about didactic poetry, despite its long native tradition and roots in the Latin poems of Lucretius (*De Rerum Natura, c.* 58 BCE) and Virgil (the *Georgics*, 37–30 BCE), as well as Horace's epistles. (Terry Eagleton observes that the "modern age is neurotically suspicious of the didactic, with its curious assumption that to be taught must be invariably unpleasant.")[3] A third reason is the relative novelty of the heroic couplet today, which, as mentioned earlier, tends to exaggerate its epigrammatic effect to modern ears. Add to these the haste with which a modern student is likely to be trying to sort out "main ideas" and the result may well be that of submitting to a somewhat unyielding lecture rather than, as Pope seems to have imagined, participating in a conversation.

In what follows I will sketch out a mode of reading that attends less to the intellectual positions of *An Essay on Criticism* than to its vocal postures. Although Pope had already published his *Pastorals* and written most of *Windsor-Forest* by 1711, *An Essay on Criticism*, which he substantially finished at the age of twenty-one and published a week before turning twenty-three, marks a kind of stage debut for the young, ambitious poet. What happens when we approach this poem not as a collection of petrified utterances but as an *experiment* in voice, a performance of several ways of speaking? "He do the Police in different voices," the sentence from Dickens's *Our Mutual Friend* that T. S. Eliot considered as a title for *The Waste Land*, might fit not only modernist pastiche and collage but also, more subtly, many of Pope's longer poems. To experience *An Essay on Criticism* as a poem, it will help to listen to how Pope's lines "do the critic" in different voices. For purposes of analysis, I will differentiate three voices in the poem: the Man about Town, the Poet-Critic, and the Artist as a Young Man. These divisions and labels are admittedly crude, but useful.[4]

The original text of *An Essay on Criticism* provides an unusually explicit guide to how Pope seems to have wanted the reader to hear and experience his work. The first and second editions (1711–12) make heavy use of capitalization and italics, following the orthography and underlining in Pope's manuscript closely.[5] The result goes well beyond the normal practice of capitalizing nouns and italicizing proper nouns. Many modern editions drop these features, and even Pope himself dropped many of them later on, perhaps coming to believe that his readers did not need such cues. Twenty-first-century readers, however, may find them instructive. Here are the opening lines as often reprinted in modern anthologies:

> 'Tis hard to say, if greater want of skill
> Appear in writing or in judging ill;
> But, of the two, less dangerous is the offence
> To tire our patience, than mislead our sense.
> Some few in that, but numbers err in this,
> Ten censure wrong for one who writes amiss;
> A fool might once himself alone expose,
> Now one in verse makes many more in prose.

But here is how they appeared in 1711:

> 'Tis hard to say, if greater Want of Skill
> Appear in *Writing* or in *Judging* ill,

> But, of the two, less dang'rous is th' Offence,
> To tire our *Patience*, than mis-lead our *Sense*:
> Some few in *that*, but Numbers err in *this*,
> Ten Censure wrong for one who Writes amiss;
> A *Fool* might once *himself* alone expose,
> Now *One* in *Verse* makes many more in *Prose*.

Modernization of line three has the unfortunate effect of ignoring Pope's meter: the line scans if "dang'rous" and "th' Offence" are each two syllables, not three. But other aspects of Pope's original typography emphasize sound and logical relationships together. Italics in this case call attention to something close to what I earlier called the "strongstress" within the lines. "*Writing*" and "*Judging*" dominate the second line, and the typography also calls attention to their antithetical relationship ("writing" here means what we call creative writing and "judging" means criticism), just as lines 4 and 5 oppose "patience" to "sense" and "that" to "this." The atypical capitalization of verbs in line 6 – "Censure … Writes" – continues the antithesis. Pope then directs the reader to perform line 7 in a manner in tension with the usual meter, slightly demoting the expected stress on "once" (the fourth syllable) and promoting "himself" (the fifth and sixth) as a spondee (two stressed syllables); the effect is to emphasize the claim that bad poets used to harm only *themselves* while now (thanks to proliferation of published criticism) a *little* bad poetry generates a *lot* of bad prose.

The tone already grows complex. The speaker has introduced a fairly demanding set of logical relationships of similarity and difference: in one column go bad poetry, tried patience, a relatively small number of writers, and isolated self-exposure; in the opposing column go bad criticism, corrupted sense, a large number of censurers, and collective foolishness. But all of this is proposed with an air of insouciance bordering on flippancy ("'Tis hard to say …"). We can think of this speaker as the Man about Town, and the next couplet underscores his urbanity:

> 'Tis with our *Judgments* as our *Watches*, none
> Go just *alike*, yet each believes his own.

But the next four lines begin to introduce another speaker, the Poet-Critic:

> In *Poets* as true *Genius* is but rare,
> True *Taste* as seldom is the *Critick*'s Share;
> Both must alike from Heav'n derive their Light,
> These *born* to Judge, as well as those to Write.

(11–14)

He makes a very high claim for true poets *and* true critics. Both are rare, perhaps chosen (granted light "from Heav'n"), and certainly born with their uncommon gifts and vocation. Of course, the Man about Town and the Poet-Critic are really different voices of a single speaker, whose ability to be offhand and idealistic at almost the same instant has fast become part of the poem's meaning. We are at once engaged with the sort of person who can voice worldly amusement at bad poets and critics not because he is cynical about literary art but because he considers its pursuit a vocation. We seem to be in the hands of a guide deeply serious about poetry who promises not to take himself too seriously. There is a very instructive difference, for example, between the way Pope summarizes the poem's opening eight lines in the prefatory table of contents – "That 'tis as great a fault to judge ill, as to write ill, and a more danger-ous one to the public" – and the poetry itself.[6] Danger "to the public" is a fairly somber affair. "Public" as a noun had only been in use for about a century and generally connoted something closer to the citizenry or population at large than to the more specialized "reading public," a phrase that would not come into use for another century. The tonal range from the underlying warning of potential public danger to bemused head-scratching over whether bad poets or critics are "greater" in their badness will span the entire poem.

Humorous passages from six to forty-six lines, not including scattered one-liners, make up roughly one-fourth of the poem. The humor ranges from slight to sharply satirical, and boundaries often blur, but we can get a good sense of the poem's tonal structure by thinking about where the primarily humorous passages occur and what work they do. The following summaries are meant to refresh the memory of the reader familiar with the poem. To the reader who is not, I suggest pausing here to read over just these sections before tackling the whole. Most readers will read these 200 lines of pentameter aloud in about ten to twelve minutes, and taking the time to do so will permanently bring home the fact that the *Essay* is not a treatise but a performance. The passages are these:

1. lines 26–45: many critics are mental coxcombs, eunuchs, mules, or "equivocal" insects;
2. lines 104–17: unable to win the lady (poetry), aspiring writers wooed her maid and became critics; like modern "Pothecaries" (pharmacists), these critics want to supplant those rightly above them and hope to write poetry by "receipt" (recipe or prescription);
3. lines 205–10: pride fills empty heads, as "wind" fills unhealthy bodies and nature a vacuum;
4. lines 267–84: Don Quixote, exemplifying critics blinded by pet enthusiasms,

    gravely demands that a theater be altered to accommodate a play's battle scene rather than the other way around;

5.   lines 305–61: "language" critics and others judge surface alone, including sound patterns; examples of awkward versification;

6.   lines 414–45: critics dependent on received opinion, wealth, or whim treat the muse like a mistress alternately idolized and abused, and they justly earn the same "cobweb" fate as the medieval "School-Divines" whose works sleep unread;

7.   lines 585–630: bad critics (like Appius) are dogmatic, incorrigible, and tireless, ready to read aloud even at the church altar: "For *Fools* rush in where *Angels* fear to tread."

As this schematic description suggests, the humorous passages describe bad writing and contrast it with positive precepts and practices. Between the first and second passages, for example, comes the demanding verse paragraph on following Nature:

> First follow Nature, and your Judgment frame
> By her just Standard, which is still the same:
> *Unerring Nature*, still divinely bright,
> One *clear*, *unchang'd* and *Universal* Light,
> Life, Force, and Beauty, must to all impart,
> At once the *Source*, and *End*, and *Test* of *Art*.
> Art from that Fund each *just Supply* provides,
> Works *without Show*, and *without Pomp* presides:
> In some fair Body thus th' informing Soul
> With Spirits feeds, with Vigour fills the whole,
> Each Motion guides, and ev'ry Nerve sustains;
> *It self unseen*, but in th' *Effects*, remains.
>
>   (68–79)

The lines are challenging intellectually and grammatically. Nature should guide critical judgment (68–9) because it is in effect the "soul" of art (76–7), but this Nature is an ideal order under or above the observable world we usually call Nature. Its two attributes in line 70 are implicitly three, because the adverb "still," meaning "always," adds permanence to Nature's unerringness and divine clarity. These three attributes are reinforced in the next line and then solidified in the next (72) as three functions: Nature is art's origin, art's goal, and art's standard ("the *Source*, and *End*, and *Test*"). These triads, however, interact with paired oppositions and parallels: Nature versus Art, Nature and Art working without show and presiding without pomp, the unseen soul versus its visible effects. One of these parallels, "Works *without Show*, and *without Pomp* presides," is tightened by chiasmus, a "crossing" or X-like syntactic structure in which two units are parallel but inverted. In this case a verb and adverbial phrase are followed by an adverbial phrase and verb:

Works	without show
without pomp	presides.

A final layer of complexity adds a *four*-part parallel to the twofold and threefold divisions: Soul/Nature *feeds, fills, guides,* and *sustains* Body/Art. The passage requires that we grasp subtle distinctions and analogies almost simultaneously. It is a kind of microcosm of the poem, which steadily moves toward the conclusion that Judgment (for Pope, as for Locke, the capacity for discerning distinctions) and Wit (discerning resemblances) are ultimately united.

But such rigorous writing is not the sort of regimen a reader is likely to sustain without relief or, more importantly, even to enter into without having first been persuaded of the speaker's sense of humor. Grounding is provided not only by the passages before and after the poem's more earnest and difficult sections but also by the brief interjections of humor I referred to as one-liners. Given Pope's use of the couplet, some of these are actually two-liners. Just after the passage on Nature, Pope observes that some people favor their wit *or* their judgment so much as to be ineffective:

> For *Wit* and *Judgment* often are at strife,
> Tho' meant each other's Aid, like *Man* and *Wife.*

> (82–3)

This couplet provides a moment of down-to-earth relief, but it has a richer effect as well. If we think about what sort of person could make this observation in just this way, we will imagine a speaker who has seen much of the world, literary and human, is amused but not without idealism (spouses are "meant" to benefit each other), and enjoys insinuation as well as blunt statement. The most direct meaning of the simile is that wit and judgment are like man and wife because both are supposed to be mutually helpful, but of course the secondary comparison clicks into place just behind it: they are also alike in quarrelling with each other. The joke is relaxed but shrewd, and central to a poem that undertakes to negotiate a better contract between critical and creative energies.

A constructed speaker implies an equally constructed reader, presumably the sort of person who shares what seem to be common-sense attitudes and who gets the jokes. In the case of the couplet above, he or she shares a sense of rueful amusement concerning marriage. But in the more earnest sections, Pope constructs his ideal reader – or appeals to the reader's ideal self – more explicitly. Having laughed at bad critics too numerous to specify ("their Generation's so *equivocal*"), Pope abruptly changes direction:

> But *you* who seek to *give* and *merit* Fame,
> And justly bear a Critick's noble Name,
> Be sure *your self* and your own *Reach* to know,
> How far your *Genius*, *Taste*, and *Learning* go …
>
> (46–9)

And he does so again just as sharply at the end of the second satiric section (104–17), constructing the reader as someone opposite to those critics who usurp the poets' place, write recipes for poems, and so on. At this point, the construction of speaker and listener becomes reciprocal. As a reader, I imagine the speaker as someone sufficiently discerning to see that I am sufficiently discerning to not want to be like those other (undiscerning) critics:

> *You* then whose Judgment the right Course wou'd steer,
> Know well each Ancient's proper *Character*,
> His *Fable*, *Subject*, *Scope* in ev'ry Page,
> *Religion*, *Country*, *Genius* of his *Age*:
> Without all these at once before your Eyes,
> *Cavil* you may, but never *Criticize*.
>
> (118–23)

More often than not, Pope's "you" seems to refer to general readers rather than professional critics; the poem is, after all, more about how to read intelligently than about what to say in a critical article. But the most fervent direct address (560–83) treats the reader as a fellow author:

> Learn then what Morals Criticks ought to show,
> For 'tis but *half* a Judge's *Task*, to *Know*.
> 'Tis not enough, Taste, Judgment, Learning, join;
> In all you speak, let Truth and Candor shine:
> That not alone what to your *Sense* is due,
> All may allow; but seek your *Friendship* too.
>
> (560–5)

As that last line suggests, however, shared authorship is a more than literary value:

> Be *silent* always when you *doubt* your Sense;
> And *speak*, tho' *sure*, with *seeming Diffidence*:
> Some positive persisting Fops we know,
> Who, if *once wrong*, will needs be *always* so;

> But you, with Pleasure own your Errors past,
> And make each Day a *Critick* on the last.

(566–71)

Before taking up other aspects of Pope's speaker, I would like to point out a further use of italics to script performance and suggest collaboration, often in wordplay. Pope highlights metaphorical puns, for example, in this couplet – "Expression is the *Dress* of *Thought*, and still / Appears more *decent* as more *suitable*" – and the play on "subjects" as people and as topics in the line continuing the clothing conceit: "For different *Styles* with diff'rent *Subjects* sort" (318–19, 322). If we follow Pope's cue to read these words more slowly and emphatically, we are likely to hear the pun. Occasionally, the wordplay is remarkably sexual but unremarked. Commentators tend to pass silently over this line, for example, on the licentiousness of Restoration comedy:

> And not a Mask went *un-improv'd* away.

(541)

"Mask" is a common synecdoche for a woman dressed for a masked ball or masquerade and, presumably, for an anonymous intrigue. But the pun is on the adjective Pope italicized. On the obvious level, the word is used sarcastically: the plays offered moral corruption, not moral improvement, so women *did* go away unimproved. The word "improved" also had a legal meaning, however, which is quietly relevant here. "Improved" land was property that had been cultivated and seeded. In this sense, a woman might not leave the Restoration playhouse without a good chance, as common parlance might continue the agricultural metaphor, of having been plowed and planted.

Puns may be part of the poem's humor, but they are also part of the identification of the speaker as a man in control of language. While Pope makes fun of critics who pay attention *only* to words, long sections of the poem demonstrate that writers who do not take words seriously write foolishly and feebly. To use the logician's distinction, well-chosen words may not be sufficient to make a good poem but they are surely necessary. This point brings us to a third aspect of Pope's speaker, his presence as a self-identified Poet-Critic. I characterized two aspects of Pope's speaker above as the Man About Town and the Poet-Critic but have said little about the latter because he is in one sense obvious in every line of the poem. The work presents itself immediately as a poetical essay, and it quickly suggests not only that the best critic will be a poet but also that the true modern will have to be a critic. But in a more self-conscious sense the Poet-Critic appears in those sections that call attention uncompromisingly to the poetic medium. The poetic side of his dual identity comes to the fore unmistakably in self-referential passages presenting the Artist as a Young Man, in a sense the Poet as *vates* or visionary. But first, the Poet as *artes*, maker of verses.

The pattern of alternating worldly blame and ardent praise that we have seen in earlier parts of the poem continues into the famous section on sound in poetry (337–83), in which the Poet-Critic not only lays out certain principles but demonstrates technical and creative power. The passage begins negatively (the first half of it is included above in the list of humorous sections) by criticizing both the critics who look only for linguistic effects and poets who handle language clumsily. Pope calls the critics "tuneful Fools" for paying so much attention to poetry's music, but he launches at once into an extended study of just that subject, leavened first by some tuneful foolery of his own:

> These *Equal Syllables* alone require,
> Tho' oft the Ear the *open Vowels* tire,
> While *Expletives* their feeble Aid *do* join,
> And ten low Words oft creep in one dull Line …

and then by deft parody of poetic clichés:

> While they ring round the same *unvary'd Chimes*,
> With sure *Returns* of still *expected Rhymes*.
> Where-e'er you find *the cooling Western Breeze*,
> In the next Line, it *whispers thro' the Trees*;
> If *Chrystal Streams with pleasing Murmurs creep*,
> The Reader's threaten'd (not in vain) with *Sleep*.
>
>   (344–53)

The difference between amateur writers and the (true) Poet will become clear by contrast. Conventional versifiers strain to end their poems ponderously:

> Then, at the *last*, and *only* Couplet fraught
> With some *unmeaning* Thing they call a *Thought*,
> A *needless Alexandrine* ends the Song,
> That like a wounded Snake, drags its slow length along.
>
>   (354–7)

The alexandrine, a six-foot line, was common in French poetry, briefly modish in English but often sluggish, and ludicrously so in this example. When Pope ends his positive demonstration of how "The *Sound* must seem an *Eccho* to the *Sense*" with an alexandrine of his making, however, it turns out to be barely perceptible:

> But when loud Surges lash the sounding Shore,
> The *hoarse, rough Verse* shou'd like the *Torrent* roar.
> When *Ajax* strives, some Rocks' vast Weight to throw,
> The Line too labours, and the Words move *slow*;
> Not so, when swift *Camilla* scours the Plain,
> Flies o'er th' unbending Corn, and skims along the Main.
>
> (368–73)

The section as a whole does more than show off the Poet-Critic's skill. The poet as *artes* merges with the poet as *vates*, as technical virtuosity modulates into awe for poetry's connection to the suprarational "*Pow'r of Musick*" (374–83). This connection underlies poetry's mysterious ability to "surprize / And bid Alternate Passions fall and rise." When Alexander the Great heard the music of Timotheus, Pope says, "the *World's Victor* stood subdu'd by *Sound*!" Praising John Dryden's lofty St. Cecelia's Day odes on the power of music for their own lyric power, Pope insists that mastery of the passions distinguishes modern as well as ancient poetry: "what *Timotheus* was, is *Dryden* now."

The voice of the Artist as a Young Man in *An Essay on Criticism* is that not of Joycean rebellion but of poetic filial piety. It emerges most strongly at the conclusion of Pope's celebration of the ancient poets (181–94), those "*Bards Triumphant*! born in *happier Days*," a section Pope summarizes in the table of contents as "Reverence due to the *Ancients*, and praise of them," and in the self-portrait that emerges at the end of the poem through the compliment to William Walsh (729–44), an early friend and adviser. In looking back to the Ancients, the Poet expresses not only reverence but ambition:

> Oh may some Spark of *your* Cœlestial Fire
> The last, the meanest of your Sons inspire,
> (That on weak Wings, from far, pursues your Flights;
> *Glows* while he *reads*, but *trembles* as he *writes*)
> To teach vain Wits a Science *little known*,
> T' *admire* Superior Sense, and *doubt* their own!
>
> (195–200)

The lines contain obligatory modesty ("last" means latest, not final, heir), but they leave little doubt that the speaker "glows" with ambition as well as admiration, and "trembles" with energy as well as trepidation.

The reading sketched here leaves much of importance in the *Essay* untouched, especially the weight the poem puts on the patient cultivation of literary "judgment" and on sympathetic generosity as a condition of reading ("The *gen'rous Pleasure* to be charm'd with Wit").[7] The poem is hardly the mere collection of commonplaces that some readers have imagined, and it repays rigorous intellectual analysis. The somewhat unorthodox approach taken here has, I hope, the foundational usefulness of helping to bring the poem to life by reminding us that it is not versified doctrine but a work of poetic art – that is, a composition that could take no other form. Voice is of course not all there is to *An Essay on Criticism* as a poem, but there is no poem without it. The fluent, flexible voice projects artistic and ethical values that go deeper than doctrine or logic. The critic whom Pope follows most closely is Horace. While Horace's principles are generally relevant to *An Essay on Criticism*, it helps most to remember just what Pope emphasizes about the *manner* of Horace's *Ars Poetica* and other epistles:

> *Horace* still charms with graceful Negligence,
> And without Method *talks* us into Sense …

(653–4)

We need to hear the talking to grasp the sense, or, as Pope might think of it, to come back to our senses.

The importance of returning to truth through memory underlies the tone as well as the tenets of *An Essay on Criticism*. More than any other of Pope's critical positions, his conviction that important truths are likelier to be recovered than invented is commonly misunderstood, and its relation to the poem's voice underappreciated. Pope's aphoristic definition of "wit" in the broad sense of imagination is frequently quoted – "*True Wit* is *Nature* to Advantage drest, / What oft was *Thought*, but ne'er so well *Exprest*" – and frequently denigrated. Samuel Johnson was among the first of many to object that this definition seems to limit wit to "happiness of language."[8] But Pope's definition deepens when we quote his complete sentence:

> *True Wit* is *Nature* to Advantage drest,
> What oft was *Thought*, but ne'er so well *Exprest*,
> *Something*, whose Truth convinc'd at Sight we find,
> That gives us back the Image of our Mind.

(297–300)

The second couplet renders the process somewhat more mysterious. I do not take it simply to mean that we react to a good poem or passage by believing that we have had the same idea a dozen times but never quite got around to putting it so deftly. Being given back the image of our mind suggests something more like deep recognition and compelling conviction. In this light, Pope's account seems more compatible with Romantic ideas of creative imagination than we might expect. Keats may have had little interest in Pope, but Pope would not have argued with Keats's belief that "Poetry should surprise by a fine excess and not by Singularity – it should strike the reader as a wording of his own highest thoughts, and appear almost a Remembrance." And while some of Ralph Waldo Emerson's phrasing might have sounded portentous in early eighteenth-century England, Pope would probably have understood also this pronouncement on knowledge as remembrance in *Self-Reliance*: "In every work of genius we recognize our own rejected thoughts; they come back to us with a certain alienated majesty."[9]

Emerson and other nineteenth-century sages often cultivate an oracular voice in proclaiming such truths, but *avoiding* the oracular is central to the decorum of *An Essay on Criticism*. We began by noting Pope's insistence on critical tact:

> Men must be *taught* as if you taught them *not*;
> And Things *unknown* propos'd as Things *forgot*.
>
> (574–5)

When we grasp the complex role of memory in the poem, this couplet becomes much more than a call to have the good manners not to condescend to one's audience. Part of how Pope "talks us into sense" involves showing how the boundary that separates remembering and inventing blurs in the most interesting areas of life. Pope's theory of poetry is epistemological as well as performative, and the poem urges the reader to respect the complex relation of memory to imagination. *An Essay on Criticism* argues that the difference between the unremembered things we don't *know* we know (already) and the things we really don't know (yet) is more mysterious in poetry than in the plain prose of common sense. And that mystery is precisely what poems can best voice.

Chapter 4

Talking in tetrameter

Butler and burlesque   *48*
Familiarity breeds tetrameter   *52*
Marvell and the meditative line   *56*
Trochaic variations   *59*
Couplet "odes" and hymns   *62*
Reading Swift's tetrameter: the *Satirical Elegy on the Death of a Late Famous General* and *Cadenus and Vanessa*   *67*

Most readers who have not ventured very far into eighteenth-century poetry are likely to think of its "tight little couplets" as heroic couplets, the kind we have been examining. But probably as many or even more poems in the period were written in shorter couplets, whose lines are called iambic *tetrameter* if one is focusing on their four-beat norm, or simply *octosyllabic* if one is indicating their length of eight syllables. Readers may have run into tetrameter couplets in the poetry of Swift, now widely anthologized and taught. Swift wrote and published poetry all through his career, from the 1690s into the late 1730s, and many of his poems are among his most engaging work. His best poetry is characteristically not "poetic." After some early, improbable attempts at writing lofty odes, Swift turned to the informal tetrameter couplet and gave it his distinct stamp in the great satiric poems of the last two decades of his writing life, including poems such as *Phyllis, or The Progress of Love* (c. 1719), *Elegy on the Death of a Late Famous General* (1722), *Verses on the Death of Dr. Swift* (1735), and *The Legion Club* (1736). He imprinted the form so memorably that we may automatically associate it with the comic mode generally and more particularly with what may be called Swift's "anti-poetry" or "pseudo-doggerel." The former term refers primarily to subject matter (unpoetic stenches and sewage, for example); the latter pertains more to versification and voice. While doggerel is poorly constructed, inept poetry, "pseudo-doggerel" involves pretended ineptitude, an imitation of bad writing in which the author's skill and cleverness peek through.[1]

Certainly, the tetrameter couplet can lend itself to burlesque humor. The closer together rhymes occur, the closer the effect may be to jingling, especially if the rhymes are somewhat forced –

> Her Milk-white hands, both Palms and Backs,
> Like Iv'ry dry, and soft as Wax …

– or feminine:

> One Argument she summ'd up all in,
> "The *Thing was done* and *past recalling*:
> And therefore hop'd she should recover
> His Favour, when his *Passion's over!*
> She valu'd not what others thought her,
> And was—his *most obedient Daughter*."[2]

Anne Finch similarly uses the shorter line and feminine rhyme to suggest mechanical behavior and clichéd speech. Her stereotypic courtier, "Sir Plausible":

> Has still some applicable story
> To gratify a Whig or Tory,
> And even a Jacobite in tatters
> If met alone he smoothly flatters …
> Greets friend and foe with wishes fervent,
> And lives and dies your humble servant.[3]

Swift, Finch, Matthew Prior, and many other eighteenth-century poets learned this brisk manner largely from Samuel Butler, whose anti-Puritan satire, *Hudibras* (1663–78), burlesqued the Dissenters' claims to inward revelation:

> 'Tis a *Dark-Lanthorn* of the Spirit,
> Which none see by but those that bear it:
> A Light that falls down from on high,
> For Spiritual Trades to cousen by:
> An *Ignis Fatuus*, that bewitches,
> And leads men into Pools and Ditches,
> To make them *dip* themselves, and sound
> For Christendome in Dirty pond;
> To dive like Wild-foul for Salvation,
> And fish to catch Regeneration.[4]

This mode's popularity and salience from the late seventeenth century through much of the eighteenth has sometimes led critics to write as if poems in tetrameter couplets are predominantly satiric. In fact, the tetrameter couplet appears in nearly every poetic genre, so that understanding the relation of this verse form to poetic voice requires a broad perspective. Actually, the question is about the relation of versification to voice*s*, plural, since the short couplet becomes the vehicle for not only satire but various meditative poems, descriptive poems, familiar epistles, "hymns" not set to music, and "odes" on religious and other topics. In trying to do justice to this range, it helps to think of the tetrameter couplet flowing into the eighteenth century not from one "source" in seventeenth-century poetry but from three equally important precedents: Samuel Butler, Andrew Marvell, and John Milton. These are not by any means the only seventeenth-century poets of note who composed significant works in tetrameter couplets: Ben Jonson, Robert Herrick, Richard Crashaw, and Edmund Waller all used the form, and many other poets (Donne, for instance) often used rhymed tetrameter lines in stanzaic groupings. But Butlerian burlesque, Marvellian rumination, and Miltonic "hymn" or apostrophe give us a good schema with which to begin.

Butler and burlesque

Burlesque writing, the opposite of mock-heroic, treats what one would normally take to be a high subject in a low style rather than in the elevated style assumed to be its due. A high style is characterized not only by lofty diction and imagery but by a deliberate *pace*, one that suggests emotional gravity and forethought. A pace suggesting neither gravity nor forethought is nearly enough by itself to lower the style, even without ludicrous diction and imagery.

When Swift characterized himself as "never having written serious couplets in my life," he meant partly that instead of the refined heroic couplets he admired in Pope (who "can in one couplet fix / More sense than I can do in six") he specialized in octosyllabic couplets that seem merely to tumble down the page.[5] Here is Swift pretending indignation at the start of *The Journal of a Modern Lady* (1729):

> It was a most unfriendly Part
> In you, who ought to know my Heart,
> Are well acquainted with my Zeal
> For all the Female Commonweal:
> How cou'd it come into your Mind,
> To pitch on me, of all Mankind,

> Against the Sex to write a Satyr,
> And brand me for a Woman-Hater?

Beyond letting the rhymes recur more quickly, the tetrameter line allows another kind of quickness. For reasons ultimately stemming from our breath rhythms, ten-syllable lines nearly always require a caesura but eight-syllable lines do not. (It is possible to read a pentameter line without pausing, but two or three unbroken lines together will usually seem clumsy and prompt the winded reader to supply caesuras, not necessarily in places that complement the meaning.) Six of the eight tetrameter lines just quoted have no caesura, and that in line 6 can nearly be ignored. The effect is to hurry us to the end of each line, as if the poet were writing as fast as we can read.

This "as-if" quality is important. The hurried pace achieved through this meter may take as much labor and revision to create as do the stateliest heroic couplets. Matthew Prior's *Alma, or The Progress of the Mind* (1718), a poem of nearly 1,700 lines that is at once philosophical and mock-philosophical, must have cost even so fluent a writer as Prior much work, but the effect is continually playful. Prior's subject is the relation of body and soul ("Alma") in the history of Western thought, a topic that one might study for years – or that one might appear to ramble through in *un*studied conversation with a friend over wine. Since grave philosophers have argued endlessly, Matt tells his friend Dick that the best response is amused skepticism:

> These diff'rent *Systems*, Old or New,
> A Man with half an Eye may see,
> Were only form'd to disagree.
> Now to bring Things to fair Conclusion,
> And save much Christian Ink's Effusion;
> Let me propose an Healing *Scheme*,
> And sail along the Middle Stream …[6]

$$(\text{I.236–42})$$

And since attempts to fix its location all run into opposition, perhaps the soul moves throughout life (thus its "progress"):

> My simple *System* shall suppose,
> That Alma enters at the Toes;
> That then She mounts by just Degrees
> Up to the Ancles, Legs, and Knees:
> Next, as the Sap of Life does rise,
> She lends her Vigor to the Thighs:
> And, all these under-Regions past,
> She nestles somewhere near the Waste:

> Gives Pain or Pleasure, Grief or Laughter;
> As We shall show at large hereafter.
> Mature, if not improv'd, by Time
> Up to the Heart She loves to climb:
> From thence, compell'd by Craft and Age,
> She makes the Head her latest Stage.

(I.251–64)

Witty, deft, philosophically sophisticated, Prior's *Alma* refines Butler's rough-and-tumble satire greatly; it represents the high end of the burlesque continuum. But the reductive humor is of a piece with less intellectually informed works. The burlesque tetrameter mode seems ideally suited for the comedy of the mechanical, in which characters seem to be operating as puppets or machines. Butler's view of Puritan "enthusiasm" (self-induced delusion) is close to what Swift satirized in prose as the "mechanical operation of the spirit." In his "progress" poems Swift presents non-religious human behavior as similarly mechanical. Poems such as *Phyllis, or the Progress of Love* (1719, published 1728), *The Progress of Poetry* (1720, published 1728), and *The Progress of Marriage* (1722 [?], published 1765) resemble William Hogarth's *Harlot's Progress* (1733) and *Rake's Progress* (1735) in presenting their protagonists as unwitting stereotypes, caught in a comic predictability they cannot see. The reader sees it, however, and *hears* it. Part of the comic atmosphere of these and other poems depicting trite behavior as mechanically regular is their deliberate use of mechanically regular rhythm. The tetrameter line is closer to the meter of ballads (alternating tetrameter and trimeter) and other popular songs than is the heroic line. Pushing it just slightly in this direction, writers often use its potentially sing-song quality, in which regularity takes precedence over flexible speech, to portray sing-song behavior.

Meter dominating matter can be an ideal analogue for conventionality dominating intelligence. And emphatic rhymes complete this puppet effect. W. H. Auden nicely observes that rhymes tend to be comic when it seems "as if they have taken charge of the situation: as if, instead of an event requiring words to describe it, words had the power to create an event."[7] Actors within the event, then, begin to look ridiculous as creations of the poem, lacking agency. The reversal Auden describes is more readily achieved in tetrameter than in pentameter simply because the rhymes come more quickly.

Burlesque poems stress the predictable through generalization. Elizabeth Tollet early in the century critiques formulaic love stories in this deliberately mechanical poem, *Written in a Book of Novels*:

> Methinks that reading these Romances
> Is just like dancing Country Dances:
> All in the same dull Measures move,
> Adventures brave and constant Love;
> Each Pair in formal Order tread
> The Steps their Predecessors led.[8]

And if behavior becomes sufficiently conventional it can be reduced to an inventory, as in Swift's *The Furniture of a Woman's Mind* (1727, published 1735) for example, or to a recipe, as in Mary Alcock's *A Receipt for Writing a Novel* (1799), which enumerates the ingredients in Gothic and sentimental fictions:

> Of love take first a due proportion—
> It serves to keep the heart in motion:
> Of jealousy a powerful zest,
> Of all tormenting passions best;
> Of horror mix a copious share,
> And duels you must never spare;
> Hysteric fits at least a score,
> Or, if you find occasion, more;
> But fainting fits you need not measure,
> The fair ones have them at their pleasure …[9]

In both cases, metronymic rhythms, decisive line endings, and emphatic rhymes all underscore the mechanical regularity of the subjects. John Wilmot, Earl of Rochester (1647–80), who wrote most of his Restoration satires in pentameter, turned to tetrameter couplets to describe social mimicry in *A Ramble in St. James's Park* (1672 [?], pub. 1680). In these lines a would-be courtier tries to imitate what he thinks he knows of fashionable conduct; but doing so without judgment, he

> Converts abortive Imitation
> To universall Affectation.
> Thus he not only eats and Talks
> But feels and smells[,] sitts down and walks,
> Nay looks, and lives, and loves by Rote
> In an old Tawdry Birthday Coat.[10]

The tetrameter couplet seems naturally suited for parodying "phrases learned by rote," whether actual utterances, as in Swift's *The Furniture of a Woman's Mind*, or non-verbal, pre-fabricated "phrases" of behavior. So much so, in fact, that we need to listen carefully to its delicate uses in modes more meditative, celebratory, and intimate.

Familiarity breeds tetrameter

While countless familiar epistles were written in heroic couplets, the tetrameter couplet frequently appealed to writers seeking a familiar voice in verse letters and narratives verging toward playfulness, or in assuming the voice of someone less educated, such as a child, a servant, or sometimes a woman. Women authors themselves often gravitate toward tetrameter, as Margaret Doody argues, because it is not associated with martial subjects, affairs of state, and the professional poetic ambition usually considered a male prerogative.[11] It has stronger associations instead with common life. We glanced at these associations in the previous section, which may be due largely to the kinship between the tetrameter line and popular songs and ballads. Some metrists would argue, further, that the four-beat line comes more "naturally" in English poetry, and that even a great deal of iambic pentameter gravitates toward four real stresses rather than five.[12] For whatever reason, tetrameter couplets constitute a very large body of eighteenth-century English poetry in a low or middle style. Most of these works, though sometimes containing low imagery, are not burlesques, and they tend toward comedy rather than satire. Many give voice to great intimacy. Swift's poems to "Stella" are among the century's highest achievements as intimate epistles, and his long autobiographical *Cadenus and Vanessa* is unmatched as a familiar narrative.

Swift's good friend Mary Barber followed his example, writing a number of poems in the voice of her son or some of his school-fellows, and an especially playful one in her own voice called *On Sending my Son, as a Present, to Dr. Swift, Dean of St. Patrick's, on his Birth-Day* (1734), which includes a deft compliment to both parties. A fine statue, Barber writes, may be valued "above its Weight in Gold," but

> A richer Present I design,
> A finish'd Form, of Work divine,
> Surpassing all the Power of Art,
> A thinking Head, and grateful Heart,
> An Heart, that hopes, one Day, to show
> How much we to the Drapier owe.
> Kings could not send a *nobler* Gift;
> A *meaner* were unworthy *Swift*.[13]

Mary Leapor follows Pope more often than Swift, but her poem *The Head-Ach. To Aurelia* mixes amused self-deprecation and friendly criticism in a Swiftian manner. The friend and Leapor both have their weaknesses – Aurelia for gossip, Leapor for poetry – and their illnesses:

Just so, *Aurelia*, you complain
Of Vapours, Rheums, and gouty Pain;
Yet I am patient, so shou'd you,
For Cramps and Head-achs are our due:
We suffer justly for our Crimes;
For Scandal you, and I for Rhymes …[14]

Leapor, like Swift, Barber, and others, also adopts the voice of less educated speakers. In *The Epistle of Deborah Dough* (1751) she imagines a neighbor puzzling over how she occupies herself (with a pun on "rime," frost):

But I've no News to send you now;
Only I've lost my brindled Cow;
And that has greatly sunk my Dairy:
But I forgot our Neighbour *Mary*;
Our Neighbour *Mary*,—who, they say,
Sits scribble-scribble all the Day,
And making—what—I can't remember;
But sure 'tis something like *December*;
A frosty Morning—Let me see—
O! now I have it to a T.
She throws away her precious Time
In scrawling nothing else but Rhyme …[15]

In the familiar mode Swift had many followers throughout the century but no superiors. Pope paid homage to the distinctiveness of Swift's manner when he published one of his Imitations of Horace (*Epistle* I.vii) with the subtitle "Imitated in the Manner of Dr. Swift." In place of the pentameter couplets Pope used in his own imitations of Horace –

St. John, whose love indulg'd my labours past
Matures my present, and shall bound my last!

(*Epistle* I.i, 1–2)

– he ventriloquizes Swift's decidedly less heroic address:

'Tis true, my Lord, I gave my word,
I would be with you, June the third;
Changed it to August, and (in short)
Have kept it—as you do at Court.[16]

Esther Johnson seems to have inspired less erotic passion but deeper friendship than the other Esther in Swift's life, Esther Vanhomrigh, the "Vanessa" of *Cadenus and Vanessa*, discussed at the end of this chapter. Biographical speculation continues. In any case, the "Stella" poems written for Esther Johnson from 1719 until shortly before her death in 1728 show a remarkable epistolary intimacy. Many of these are birthday poems, but two of the most revealing are compliments occasioned by her friendship during Swift's illnesses. The first, *To Stella, Visiting me in my Sickness*, includes an inquiry into the nature of true honor and settles on Stella as an exemplar:

> Heroes and Heroines of old,
> By *Honour* only were enroll'd
> Among their Brethren in the Skies,
> To which (though late) shall *Stella* rise.
> Ten Thousand Oaths upon Record
> Are not so sacred as her Word:
> The world shall in its Atoms end,
> Ere *Stella* can deceive a Friend.
> By *Honour* seated in her Breast
> She still determines what is best:
> What Indignation in her Mind
> Against Enslavers of Mankind!
> Base Kings, and Ministers of State,
> Eternal Objects of her Hate!
>
> (51–64)

These are hardly conventional gallantries. On the whole, the Stella poems emphasize her "manly" or androgynous virtues (as do many of Swift's compliments to women friends) and their extraordinary friendship. Stella's wit, intellect, and unflinching fortitude draw Swift's admiration, even in his peevishness, as in the 1724 *To Stella. Written on the Day of her Birth, but not the Subject, when I was sick in Bed*. Swift knows he can be a difficult patient and that Stella is often herself unwell:

> When out my brutish passions break,
> With gall in ev'ry word I speak,
> She with soft speech my anguish chears,
> Or melts my passions down with tears;
> Although 'tis easy to descry
> She wants assistance more than I;
> Yet seems to feel my pains alone,
> And is a Stoic in her own.[17]

This last passage is a good example of tone and versification working together subtly to create a music of familiarity without more than a hint – for the moment – of the ludicrous. That hint lies in the rueful acknowledgment that the male patient has been the "unmanly" actor and perhaps in the reversal of Swift's habitual ironic perspective: most of us are good most of the time at being "stoical" about others' misfortunes (the "proem" of *Verses on the Death of Dr. Swift* offers a disquisition on this theme), while Stella is stoical only about hers. The simple tetrameter couplet provides a frame for the contrast between conventional language and unconventional conduct. But Swift also complicates the metrical frame enough to keep the lines from sounding wholly predictable. Although each line of this passage can be scanned regularly, a nice tension exists between meter and sentence prosody. In lines 11, 13, 14, and 17, for example, the word "my" requires more cognitive emphasis than we might normally give putatively unstressed syllables. The same is true of "She" in line 13 and especially line 16. On the other hand, "is" in the last line, often a word given little stress, here receives it owing to the metrical momentum of the passage, and thus provides an unexpected antithesis: Stella *seems* X in one sphere but *is* Y in another.

Swift's final birthday poem, for 1727, written when they both must have suspected Esther was mortally ill, is the most poignant of the Stella poems. It is a quiet tour de force in which Swift combines the roles of birthday laureate (still celebrating Stella annually, as the official Poet Laureate writes birthday odes to the king), old friend, and clergyman. The roles fuse as he asks that she "From not the gravest of divines / Accept for once some serious lines." The word "serious" refers in part to the poem's brooding on mortality, but it also refers to the counsel and spiritual comfort Swift offers as a priest to a member of his congregation who appears depressed and doubtful of the worth of the life she has led. Swift enumerates for her the virtuous acts of a "life well spent," arguing that they nourish her now ("is not virtue in mankind / The nutriment that feeds the mind …?"), and will sustain her in death:

> For Virtue, in her daily race,
> Like Janus, bears a double face;
> Looks back with joy where she has gone
> And therefore goes with courage on:
> She at your sickly couch will wait,
> And guide you to a better state.

We attribute such poetic achievement to Swift's genius, the pathos of a long friendship, and Stella's merits. No doubt the poem would not exist without these. But the point of this section is that it would also not exist apart from the versatility of the tetrameter couplet that allows for the traces of low humor (pills and eyeglasses are "mortifying stuff" to be talked of another day), familiar language, strong rhythm, and lines of lapidary simplicity: "The nutriment that feeds the mind," "And guide you to a better state"). If most poets were less skillful than Swift in the arts of familiarity, scores of lesser ones were able to benefit from the familiar line he adopted and made still more flexible.

Marvell and the meditative line

Readers of Marvell's *To His Coy Mistress*, *The Nymph Complaining for the Death of her Faun*, *A Dialogue between the Soul and Body*, or *Bermudas* often do not remember, or perhaps notice, that those poems are in tetrameter couplets, a fact difficult to ignore in the case of Butler or Swift. Many more of Marvell's best-known poems – *The Garden*, *Upon Appleton House*, *The Unfortunate Lover*, for example – are also in tetrameter couplets, though grouped in eight-line stanzas rather than verse paragraphs. It may not be accurate to consider Marvell the pioneer in the "serious" use of the short couplet. Ben Jonson (*On My First Daughter*) and Richard Crashaw (*Upon the Death of a Gentleman* and *Upon the Death of the Most Desired Mr. Herrys*) used it for elegy in the seventeenth century, and Robert Herrick used it not only in rural celebrations such as *The Country Life* and *His Content in the Country* but also in at least one religious poem, *To Find God*. But the concentrated force of Marvell's example is instructive. Marvell left strong works in tetrameter of witty philosophical argument, contemplation of place, and an epistolary mode more public and ruminating than intimate (we learn nothing of the mistress other than that she is "coy" but much about temporality and haunted pleasures). Some notable eighteenth-century poems that, loosely speaking, extend Marvell's mode include Lady Mary Chudleigh's *To the Ladies*, *Dear to the Gods Ambrosia Prov'd*, and her two dialogues, *The Inquiry* and *The Choice* (1710); Anne Finch's *The Tree* and *The Bird* (1713); Thomas Parnell's *Night-Piece on Death* (1722) and several of his more directly religious poems (published in 1758, long after Parnell's death in 1718), such as *The Soul in Sorrow*, *The Happy Man*, and *The Way to Happiness*; Dyer's *The Country Walk* (1726); and Elizabeth Tollet's *On a Death's Head* (1724), *The Winter Song* (1755), and *Psalm CX* (1756).

Chudleigh's *To the Ladies* is becoming well known because its argument that "Wife and Servant are the same, / But only differ in the Name" captures an early feminist perspective. But *Dear to the Gods Ambrosia Prov'd*, the lovely twenty-line poem that forms part of her essay *Of Solitude*, better illustrates Chudleigh's tetrameter versification and analogical wit. The opening lines establish the conceptual parallel, that ambrosia is to gods what books are to mortals:

> Dear to the Gods *Ambrosia* prov'd,
> As dear are Books where they're belov'd;

They're still the Mind's delicious Treat,
Its healthful, most substantial Meat;
The Soul's ennobling, sprightly Wine,
Like Nectar sweet, and as Divine …[18]

Before pursuing Chudleigh's development of the conceit, let us listen more closely to these lines with an ear toward performance. Two things are marked typographically below: the probable strongest stress of each line (indicated in bold) and the caesura (indicated by spacing). As noted earlier, tetrameter lines do not require a caesura as decisively as do pentameter lines, but most have one; in this instance, all but line 3 allow for at least a slight pause between phrases:

Dear to the Gods   *Ambrosia* prov'd,
As dear are **Books**   where they're belov'd;
They're still the **Mind's** delicious Treat,
Its healthful,   most sub**stan**tial Meat;
The **Soul's** ennobling,   sprightly Wine,
Like Nectar sweet,   and as Di**vine** …

The lines are heavily end-stopped, but Chudleigh varies the placement of the caesura artfully: it follows the fourth syllable (arguably the "default" position for tetrameter) in lines 1, 2, and 6, the third syllable in line 4, and the fifth in line 5. And the position within the line of the "strongstress" ranges from relatively late (lines 1 and 4), to medial (lines 2 and 3), to early (line 5), falling on the terminal or rhyme position only in the last line of the passage. In addition to avoiding monotony, these movements of emphasis underscore the view of books as substantial food for the human mind and soul, conferring on mortals something of divinity.

The divine gift communicated through books is both inspiration and aspiration, as elevating as the water of the muses' spring and capable of endowing humans with the ambition of demigods:

Castalian Springs did ne'er produce
A richer, more spirituous Juice.
When by't inspir'd, we fearless rise,
And, like the Giants, brave the Skies.
Pelion on *Ossa* boldly lay,
From thence both Earth and Sea survey:
On them the huge *Olympus* throw,
Then to the tow'ring Summet go,
Thence take a View of Worlds on High,
From Orb to Orb with Pleasure fly …

(7–16)

Books take modern readers even higher, beyond the transcendent insights of ancient polytheism to the truths of scientifically informed theism. Comic novelty leavens her sarcasm, as the moderns pile not only Mount Pelion atop Mount Ossa (as in Greek myth the giants Otus and Ephialtes had done in trying to reach the gods) but Mount Olympus on both. Thanks to such towering ambition, now lovers of books can

> Still upward soar, until the Mind
> Effects does in their Causes find,
> And them pursue till they unite
> In the bless'd Source of Truth and Light.

(17–20)

Chudleigh's mixture of extravagance, intellectual ardor, and piety exploits and extends the range of the quick tetrameter couplet. Her last line gives a deeper meaning to the phrase "light verse."

Parnell's *Night-Piece on Death* reaches a pious acceptance of Death, who speaks the last thirty lines, but it begins with a wryly learned, Marvellian bemusement at the limitations of bookishness. Commonly anthologized and referred to as a precursor of the "graveyard poetry" of the mid-century, the *Night-Piece* combines urbane rapidity with an earthy Elizabethan pun. (Some preliminary notes: a candle's blue flame indicated the presence of ghosts – or a lack of fresh air; the Schoolmen are the medieval philosophers and theologians whom Parnell read in his studies in divinity; and the Sages are the ancient philosophers.)

> By the blue Tapers trembling Light,
> No more I waste the wakeful Night,
> Intent with endless view to pore
> The Schoolmen and the Sages o'er:
> Their Books from Wisdom widely stray,
> Or point at best the longest Way.
> I'll seek a readier Path, and go
> Where Wisdom's surely taught *below*.[19]

The category "wisdom below" would usually mean wisdom on earth as opposed to heavenly knowledge, but the poem proceeds to contemplate those *within* the earth, digging below the surface of the earth to recover transcendent meaning.

Many writers used the tetrameter couplet for religious verse, and it is also a common choice for reverential poems of other kinds, particularly poems celebrating nature, by addressing either creatures or places. Finch's *The Bird* and *The Tree* are good examples of the former, John Dyer's *The Country Walk* and *Grongar Hill* (1726) of the latter. But as we will see, the line is often faint between such celebratory meditations and the more exalted celebrations treated below as "odes." Like many apostrophes, for instance, Finch's *The Bird* approaches prayer –

> Kind bird, thy praises I design,
> Thy praises, like thy plumes shou'd shine,
> Thy praises, shou'd thy life outlive,
> Cou'd I, the fame I wish thee, give.

– as *The Tree* does even more closely, in a litany of gratitude:

> Fair *Tree*! for thy delightful shade
> 'Tis just that some Return be made;
> Sure, some Return is due from me
> To thy cool Shadows, and to thee.

All of the tree's many beneficiaries, human and animal, Finch imagines, sing their thanks:

> Shall I then only Silent be,
> And no Return be made by me?
> No; let this Wish upon thee wait,
> And still to flourish be thy Fate.
> To future Ages may'st thou stand
> Untouch'd by the rash Workman's hand ...[20]

The language of petition – "let this wish ..." – wholly constitutes one of Finch's most ambitious poems, *The Petition for an Absolute Retreat*. All but the first seven lines of this 293-line poem are in tetrameter couplets, but with a metrical difference that brings us to a large boundary between something like conversation and something like prayer or incantation.

Trochaic variations

The metrical difference between ritualized and conversational verse lies in omitting the first, unstressed syllable, yielding lines of seven rather than eight syllables. Before looking more closely at the technical variations, let us listen to the performative effect of two representative passages. Here is Finch wishing for the wholesome abundance of Eden:

> Grapes, with Juice so crouded up,
> As breaking thro' the native Cup;
> Figs (yet growing) candy'd o'er,

By the Sun's attracting Pow'r;
Cherries, with the downy Peach,
All within my easie Reach;
Whilst creeping near the humble Ground,
Shou'd the Strawberry be found
Springing wheresoe'er I stray'd,
Thro' those Windings and that Shade.

(*Petition for an Absolute Retreat*, 38–47)

All but lines 39 and 44 begin with a stress and are seven syllables long, as are all of the first ten of Dyer's *Grongar Hill*. Here Dyer invokes the sister muses of painting and poetry to help describe his landscape (a "van" is a summit):

Silent Nymph, with curious eye,
Who the purple ev'ning lie
On the mountain's lonely van,
Beyond the noise of busy man,
Painting fair the form of things,
While the yellow linnet sings;
Or the tuneful nightingale
Charms the forest with her tale;
Come, with all thy various hues,
Come, and aid thy sister Muse …

(*Grongar Hill*, 1–10)

Finch, Dyer, and other eighteenth-century poets also use the seven-syllable line in combination with regular tetrameter. Twenty of the 156 lines of Dyer's *The Country Walk* are shortened, allowing all three possible combinations: a shorter line 1) beginning the couplet, 2) ending it, or 3) both:

1)   Sweetly shining on the eye,
     A riv'let gliding smoothly by …
2)   An old man's smoky nest I see
     Leaning on an aged tree …
3)   Oh! how fresh, how pure the air!
     Let me breathe a little here.

What to call these seven-syllable, four-beat lines? Here, literary critics frequently pass by in silence and students of prosody frequently disagree. Lines conforming to a pattern of stress/unstress would seem to be trochaic. The best-known trochaic line is probably the opening of Blake's *The Tyger*:

Tyger, tyger burning bright—

Though strictly speaking a trochaic line would end with an unstressed syllable –

> Tyger, tyger burning brightly.

(The weakness of my metrical "improvement" suggests why purely trochaic lines are rare in English poetry. An unstressed final syllable would commit the poet either to barely perceptible rhymes or to a series of feminine ones: "Tyger, tyger burning brightly / In the forest nearly nightly …") Some students of prosody would not regard Dyer's shorter lines as trochaic at all: because the lines occur in a dominant pattern of iambic meter, this argument runs, the seven-syllable lines are technically "acephalous iambic tetrameter," that is, they are "headless" because missing their first syllable.

As always, the problem of terminology is only interesting for what it allows us to communicate to each other and, more often than we realize, what it allows us to *notice*. The first thing is to make sure we hear and can begin to explain why Blake's "Tyger, tyger burning bright" sounds so unlike Frost's "Whose woods these are I think I know." Whether we can best describe Blake's lines or those of Finch and Dyer above as metrically trochaic or (acephalous) iambic – that is, as moving in "falling" or "rising" rhythm – will depend on how we experience them. And that will depend on context. In the poems above, where line after line begins with a trochaic foot and continues thus until the final syllable, we experience the line as trochaic, or, if we wish to be exact, as a truncated trochaic line, shortened by a syllable at the end. If, on the other hand (or foot), the pattern of iambic meter is established initially, then shorter lines might be felt and best described as iambic lines that have been shortened at the front.

In the clearly trochaic passages above from Finch's *Petition* and Dyer's *Grongar Hill* one feels from the outset a rhythm more insistent, stylized, and conspicuous than in iambic verse. Whether that is because English is "naturally" an iambic language, as is sometimes said, is debatable. As a Germanic language, English has a higher proportion of words that are accented on the first syllable and a much greater percentage of monosyllabic words than do many other languages; but the presence of articles in English and its normal word order make for many *phrase* units that are iambic or more nearly so than trochaic. A verb like "speeding" is trochaic by itself, but it is likely to occur in an iambic environment: "A car went speeding by." For whatever reason, speakers of English have tended to associate speech with iambic poetry, whether the "high" speech of Renaissance and later drama or the more colloquial speech of conversation poems and dramatic monologues. Correspondingly, we associate trochaic verse with special uses of language, such as, at the extreme, magic charms, spells, incantations. Most of the three witches' speech in *Macbeth* is trochaic tetrameter: "Double, double, toile and trouble; / Fire burne, and Cauldron bubble …"

Once a strong trochaic meter establishes itself and the "reversal of expectations"[21] for iambic rhythm is clear, the poetic pattern seems to dominate, or even replace, normal sentence prosody. Having read "**Tyg**er, **tyg**er **burn**ing **bright**," we are pushed onward to perform the second line as "**In** the **for**est **of** the **night**," even though "in" and "of" would in most contexts be unstressed (as in the sentence "The squirrels thrive in forests of oak"). And so in Finch's *Petition*, less flamboyantly than in *The Tyger* but no less surely, the trochaic line "Figs (yet growing) candy'd o'er" leads us to read the next as "**By** the **Sun's** at**tract**ing **Pow'r**," just as the last line quoted above (p. 60) becomes "**Thro'** those **Wind**ings **and** that **Shade**." We can see the same promotion of normally unstressed words in Dyer, as a pronoun, preposition, and conjunction – "Who," "On," and "Or" – at the start of the line suddenly gain prominence. This elevation of pattern over ordinary sentence sound helps account for our association of trochaic meter with irrational or suprarational expression.

Eighteenth-century poets, of course, did not invent trochaic tetrameter couplets (or acephalous iambic ones), nor the mixing of seven- and eight-syllable lines. For the latter, especially, they were indebted to Milton's *L'Allegro* and *Il Pensoroso*. Much has been written about the influence of Milton on the eighteenth century, but in the case of his early poems more attention has gone to mid-century poets' use of Milton's atmosphere and diction, in *Il Pensoroso* particularly, than to the importance of his metrical experiments. Although more of Milton's lines are regularly iambic in these poems than not ("But come thou Goddess fair and free"), trochaic lines keep breaking in, and in some parts take over:

> Haste thee nymph, and bring with thee
> Jest and youthful Jollity,
> Quips and Cranks, and wanton Wiles,
> Nods, and Becks, and Wreathed Smiles.

> (*L'Allegro* 25–8)

Milton's virtuoso apostrophes to the personifications Mirth and Melancholy bring us from mediation to the kind of tetrameter poem that many eighteenth-century poets called hymns or odes.

Couplet "odes" and hymns

Most of the odes written in the eighteenth century and all of its most famous ones, those of Gray and Collins, use stanzaic patterns, sometimes – with Pindar or Horace in mind – very elaborate ones with complicated rhyme schemes. Probably most hymns for singing are in simple quatrains with interlocking rhymes (*abab*). Stanza forms will be discussed in the next section. But many poets also used the familiar, flexible tetrameter couplet to write so-called odes and hymns *to* or *on* various entities, states of being, or states of mind. Some of these are explicitly religious, like Elizabeth Tollet's *Sacred Ode* and Addison's *The Spacious Firmament on High*. Tollet uses the taut trochaics we saw in Milton, Finch's *Petition*, and Dyer's *Grongar Hill*:

> Heav'nly Muse! my Soul inspire,
> Tune my Voice, and string my Lyre:
> Higher yet, and yet more high
> Lift the mutual Harmony.
> Wake me from delusive Dreams;
> Vain imaginary Themes:
> Lift my Voice to him above;
> Wisdom, Word, and heav'nly Love.
>
> (*Sacred Ode*, 1–8)

The meter is difficult to sustain, but Tollet gamely stays with it to the concluding triplet, in which the song of the angels welcomes Christ back to heaven:

> Open on your Hinges fly,
> Azure Portals of the Sky!
> To the King of Majesty.
>
> (65–7)

Addison, on the other hand, cultivates a slower pace in the ode he said was inspired by the "bold and sublime manner of thinking" of the Psalmist. His poem actually builds on both Psalm XIX ("The heavens declare the glory of God: and the firmament sheweth his handy worke ...") and the expanded universe of Newtonian science. The deliberate movement of Addison's contemplation of vastness is conveyed through regular iambic tetrameter and underscored by the division of the poem, in Marvellian fashion, into eight-line sections:

> The spacious firmament on high,
> With all the blue etherial sky,
> And spangled heav'ns, a shining frame,
> Their great Original proclaim:
> Th' unwearied Sun, from day to day,
> Does his Creator's power display,
> And publishes to every land
> The work of an Almighty hand.

Readers looking for the language of the King James Bible or a familiar hymnal sometimes mistakenly assume that Addison's religious feeling is lukewarm. Instead, it is calm – or, more accurately, the voice scripted by the poem is calm. The voice feels calm because the opening sections consist of declarative sentences rather than imperatives or exclamations, as in Tollet's poem or in much of the religious poetry of Christopher Smart. And the sentences are declarative because Addison is stating the creation's testimony to the Creator as an intellectual certainty rather than a merely pious belief. The third section asks how faith and intellect are to be reconciled. Since the heavenly bodies are now silent – in the modern scientific worldview they no longer make medieval music – how can they be said to "proclaim" God? The answer lies in knowledgeable contemplation; we can "hear" the true music of the spheres through informed rationality:

> What though, in solemn silence, all
> Move round the dark terrestrial ball?
> What tho' nor real voice nor sound
> Amid their radiant orbs be found?
> In Reason's ear they all rejoice,
> And utter forth a glorious voice,
> For ever singing, as they shine,
> "The hand that made us is divine."

(17–24)

The unusual caesura just before the end of line 17 puts heavy emphasis on the word immediately following it, and "all" the celestial bodies then move without pause through the next line, as in their circuits. Line 20 speeds up, completing the couplet by paralleling sight and sound: the orbs are voiceless but "radiant." The last four lines turn on this parallel by endowing "Reason's ear" with the power of hearing the meaning of what the eye and mind can see. The last line epitomizes the poem's religious tact – a matter of impersonality, not indifference – by moving the ultimate profession of faith from the poet's visionary voice to the voice of the whole visible creation. Addison's hymn shows the tetrameter line at the opposite end of the spectrum from burlesque. Instead of conveying colloquial rapidity, Addison's four-beat lines achieve the settled brevity of lapidary inscription.

Thomas Parnell wrote several "hymns" that are conventionally religious, including a prayerful series for Morning, Noon, and Evening, but his *A Hymn to Contentment* is better known.[22] That description is relative because Parnell is under-represented in anthologies, and the mixture of secular and sacred in *A Hymn to Contentment* suggests one reason his work has resisted easy characterization. This poem addresses a secular personification, Contentment, who in turn briefly addresses the poet, inspiring him to declare his vocation as a religious poet. Later on we will look more closely at personification, but for now these three stages of the poem show three different kinds of voice and versification within the reverential tetrameter couplet.

The first is invocatory, as Parnell begins the *Hymn* with three trochaic lines meant to conjure Contentment –

> Lovely lasting Peace of Mind,
> Sweet Delight of human kind!
> Heav'nly born, and bred on high …

– before slowing to elaborate:

> To crown the Fav'rites of the Sky
> With more of Happiness below,
> Than Victors in a Triumph know …

The speaker establishes an idea of Contentment partly through description and partly through differentiation – from Ambition, Avarice, even Solitude, since without Contentment "Solitude's the Nurse of Woe" (24) – and then resumes his invocation: "Lovely, lasting Peace appear …" (33).

The second stage of the poem reveals that the first occurred at some unspecified earlier time, when "as under Shade I stood, / I sung my Wishes to the Wood" (37), and that the first 36 lines are essentially self-quotation. The second section quotes "Contentment," characterized in a productive pun as a "Grace" (42). In classical mythology the Graces represent aesthetic energy, but Parnell has Christian salvation very much in mind as well:

> —Go rule thy Will,
> Bid thy wild Passions all be still,
> Know God—and bring thy Heart to know,
> The Joys which from Religion flow;
> Then ev'ry Grace shall prove its Guest,
> And I'll be there to crown the rest.
>
> (43–8)

Contentment begins her speech emphatically: of her first thirteen words set off in dashes, one might plausibly stress all but "be" and the second syllable of "Passions." The slight understressing in line 46 ("The **Joys** which from Re**lig**ion **flow**") compensates for the initial heaviness, and the regularity of her last two lines expresses the tranquility Contentment promises.

The third stage of the poem, in which the speaker confirms his vocation as religious celebrant, uses the tetrameter couplet cumulatively, as the poet amasses a catalogue of his new subjects, God's creations. Parnell exploits the tetrameter's ability to function without a caesura in most of these gathering lines:

> The Sun that walks his airy Way,
> To light the World, and give the Day;
> The Moon that shines with borrow'd Light,
> The Stars that gild the gloomy Night;
> The Seas that roll unnumber'd Waves;
> The Wood that spreads its shady Leaves;
> The Field whose Ears conceal the Grain;
> The yellow Treasure of the Plain ...

(63–70)

The headlong parallelism of these lines is underscored by the sudden return to a more conversational syntax in the poet's confident resolution. The final four lines of this section comprise two short sentences (punctuation aside) and contain five caesuras (marked in the first two lines, following "Maker" in the third, and, in the fourth, following both "want" and "ask"):

> All of these, and all I see,
> Wou'd be sung, and sung by me:
> They speak their Maker as they can,
> But want and ask the Tongue of Man.

(71–4)

The versatile versification within Parnell's *Hymn* suggests in miniature the range of possibilities for the tetrameter couplet that we have surveyed thus far. Performing these couplets demands as much of our aural attention as does the more commonly discussed heroic couplet. Its meter and quickly recurring rhymes can reinforce modes from the ridiculous to the sublime. I will take up formal odes in the next chapter, but it is worth noting here that substantial parts of some of William Collins's loftiest odes (*The Passions*, *Liberty*, and *Ode on the Poetical Character*, for example) are in tetrameter couplets. Tetrameter could bring quickness and concision to the sometimes lumbering ode. In one case it even provided a salutary alternative to the ode altogether. Curiously, John Dyer wrote *Grongar Hill* as an ode before revising it into the familiar form in which we encountered it above. In the process, he abandoned some cumbrous lines such as these:

> The Princes Tenure in his Roofs of Gold,
>   Ends like the Peasant's homelier Hold;
> Life's but a Road, and he who travels right,
> Treats Fortune as an Inn, and rests his Night ...[23]

Dyer instead refined them into taut memorability:

> A little Rule, a little Sway,
> A Sun-beam in a Winter's Day,
> Is all the Proud and Mighty have
> Between the Cradle and the Grave.

(89–92)

Well handled, the tetrameter couplet provides much to listen for. At its best, its casual concision and quick rhymes combine two qualities usually thought of as opposed: the intimacy of talk and the impersonality of inscription. A modern reader is more likely to find that interesting combination in the poetry of the eighteenth century than anywhere else.

Reading Swift's tetrameter: the *Satirical Elegy on the Death of a Late Famous General* and *Cadenus and Vanessa*

The *Satirical Elegy*

Two of Swift's most powerful poems, one short, one long, might be called counter-elegies, poems in which he imagines the unofficial reactions of various speakers to the subject's death. The longer of these, *Verses on the Death of Dr. Swift*, will be taken up in Chapter 6 as a superb instance of first-person poetic satire. In Swift's much briefer counter-elegy, the subject is the recently departed Duke of Marlborough, a great man for many and clearly not one for Swift. The *Satirical Elegy on the Death of a Late Famous General* is not a vocal tour de force like *Verses on the Death of Dr. Swift*, but its brevity and simplicity make it ideal for examining Swift's play of talking voices.

Written shortly after the death of John Churchill, Duke of Marlborough, in June 1722, *A Satirical Elegy* was so topically explosive that it was not published until two decades after Swift's own death.[24] Topicality in this case is not much of a barrier for modern readers. All we really need to know of its context is that Marlborough was seen by Swift as no hero. Indeed, Swift has virtually no military heroes: a few years later in *Gulliver's Travels* a soldier is defined as "a Yahoo hired to kill in cold Blood as many of his own Species, who have never offended him, as he possibly can" (Part IV, chapter 5). Swift considered Marlborough moreover as a manipulative politician and war profiteer, whose death would inevitably be greeted in official quarters with an elaborate public funeral and a host of eulogistic orations and poems. Here is the opening of one such poem, by Nicholas Amhurst:

> Churchill is dead! And in that Word is lost
> The bravest Leader of the bravest Host;
> A veteran Chief, that in the bloody Field
> For forty rolling Years untaught to yield;
> Through half the sever'd Globe obtain'd Renown
> And with its brightest Gems adorn'd the *British* Crown …²⁵

Swift's opening line could be a deliberate echo of Amhurst's:

> His Grace! impossible! what, dead!
> Of old age too, and in his bed!
> And could that Mighty Warrior fall,
> And so inglorious, after all?
> Well, since he's gone, no matter how,
> The last loud trump must wake him now:
> And, trust me, as the noise grows stronger,
> He'd wish to sleep a little longer.

These eight lines set up a counterpoint of two voices that will shape the first three-fourths of the poem. The first implied speaker, apparently neutral or perhaps a Marlborough partisan, asks a question (as in lines 1–4), which a second, indignantly sarcastic speaker then answers (as in 5–8). The second time this happens the questioner throws in an apparent compliment, since Marlborough died at seventy-two, not sixty:

> And could he be indeed so old
> As by the news-papers we're told?
> Threescore, I think, is pretty high …

which leads to this increasingly disgusted rejoinder (suggesting that sixty years would have been ample):

> 'Twas time in conscience he should die.
> This world he cumber'd long enough;
> He burnt his candle to the snuff;
> And that's the reason, some folks think,
> He left behind *so great a s—k*.

(12–16)

The conspicuously concealed word *stink* plays on the olfactory image of a candle made of tallow that, unlike wax, would smell unpleasantly, especially toward the end. It is a metaphor for both a sick room of stale linen and bed-pans and, more broadly, a foul life and legacy. *Stink* is of course a word of disgust, but one can also hear it being uttered with comic satisfaction.

The final exchange is angrier still. To the first speaker's observation and question –

> Behold his funeral appears,
> Nor widows' sighs, nor orphans' tears,
> Wont at such times each heart to pierce,
> Attend the progress of his he[a]rse.
> But what of that …

(17–21)

– the skeptic makes a darkly ironic reply. Catching its tone involves heavily stressing two normally insignificant words, as Swift's meter encourages:

> his friends may say,
> He had those honours **in** his day.
> True to his profit and his pride,
> He made them weep be**fore** he died.

(21–4)

The poem's third and ultimate voice is prophetic, pronouncing the epitaph that will never be written for Marlborough in a militaristic culture but which should be inscribed on his tomb:

> Come hither, all ye empty things,
> Ye bubbles rais'd by breath of Kings;
> Who float upon the tide of state;
> Come hither, and behold your fate.
> Let pride be taught by this rebuke,
> How very mean a thing's a Duke;
> From all his ill-got honours flung,
> Turn'd to that dirt from whence he sprung.

This voice of finality differs from the second, skeptical speaker in moving toward generalization and abandoning sarcasm for moral imperative. The subject is now not the Marlborough of this moment, since there is hardly any point in satirizing the dead, but any royal favorite. And the audience is anyone, now or later, who should stop by this imaginary gravesite: "Come hither … Come hither." The last line focuses its contempt for Marlborough into ethical indignation. Seen in proper perspective, through the lens of universal mortality, Marlborough was a mushroom that "sprung" up in dubious soil and that now should be "flung" from the respect of a knowing citizenry: dust to dust. Perhaps worse than dust, since the insistent tetrameter rhymes of "flung" and "sprung" subliminally pull the "dirt" between them in the direction of "dung."

Cadenus and Vanessa

Written in 1713 and published in 1726, Swift's *Cadenus and Vanessa* is a work much discussed by Swiftians and little known by general readers. Nearly 900 lines long, it resists anthologizing but is irresistible once found, as it may be now in various inexpensive texts. The poem compellingly chronicles what was, if not a love affair, at least a tempting infatuation between Esther Vanhomrigh and Swift. (Swift made up the name "Vanessa" from "Essa," a diminutive of Esther, and the beginning of her surname; "Cadenus" is an anagram for "*decanus*," Latin for "dean," Swift's church position.) Its manner can be grasped briefly here through one example. Swift establishes Vanessa's extraordinary combination of beauty and intellectual character through a creation fable in which Venus, determined to restore love's dominion in society, tricks Pallas Athena into endowing the new-born Vanessa with enough "male" virtues to attract even the jaded moderns:

> Wisdom's above suspecting Wiles;
> The Queen of Learning gravely smiles,
> Down from *Olympus* comes with Joy,
> Mistakes *Vanessa* for a Boy;
> Then sows within her tender Mind
> Seeds long unknown to Womankind:
> For manly Bosoms chiefly fit,
> The seeds of Knowledge, Judgment, Wit.[26]

The narrator's voice is but one of many in this uniquely complex yet paradigmatic work. In fact, a careful reader of this longest of Swift's poems (*Cadenus and Vanessa* is nearly twice the length of *Verses on the Death of Dr. Swift*) will experience one of the richest constructions of polyphony in English poetry. In it Swift creates a virtual closet drama, with at least nine explicitly designated speakers and several others implied. Not just Swift's multiplicity of speakers but his different levels of discourse in the poem offer a model of vocal interplay and comic narrative psychology perhaps unparalleled before the nineteenth-century novel. Much discussion of *Cadenus and Vanessa* has, understandably, centered on biographical questions about the nature of the relationship between Swift and his friend, a relationship presented in the poem in part as between tutor and student. But it is difficult, and for our purposes irrelevant, to go beyond recognizing that the story of Vanessa's ardor and Cadenus's embarrassed insistence that the relationship remain Platonic is told with humor, pathos, and, finally, determined equivocation:

> But what Success *Vanessa* met,
> Is to the World a Secret yet:

> Whether the Nymph, to please her Swain,
> Talks in a high romantick Strain;
> Or whether he at last descends,
> To act with less Seraphick Ends;
> Or, to compound the Business, whether
> They temper Love and Books together;
> Must never to Mankind be told,
> Nor shall the conscious Muse unfold.

(826–35)

Speculating about what the poem reveals or conceals is less helpful than trying to hear what it performs. Most of this poem requires a narrator, but roughly a fourth of the lines are spoken by its cast of characters. The story begins with a trial to determine whether men or women are to blame for the modern debasement of love, in which deep feeling has "dwindled to Intrigue / And marriage grown a Money-League" (13–14), and immediately we hear lawyers plead on both sides (7–19, 27–66). To the voices of the narrator and these two attorneys are soon added those of Venus herself (85–90, 142–53, 180–3, 188–97, 867–91), Athena (288–303), Cupid (498–509), and Vanessa (622–31, 686–719, 801–25). These line numbers are approximate: early editions of the poem set no speeches in quotation marks or do so very inconsistently, making it sometimes difficult to tell where narration ends and speech begins.

The boundaries are all the more difficult to discern because Swift combines direct discourse (quoted speech), indirect discourse (reported speech), and, most surprisingly, free indirect discourse (the character's thoughts presented in the character's idiom, also called free indirect style). The last is surprising because it is usually associated with Austen in early nineteenth-century England and Flaubert in mid-nineteenth-century France, but we will see it at work toward the end of *Cadenus and Vanessa*. First, to clarify these terms, let us begin with an example of indirect discourse, as Vanessa speaks to Cadenus:

> Had he employ'd his Time so long
> To teach her what was Right and Wrong;
> Yet could such Notions entertain
> That all his Lectures were in vain?
> She own'd the wand'ring of her Thoughts;
> But he must answer for her Faults.
> She well remember'd, to her Cost,
> That all his Lessons were not lost.
> Two Maxims she could still produce,
> And sad Experience taught their Use ...

(606–15)

In direct speech the first two lines (for example) would read: "Have you employed your Time so long / To teach me what is Right and Wrong …?" The narration soon carries us in this direction:

> Now, said the Nymph, to let you see
> My Actions with your Rules agree;
> That I can vulgar Forms despise,
> And have no Secrets to disguise;
> I knew, by what you said and writ,
> How dang'rous Things were Men of Wit …

(622–7)

Most speech in the poem is either directly quoted or indirectly reported, but after Vanessa argues persuasively that her love is rational, and thus by implication should be reciprocated, the narrator uses free indirect discourse to present Cadenus's private rationalization in what seem his own words. Cadenus

> Insensibly came on her Side:
> It was an unforeseen Event,
> Things took a Turn he never meant.
> Howe'er it came, he could not tell,
> …
> But sure she never talk'd so well.
> His Pride began to interpose;
> Preferr'd before a Crowd of Beaux:
> So bright a Nymph to come unsought,
> Such Wonder by his Merit wrought:
> 'Tis Merit must with her prevail,
> He never knew her Judgment fail:
> She noted all she ever read,
> And had a most discerning Head.

(737–9, 756–65)

Free indirect discourse represents unspoken thoughts, which is why we generally associate it with the emphasis placed on private experience by later novelists. The section of *Cadenus and Vanessa* dealing with Cadenus's reaction to Vanessa's declaration is the most personal part of the poem. I do not mean that it is necessarily the most reliably autobiographical but that it probes internal consciousness, not without irony. Swift announces the transition from free indirect discourse back to direct discourse clearly: "So when Cadenus could not *hide*, / He chose to *justify* his pride" (770–1, my emphasis). This differentiation of what psychologists today call "inner speech" from actual speech is an important part of the poem. In words hidden from all but ourselves, we can rationalize; but in Swift's narrative to try to "justify" is to speak publicly.

Cadenus and Vanessa may be unique for a poem written so early in its sustained use of free indirect discourse (734–65), but its combination of stylistic impetuosity, ironic revelation, and comic exposure of characters through their own words is representative of much eighteenth-century poetry. As in the case of any major work, there is nothing inevitable about the creation of *Cadenus and Vanessa*; its fine achievement seems almost improbable. But it could only have come into being in the eighteenth century and in the tetrameter couplet, the period's uniquely flexible verse form.

Chapter 5

Blank verse and stanzaic poetry

Blank verse   *74*
Stanzaic poems   *81*

Blank verse

It has often been observed that a lot of bad blank verse was written during the eighteenth century, and Milton's influence is usually blamed. It is not often enough observed that a lot of bad blank verse has been written in every period from the Renaissance on, with and without Milton's help. Milton's originality and particular influence lay in having appropriated blank verse for non-dramatic poetry and having written a great epic. His success no doubt influenced many would-be epic poets to flap toward the heavens when they had better stayed at home. But for the reader new to the period, who is in little danger of wading into its failed epics or long poems on agriculture, the question is what to listen for in the major achievements in blank verse by accomplished poets such as James Thomson, Anna Laetitia Barbauld, and William Cowper.

The story of blank verse through much of the eighteenth century is one of growing flexibility, until by the 1780s and 1790s it has grown quiet enough to become a supple and subtle medium for conversational meditation. Although early in the century both the heroic couplet and blank verse were associated with lofty speeches – in epic, heroic drama, and tragedy – the couplet was adapted for conversation much more quickly. It was to couplets, as we have seen, that many writers throughout the century turned for colloquial discourse and couplets that Finch, Parnell, Tollett, Johnson, and Goldsmith adopted for rumination. The best explanation may be Pope's own. Speaking with Joseph Spence in June of 1739, Pope remarked, "I have nothing to say for rhyme, but that I doubt whether a poem can support itself without it in our language, unless it be stiffened with such strange words as are like to destroy our language itself." In other words, blank verse encourages exotic diction and a grandeur at odds with a middle style: "The high style," Pope continues, "that is affected so much in blank verse would not have been borne even in Milton, had not his subject turned so much on strange out-of-the-world things as it does."[1]

The association of blank verse with the stage, with Milton, and thus with sublimity, made conversation difficult. Perhaps Matt Bramble of Smollett's *Humphrey Clinker* (1771) has its grandiloquent associations in mind as he describes young Wilson's response when warned to stop pursuing Liddy: "he replied in blank verse, and a formal challenge ensued." Edward Young seems to have felt that because his long poem *Night-Thoughts* (1742–5) centered on "out-of-the-world things" – the poem's subtitle is "*On Life, Death, and Immortality*" – his blank verse could affect a very high style indeed. Young's verse tends often to be histrionic and self-consciously sublime:

> *This* is the Desert, *this* the Solitude:
> How populous, how vital is the grave!
> *This* is Creation's melancholy Vault,
> The Vale funereal, the sad *Cypress* gloom;
> The land of Apparitions, empty Shades.
>
> (I.115–19)[2]

And it remains heavily influenced by the couplet, often falling into unrhymed two-line epigrams:

> If there is Weight in an ETERNITY,
> Let the *Grave* listen;—and be *graver* still …
>
> (VII.1479–80)

and occasionally even into a rhymed couplet:

> Mark well, as foreign as *These Subjects* seem,
> What close Connection ties them to my Theme.
>
> (VI.234–5)

Night-Thoughts was vastly popular for a century, but its mixture of "graveyard" self-dramatization and Christian didacticism has not worn well since George Eliot dismissed it in 1857 as "egoism turned heavenward." Much of it is better than that, however, and most readers who give it a few hours will at least agree with Samuel Johnson that the "wild diffusion of the sentiments, and the digressive sallies of imagination, would have been compressed and restrained by confinement to rhyme" and that its strength "is not exactness, but copiousness."[3] Although champions of blank verse since Milton have claimed freedom from restraint and confinement, they have not always been able to achieve freedom from bombast and "high style."

Some of the earliest non-dramatic uses of blank verse in the century are in fact parodic, using Miltonic mannerisms for comic effect. In *The Splendid Shilling* (1701, rev. 1705), John Philips sings the woes of a student deep in debt and hounded by the bill collector ("dunn"):

> Thus while my joyless Minutes tedious flow
> With Looks demure, and silent Pace, a *Dunn*,
> Horrible Monster! hated by Gods and Men,
> To my aerial Citadel ascends;
> With Vocal Heel thrice thund'ring at my Gates,
> With hideous Accent thrice he calls ...[4]

But the mock-heroic humor does not prevent Philips from using blank verse seriously a few years later in *Cyder* (1708), a georgic poem on the care of orchards and the making of cider, which, in the manner of Virgil's *Georgics*, is as much about the culture of the nation as about the cultivation of a crop. John Gay follows Philips's hints a year later, in *Wine*, a poem more comic than georgic (perhaps since England is known for drinking wine rather than producing it):

> *Bacchus* Divine, aid my *adventrous* Song,
> That with no middle flight intends to soar.
> Inspir'd *Sublime* on *Pegasean* Wing
> By thee upborn, I draw *Miltonic* Air.

(12–15)

Several decades later, Christopher Smart would turn to blank verse for his georgic, *The Hop-Garden* (1752), announcing that the cultivation of hops is a more proper English subject than viniculture, a lore he will "teach in verse Miltonian."[5]

Not all who chose blank verse followed Milton. As early as 1706 Isaac Watts said that in his own blank verse poems he sought to avoid the breathless length of Milton's sentences "and sometimes of his Parentheses," as well as his "Roughness and Obscurity." Nor would he adopt "Archaisms, Exoticisms, and a quaint Uncouthness of Speech in order to become perfectly *Miltonian*."[6] In *The Seasons*, James Thomson, the most important blank verse poet of the century's first half, usually avoids these peculiarities but not always the temptation to oratorical expansiveness. Thomson often moves from sublime description to patriotic rhetoric, as in this passage on boosting productivity and besting the Dutch in fishing:

> Oh! is there not some Patriot, in whose Power
> That best, that godlike Luxury is plac'd,

Of blessing Thousands, Thousands yet unborn,
Thro' late Posterity? some, large of Soul,
To cheer dejected Industry? to give
A double Harvest to the pining Swain?
…
                    with venturous Oar
How to dash wide the Billow; nor look on,
Shamefully passive while *Batavian* Fleets …
Defraud us of the glittering finny Swarms …[7]

Passages of this kind of high style in *The Seasons* bring to mind Johnson's diagnosis of heroic drama: "Declamation roar'd, while Passion slept."[8] But Thomson achieves a more intimate tone in much of *The Seasons*. In fact, within a few lines of the passage just quoted he turns from British nationalism to the scene at hand, and in doing so turns down the volume:

MEAN-TIME, light shadowing all, a sober Calm
Fleeces unbounded Ether: whose least Wave
Stands tremulous, uncertain where to turn
The gentle Current: while illumin'd wide,
The dewy-skirted Clouds imbibe the Sun,
And through their lucid Veil his soften'd Force
Shed o'er the peaceful World. Then is the Time,
For those whom Wisdom and whom Nature charm,
To steal themselves from the degenerate Croud,
And soar above this little Scene of Things:
To tread low-thoughted Vice beneath their Feet;
To soothe the throbbing Passions into Peace;
And woo lone *Quiet* in her silent Walks.

(Autumn, 955–67)

These lines move more softly for reasons that go beyond diction to syntax and the relation of sentence structure to versification. Of course, words like *soften'd, calm, gentle, soothe*, and *Quiet* (herself) are atmospheric, but they function within two sentences that unfold easily and slowly. The rhetorical questions of the earlier passage give way to declarative utterances. The first (from "Meantime" to "the peaceful World") describes Evening as a collaboration of the sun, ether, and clouds. It builds an elusive but impressive large-scale image phrase by phrase. What we might call the cognitive pacing – the sequence in which information is presented to the reader – is leisurely: a calm breeze 1) lightly shadows the scene ("light" is a punning adverb here) because it 2) "fleeces" the sky (ether) with clouds, which in turn 3) drink up the direct sunlight and then 4) convey ("shed") it in milder form over the landscape. The strong enjambment of the first three lines and the sixth (especially strong owing to the inversion of verb, "shed," following the direct object, "force") nicely reinforces the idea that these things are all happening at once, although we have experienced them sequentially. The second sentence, beginning "Then is the Time," builds on the lovely suspension already established. It moralizes the landscape but does so gently, managing to remain descriptive and to remain a simple declarative sentence despite the opportunities for rhetorical questions and exhortation. (Imagine, instead, "Is not the time / At hand for Britons all …?") Moments like these contribute as much, perhaps more, to the greatness of *The Seasons* as do its howling snowstorm and "repercussive roar" of summer thunder.

Anna Barbauld ranks among the most important writers of blank verse in the later eighteenth century. She is not widely recognized as such, primarily because she is still not known enough generally and because she wrote in so many other forms. But she wrote at least ten accomplished blank verse poems. Seven of these fall within the century proper, ranging from the early *Corsica*, 1769, to what may currently be her most anthologized poem, *Washing Day*, and *To Mr. S. T. Coleridge* (both 1797). Looking at *A Summer Evening's Meditation* will be instructive for three reasons: it is relatively early (1773), distinctly beautiful, and all the more remarkable for its distance from the blank verse poem that seems to have inspired it, Young's *Night-Thoughts*.

Barbauld takes her epigram – "One sun by day, by night ten thousand shine" – from the last of Young's "Nights," a survey of the night sky. Both the precedent of Youngian sublimity and the "aesthetics of the infinite" invariably associated with astronomical prospects might be expected to pull the young poet's verse into rhapsodic excess. Moreover, Barbauld's one earlier work in blank verse, *Corsica*, had flown high in the clouds of public oratory. But in *A Summer Evening's Meditation* and subsequent blank verse poems, Barbauld creates a sense of meditative process and personal discovery:

> 'Tis now the hour
> When Contemplation from her sunless haunts,
> The cool damp grotto, or the lonely depth
> Of unpierc'd woods, where wrapt in solid shade
> She mused away the gaudy hours of noon,
> And fed on thoughts unripen'd by the sun,
> Moves forward; and with radiant finger points
> To yon blue concave swelled by breath divine,
> Where, one by one, the living eyes of heaven
> Awake, quick kindling o'er the face of ether
> One boundless blaze …[9]

(18–28)

With Young as precedent, we might think of Barbauld's blank verse as anti-ep-igrammatic. The first long clause runs over six lines ("'Tis now the hour / When Contemplation … Moves forward"), its periodic construction pulling the reader through the mixture of mildly end-stopped and strongly enjambed lines. Admiration grows but no exclamation points start up, real or virtual. The second half of this excerpt does contain an exclamation and rhetorical questions, but even here Barbauld's voice is intense rather than histrionic, as we can appreciate by juxtaposing lines 42–50 with the passage in Young from which Barbauld drew her epigraph. Here is Young, making his "Moral Survey of the Nocturnal Heavens":

> This Theatre!—what Eye can take it in?
> By what divine Enchantment was it rais'd,
> For Minds of the first Magnitude to launch
> In endless Speculation, and adore?
> *One* Sun by Day; by Night *Ten thousand* shine;
> And light us deep into the DEITY,
> How boundless in Magnificence and Might!
> O what a Confluence of ethereal Fires,
> From Urns un-number'd, down the Steep of Heav'n,
> Streams to a Point, and centres in my Sight?[10]

By comparison, Barbauld's exclamation is muted and her questions less rhetorical:

> Nature's self is hush'd,
> And, but a scatter'd leaf, which rustles thro'
> The thick-wove foliage, not a sound is heard
> To break the midnight air; tho' the rais'd ear,
> Intensely listening, drinks in every breath.
> How deep the silence, yet how loud the praise!
> But are they silent all? or is there not
> A tongue in every star, that talks with man,
> And woos him to be wise?
>
> (42–50)

Whether there is a tongue in every star may not be entirely an open question for the devoutly Unitarian Barbauld. But the question does seem to emerge sometime after the word "breath," in line 46, rather than to have been waiting in the wings all along. As we meet first the deep silence, then the paradox of silence giving praise loudly, then the musing redefinition of terms, we are following a mind in process.

The spontaneity of the mind's processes is the foundational theme of Cowper's greatest long poem, *The Task* (1785), and some of its finest moments trace the movements of consciousness closely. Having said that a fire in the winter parlor is congenial to the "unthinking mind," the poet defends the notion of such a mind against "ye" who "never feel a stupor" – or experience poetic reverie:

> I am conscious, and confess
> Fearless, a soul that does not always think.
> Me oft has fancy ludicrous and wild
> Sooth'd with a waking dream of houses, tow'rs,
> Trees, churches, and strange visages express'd
> In the red cinders, while with poring eye
> I gazed, myself creating what I saw.
> Nor less amused have I quiescent watch'd
> The sooty films that play upon the bars
> Pendulous, and foreboding in the view
> Of superstition prophesying still
> Though still deceived, some stranger's near approach.[11]

This passage colored Coleridge's memory of fire-gazing in *Frost at Midnight* (1798). The film fluttering on the coal grate reminds Coleridge of his "early school-boy days" when with "superstitious wish / Presageful" he "gaz'd upon the bars, / To watch the *stranger* there!"[12]

But here we may look backward from Cowper rather than ahead. The passage from *The Task* shares some of the oratorical proclivity of Young: an oppositional group is conjured up – a wrongheaded "ye" – and confuted. For Young, this group is the grave "foes to song" who regard religious poetry suspiciously. For Cowper it is practical-minded people who imagine they are always thinking and believe everyone else should do likewise. But Cowper seems much less interested in refutation. After the first sentence, the rhetorical opponent immediately fades away and the entertainment of reverie becomes the real subject. After two short sentences, two longer ones explore fireside musing with leisurely expansiveness. By Cowper's "entertainment of reverie" I mean both that he considers it as enjoyment and examines it as an arresting phenomenon. The relation of line to sentence is flexible and relaxed, reinforcing the slight hint of mock-heroic that Cowper often uses in *The Task* to keep his blank verse at ordinary ear-level. The playful Miltonism near the end – the film of flame playing upon "the bars / Pendulous, and foreboding" – is a quietly witty bit of lineation in which "pendulous" *depends* from one line to the next. Wit plays too in the contrast of Latinate words such as "pendulous," "quiescent," "ludicrous," and "superstition" with the homely red cinders and sooty film. A subdued internal dialogue runs through the passage, in which learned disapproval speaks in Latinate diction and folk belief in Anglo-Saxon.

Thomson in his quieter moments, Barbauld, and Cowper help broaden blank verse expectations from those of epic and drama – or, worse, declamatory miniatures of epic and drama – to those of lyric consciousness. The change is one of generic inclusion rather than wholesale migration. Blank verse remained linked to drama and epic, as works by several eighteenth-century and Romantic poets remind us, and Cowper himself used blank verse not only for *The Task* but also for his translations of Homer in the early 1790s. But by then he and others had already done much to create a blank verse unlike any Pope could imagine in the 1730s when he spoke of Milton's "out-of-the-world" idiom. At its best, eighteenth-century blank verse grows as free as rhymed poetry from the "stiffening" of "strange words" and affectations of the "high style," making its music of *in*-the-world things. Edward Young in 1759 grandly proclaimed that "what we mean by blank verse, is verse unfallen, uncurst; verse reclaim'd, reinthron'd in the true *language of the Gods*."[13] Blank verse had to be wrested from the hands of some of its enthusiasts to become the language of men and women.

Stanzaic poems

Although couplet poetry could offer freedom from the constraints of stanzaic patterns, stanza forms continued to offer real attractions. The most common stanzas are quatrains of various kinds. Many poets also used six-line stanzas, and a few poets adopted more intricate stanza forms, such as the Spenserian stanza (eight iambic pentameter lines and a concluding hexameter, rhyming *ababbcbcc*). Those who wrote odes often adopted stanzas of irregular rhyme scheme and line length. Finally, during the second half of the century, the sonnet began to reappear, after more than a century of dormancy. Surveying all of these developments, we need to keep in mind that terminology in the period was fairly loose. "Sonnet" in a poem title *might* mean what we would call a sonnet but often meant merely a short song, just as "ode" might or might not mean a poem with a recognizable Greek or Roman precedent, and "hymn," as we have seen, might or might not mean a poem suitable for singing. A short survey of common forms follows.

Quatrains

Readers will encounter quatrains, usually rhyming *abab*, more frequently than other stanzaic patterns, so I will start with them. The three most important kinds of quatrains are these:

1) the *heroic quatrain*, in iambic pentameter;
2) the *long meter quatrain*, in tetrameter;
3) the *common meter quatrain*, in alternating tetrameter and trimeter.

All three were popular to the end of the century, as illustrated by these opening lines of three poems by Anna Barbauld.

1) Heroic quatrain:

> Yes, injured Woman! rise, assert thy right!
> Woman! too long degraded, scorned, opprest;
> O born to rule in partial Law's despite,
> Resume thy native empire o'er the breast!
>
> (*The Rights of Woman*, c. 1795)

2) Long meter:

> Rise mighty nation! in thy strength
> And deal thy dreadful vengeance round;
> Let thy great spirit rous'd at length,
> Strike hordes of Despots to the ground.
>
> (*On the Expected General Rising of the French Nation in 1792*)

3) Common meter:

> Oh! hear a pensive captive's prayer,
> For liberty that sighs;
> And never let thine heart be shut
> Against the prisoner's cries.
>
> (*The Mouse's Petition*, 1773)

The *heroic quatrain* is not the most common stanza in the eighteenth century ("common meter" does in fact live up to its name), but it may be the most familiar as the building block of the best-known poem of the period, Gray's *Elegy Written in a Country Church Yard*. In fact, the association of the heroic quatrain with Gray's elegy quickly became so strong that it is sometimes called the "elegiac stanza." Just as heroic couplets tend toward slower, statelier movement than tetrameter couplets, so the heroic quatrain can lend itself to more deliberate pacing than quatrains of shorter lines. Oliver Goldsmith declared it the "slowest movement that our language admits of."[14] Barbauld uses it in *The Rights of Woman* more for loftiness than languor, but for Gray the longer pentameter line and the separation of the rhymes by twenty syllables offer a subdued, processional measure:

> The Curfew tolls the knell of parting day,
> The lowing herd wind slowly o'er the lea,

The ploughman homeward plods his weary way,
And leaves the world to darkness and to me.

(Elegy, 1–4)

Much of the sound of this passage derives from resources other than rhyme pattern and line length (for example, the rich alliteration of "w" and repetition of "l" sounds), but let us concentrate on those for the moment. One reason for the sonorous quality of Gray's lines is their lack of clearly marked caesuras. They lack not only guiding punctuation but also the phrasing that alerts readers to internal pauses. Syntax pulls a reader to the end of each line, thus making the break *between* lines more marked. The simple subject-verb-object structure of the first line requires processing as a single unit (the curfew tolls the knell), with just the bare possibility of pausing slightly to assimilate the specification (the knell – of parting day). The same is true of the adverbial phrase (o'er the lea) at the end of the second line, but a reader will feel a slight tension here because two other possibilities are equally attractive. We can take all the adverbial modification as a single piece (slowly o'er the lea) or take the whole predicate together (wind slowly o'er the lea). Something similar occurs in the third line, where the slight complication of structure over line one (now subject-*adverb*-verb-object) does not decisively invite us to pause; yet "plowman homeward plods" is enough of a mouthful to encourage stopping for breath and thus to be in tension with the syntactic flow. Most readers will, I think, respond to the syntax more than to the slight discomfort of reading line 3 through to the end. But having *not* paused there, we are likely to experience the need to pause in line 4 as almost physiological. The resulting performance underscores Gray's solitary voice more effectively than would heavy-handed punctuation or typography. Aided by the delayed but inevitable final rhyme, most readers will produce the fourth line thus: "And leaves the world to darkness—and to **me**."

We will consider other features of Gray's *Elegy* later, but here we can appreciate the cooperation of versification and voice by thinking of the heroic quatrain – like the heroic couplet – as both self-contained and part of a larger whole. The integrity of the whole becomes obvious if we try the experiment of moving any of Gray's quatrains. But it is also important to our reading experience that nearly all of the poem's thirty-two quatrains are syntactically independent, comprising a complete sentence or, typically, two or more parallel sentences:

Full many a gem of purest ray serene
The dark unfathomed caves of ocean bear:

> Full many a flower is born to blush unseen
> And waste its sweetness on the desert air.

(53–6)

Parallelism is as important in Gray's quatrains as in Pope's couplets, but it is given more room to turn in. Gray's parallel units tend to be whole "couplets" (unrhymed), rather than single lines or half-lines:

> Far from the madding crowd's ignoble strife
> Their sober wishes never learned to stray;
> Along the cool sequestered vale of life
> They kept the noiseless tenor of their way.

(73–6)

The extra room may allow for unexpected complication. Each of these two statements about the villagers buried in the churchyard opens with a modifying phrase and then proceeds to subject and predicate. The second sentence sounds so much like the first as to seem merely a reassuring restatement of it. Actually it complicates the first proposition, which is negative (telling us where the villagers did *not* live, even in imagination), by changing perspective and describing what sounded like privation as essentially positive (they *did* live in the "cool sequestered vale").

The relation of voice, syntax, and quatrain versification may be felt by subjecting Joseph Warton's variant heroic quatrain (rhyming *abcb*) to rewriting as heroic couplets. Here is the fourth quatrain from Warton's *Ode to Evening* (a poem Gray knew well):

> To the deep wood the clamorous rooks repair,
> Light skims the swallow o'er the wat'ry scene,
> And from the sheep-cotes, and fresh-furrow'd field,
> Stout plowmen meet to wrestle on the green.

(13–16)

Here is my recasting of it as couplets:

> To the deep wood the clamorous rooks repair,
> Light skims the swallow through the placid air,
> And from the sheep-cotes, and fresh-furrow'd scene,
> Stout plowmen meet to wrestle on the green.

The couplet version of these four lines still comprises three sentences, but the sentences now seem more detached from each other. Without the interlocking rhyme of the second and fourth lines the gathering of the plowmen on the village green feels less integral, less like the completion of a process that began with the birds' movement.

No one *sings* in pentameter, nor even very easily in uninterrupted tetrameter. The heroic quatrain is well suited for slow speech, its long lines bending toward dramatic utterance. *Long meter* sometimes moves more rapidly than pentameter, but it tends to work well in deliberative, meditative contexts. It can be rendered stately enough for elegy, as in this opening quatrain from Collins's *Ode Occasioned by the Death of Mr Thomson* –

> In yonder grave a Druid lies,
>> Where slowly winds the stealing wave!
> The year's best sweets shall duteous rise
>> To deck its poet's sylvan grave!

– or in these lines from Johnson's *On the Death of Dr Robert Levet*:

> When fainting nature call'd for aid,
>> And hov'ring death prepar'd the blow,
> His vig'rous remedy display'd
>> The power of art without the show.
>
> (13–16)

Although many poets declare "I sing" in poems in pentameter and tetrameter, the combinations of tetrameter and shorter trimeter lines called **common meter** are the overwhelming choice for poems that might actually be sung, such as hymns and ballads, and for spoken poems meant to evoke song. At both ends of our period Isaac Watts and William Cowper contribute scores of fine hymns in common meter to English poetry and English piety. This is the opening of Watts's familiar version of Psalm 90:

> Our God, our help in ages past,
>> Our hope for years to come,
> Our shelter from the stormy blast,
>> And our eternal home.

But common meter can readily sing another tune when out of church. Here is the close of a very different work in common meter, David Mallet's *Margaret's Ghost*, in which the guilty lover dreams so vividly of the woman he wronged that he is compelled to visit her grave, with dire results:

> He hyed him to the fatal place,
>> Where Margaret's body lay;
> And stretch'd him on the grass-green turf,
>> That wrapt her breathless clay:
>
> And thrice he call'd on Margaret's name,
>> And thrice he wept full sore:

> Then laid his cheek to her cold grave,
>   And word spake never more.

Mallet's poem is more ballad than hymn. In fact, the term *ballad stanza* is sometimes used interchangeably with *common meter*, but it may also refer specifically to the variant of common meter with the rhyme scheme *abcb*. In this looser form it appears less frequently in literary poetry than in the oral tradition.

In all of these cases the closure of the quatrain is emphatic and significant. The 28 syllables of common meter quatrains (8–6–8–6), the 32 syllables of long meter quatrains (8–8–8–8), or the 40 syllables of heroic quatrains (10–10–10–10) become clear-cut blocks of meaning. Considering couplets in Chapter 2, we saw the importance of being alert simultaneously to the larger unit, the verse paragraph, which may vary greatly in length according to sense and syntax. But in stanzaic poetry there is typically no intermediate larger unit between the rhymed section and the whole poem. The stanza, so to speak, *is* the verse paragraph.

Short observations on longer stanzas

Discussion of eighteenth-century odes often leads to technical considerations of Greek and Roman practices that are unlikely to be of much help or interest to the modern reader not already familiar with Pindar and Horace. As we have seen earlier in the instance of Collins's "ode" on Thomson in simple quatrains or in the tetrameter couplet "odes," the word had acquired a much looser meaning in the period than Ben Jonson or Dryden would have countenanced. Some eighteenth-century odes – Gray's pre-eminently and some of Collins's – are indeed elaborately Pindaric in their stanzaic patterns. But chiefly, a twenty-first-century reader needs to understand that the loftier odes of the eighteenth century were often associated with sublimity, difficulty, abrupt or absent transitions, and distance from ordinary speech. Greek odes were composed for choral performance, probably closer to chanting than actual singing but conspicuously stylized and *un*conversational. What we may miss is that the elaborate stanzas tended to announce themselves to eighteenth-century readers as public, ceremonial poetry. Many of Pindar's odes celebrated Olympic victories. Reading backward to the eighteenth century through Wordsworth's "Intimations Ode" and the odes of Keats and Shelley, the modern reader may expect private rumination where readers of Gray and Collins would have instead been listening for something closer to a collective language of lay liturgy.

As the ode illustrates, a stanzaic form can operate as much through the expectations it arouses in its historical context as through intrinsic properties. The *Spenserian stanza* is an interesting case in point. This invention of Spenser's consists of eight iambic pentameter lines and a ninth in iambic hexameter (a line of six feet, also called an alexandrine). The form was so fully identified with Spenser by the eighteenth century that any poet adopting it immediately announced that he was writing in imitation of *The Faerie Queen* (1590–6). Spenser was much admired in the period, not only by mid-eighteenth-century poets such as Thomas Warton, who in *The Pleasures of Melancholy* (1747) praised him in opposition to Pope, but also by Pope himself. Still, his archaic poetic diction – self-consciously antique even in the 1590s – had come to seem somewhat quaint by the eighteenth century, and to adopt his stanza was usually to adopt the language of his romance, with some humorous sense of incongruity or displacement.

Interestingly, this is a decidedly historical development, which seems not to have yet occurred in the middle of the seventeenth century when Sir Richard Fanshawe published his *Canto of the Progresse of Learning* (1648) in Spenserian stanzas. But when Pope imitated Spenser in his youthful poem *The Alley* (published in 1727 but probably written by 1709), he underscored the disparity between Spenser's poetry and modern reality:

> And on the broken Pavement here and there,
> Doth many a stinking sprat and Herring lie;
> A Brandy and Tobacco Shop is near,
> And Hens, and Dogs, and Hogs are feeding by;
> And here a Sailor's Jacket hangs to dry:
> At ev'ry Door are Sun-burnt Matrons seen,
> Mending old Nets to catch the scaly Fry;
> Now singing shrill, and scolding eft between,
> Scolds answer foul-mouth'd scolds; bad neighbourhood I ween.[15]

Pope uses Spenser here somewhat as T. S. Eliot would two centuries later in *The Waste Land*, to help construct an ironic urban realism. The effect is not really one of parody so much as contrast and dialogue, between poetries of pastoral innocence and polluted experience.

The simplicity and innocence that came to be imputed to Spenser (despite his obvious sophistication as poet and political figure) could be invoked through imitation in the service of nostalgia, quaintness, and mild comedy. William Shenstone's *The School-Mistress. A Poem. In Imitation of Spencer's Stile* (1737, rev. 1742) at once pays homage to and marks its distance from *The Faerie Queen*, as Shenstone constructs the small-village life of his childhood for London readers. Here, frightened children witness a schoolmate's corporal punishment:

> The other Tribe, aghast, with sore Dismay,
> Attend, and conn their Tasks with mickle Care:
> By turns, astony'd, ev'ry Twig survey,
> And, from their Fellow's hateful Wounds, beware;
> Knowing, I wist, how each the same may share;
> Till Fear has taught 'em a Performance meet,
> And to the well-known Chest the Dame repair;
> Whence oft with sugar'd cates she doth 'em greet,
> And Gingerbread y-rare; now, certes, doubly sweet.[16]

This stanza epitomizes Shenstone's attitude toward his village dame, who is recalled with fondness as well as fear but above all as a figure belonging unmistakably to the past, like Spenser.

The two other most interesting Spenserian poems of the century, James Thomson's *Castle of Indolence* (1748) and James Beattie's *The Minstrell* (1771–4), invoke Spenser less for his antiquity than for his association with imagination, sensuous beauty, and magic. Thomson's poem (of which more in Chapter 11) and Beattie's both use Spenser to explore the realm of "Fancy" and poetic creation. *The Minstrell* is a sort of proto-*Prelude* in which the growth of the young Edwin's mind feeds on "Whate'er lore tradition could supply / From Gothic tale, or song, or fable old" – the very elements Beattie means for his Spenserian form to conjure.[17]

A final observation on the importance of associations and expectations in our responses to various stanzas is in order here. If we are predisposed toward certain ways of reading when we see a poem in ballad form, it is not because the ballad stanza *must* carry only certain kinds of poetic experience but because we have read or heard many ballads that share certain subjects and moods. These are matters of convention, not brain circuitry. When a stanza is not so commonly used as to convey any particular expectations, we may respond in very different ways to the same form. A poem's effects are achieved *through* the form adopted, but we should be skeptical about attributing any effects *to* the form itself. One set of examples may illustrate the point.

The six-line stanza that Christopher Smart uses for *A Song to David* in 1763 – with lines of 8, 8, 6, 8, 8, and 6 syllables, rhyming *aabccb* – seems particularly suited for a religiously sublime ode:

> For ADORATION all the ranks
> Of angels yield eternal thanks,
>   And DAVID in the midst;
> With God's good poor, which, last and least
> In man's esteem, thou to thy feast,
>   O blessed bride-groom, bidst.[18]

And in fact the Scottish poet William Mickle would put the same stanza to work in the service of adoration in his *Knowledge. An Ode*. Here the narrator, who has been taking pride in scientific advances, is told by an ancient sage that the stars are a reminder of human limits:

> "Th'immense ideas strike the soul
> With pleasing horror, and controul
>   Thy Wisdom's empty boast,
> What are they?—Thou can'st never say:
> Then silent adoration pay,
>   And be in wonder lost."[19]

But at the beginning of the century Isaac Watts had used the same stanza not for any of his exalted religious poems such as his *The Day of Judgment, An Ode* (1706), but for a poem on marital discord, *Few Happy Matches* (1709), where he saw comic potential in the brisk final line:

> Not minds of melancholy Strain,
> Still silent, or that still complain,
>   Can the dear Bondage bless:
> As well may heav'nly Consorts spring
> From two old Lutes with ne'er a String,
>   Or none besides the Bass.[20]

And in the 1740s Thomas Gray used it in a humorous poem that has been popular since its first appearance, *An Ode on the Death of a Favorite Cat*, a poem that manages to achieve a mock-heroic and poignant tone simultaneously:

> Eight times emerging from the flood
> She mewed to ev'ry watery God,
>   Some speedy aid to send.
> No Dolphin came, no Nereid stirr'd:
> Nor cruel *Tom* nor *Susan* heard.
>   A Fav'rite has no friend![21]

These examples are not meant to imply that any voice is possible in any form. It is hard to imagine an epistolary or didactic poem, for example, succeeding in this lyric stanza, just as it is hard to envision a non-parodic blank verse satire. But the range of possibilities within a given form is always broader than the experience of a few poems would suggest.

Part II

Poetic consciousness

Chapter 6

Satiric poetry

Formal verse satire   95
Pope's *Epistle to Dr. Arbuthnot* and Swift's *Verses on the Death of Dr. Swift*   100
Formal verse satire after Pope: Samuel Johnson, Mary Jones, Mary Leapor, Charles Churchill, William Cowper   *107*

The term "satiric poetry" seems preferable to "verse satire" as a general rubric for the major poetic satires of the eighteenth century because "verse" now usually implies something less than genuine poetry, as in "light verse." That latter category will hardly contain poems such as Dryden's *MacFlecknoe* or *Absalom and Achitophel*, most of Pope's work, Johnson's *London* and *Vanity of Human Wishes*, and several others to be considered here. "Satiric poetry" challenges the suggestion that poetry and satire are mutually exclusive and insists on the status of the works as poems, on the same model as "elegiac poetry" or "lyric poetry." By doing so we can best approach our subject as a kind of poetry – appreciating it fundamentally as poetry that shares many of the resources of other kinds of eighteenth-century poetry – rather than as satire that happens to have been poured into a poetic mold. Satiric poetry is most usefully seen as part of a poetic continuum.

Enough of the period's most interesting poems take the form of satire to call for sustained attention to this poetic variety and for at least a working definition of satire as we proceed. Of the scores of books on satire, one of the few to offer a concise definition is *Swift and the Satirist's Art* by Edward W. Rosenheim, Jr., and it seems to me the most satisfactory: "satire consists of an attack by means of a manifest fiction upon discernible historic particulars." Somewhat surprisingly, Rosenheim does not include the word "comic," which quickly comes to mind in thinking of many satires. But in his view, the element of "manifest fiction" – that is, fiction meant to be recognized as such – differentiates satiric works from straightforward attacks, just as the inclusion of "historic particulars" differentiates satires from criticism of universal human

limitations. Rosenheim posits a "satiric spectrum," recognizing the large differences in tone, for example, between mild "persuasive" satires and harsh
"punitive" ones.[1] We might also recognize that some works lean more heavily
on particulars than others (Pope's *Dunciad* compared to Johnson's *The Vanity
of Human Wishes*, for example), and that the fictional element might be a full-
blown narrative or merely conspicuous exaggeration.

The problem of whether to consider satire a mode or a genre is complicated
not only by the heterogeneity of the works we call satire but also by the difficulty of defining "mode" and "genre" themselves. We can get only so far with
the distinction that a mode is a manner or attitude (as we might speak of a
satiric tone, for instance), while a genre is a distinct kind of literature, usually
with recognizable formal features (prose narrative, say). In many cases, the
boundaries between tone, subject matter, and even medium can blur. Increasingly, critics prefer to think of genre as a set of reading conventions and readers'
expectations rather than formal properties of a work itself. This reorientation
has the advantage of recognizing the social dimension of literary experience:
the person picking up a comedy or a detective story brings to the experience
expectations and kinds of attention that have been learned culturally – from
others and through time. No reader is an island, and eighteenth-century readers came to poems, including satiric poems, with historically shaped generic
expectations.

These questions bear on eighteenth-century satiric poetry particularly
because one of its two major branches is indeed a genre of its own, while the
other branch comprises various "paragenres." The prefix "para" means "beside,"
and I include under this latter term various kinds of satiric poems that respond
to pre-existent genres, often as parodies ("para" + "ode," originally an ode put
next to another one). The branch of satiric poetry that is its own genre is *formal verse satire*, largely a Roman invention. This is the kind of writing the
Roman rhetorician Quintilian (*c.* 35–100 CE) seems to have had in mind when
he wrote "*satura quidem tota nostra est*," that is, satire at least is entirely ours,
or, only satire is a Roman invention, rather than something inherited from
the Greeks.[2] Its most influential practitioners for English authors were Horace
(65–27 BCE) and Juvenal (*c.* 60–130 CE), although many scholars argue for
the importance of Persius (34–62 CE) as well. Their poems are usually in the
first person, combining exposition and episode. Such narrative as they contain
is anecdotal rather than sustained. The first-person speaker of these works is
better regarded performatively than confessionally, a persona rather than a
strictly autobiographical subject. The performance may in fact include several
versions of a self (as we saw in Pope's epistolary poetry), despite the satirist's
typical insistence on his simplicity and integrity. Roman formal verse satires

tend to be inflected by the language of the city street, their typical setting, and the temporal frame is typically the present historical moment, not the heroic Back Then of epic or the Timeless Now of lyric.

Quintilian could speak of this satire as "ours" because there was no non-dramatic poetry quite like it. By the beginning of the eighteenth century Horace and Juvenal had been translated and imitated several times, and Dryden and others had written thoughtful criticism distinguishing their voices and themes, thus helping promote formal verse satire to a higher literary status than it enjoyed in the Renaissance. But the other main branch of satiric poetry that flourishes in the Restoration and eighteenth century, the "mock" form, is often distinctive not for being unlike other kinds but by being so conspicuously *like* several genres that are officially more prestigious. We find satires that are like epics, like pastoral eclogues, like georgics, adopting parodically the kinds of diction and conventions appropriate to the other genres. They may contain more sustained narrative, and the first-person speaker tends to disappear or greatly recede. The two greatest narrative poetic satires of the period are *The Rape of the Lock* and *The Dunciad*, both mock-heroics. Since I discuss these poems at some length elsewhere in this book, this chapter will concentrate on the particular eighteenth-century achievement of first-person satiric poetry.

Formal verse satire

Dryden's comparison of Horace and Juvenal in his "Discourse concerning the Original [origin] and Progress of Satire" (1693) set the terms in which they were often opposed: Horace's "urbanity, that is, his good manners, are to be commended; but his wit is faint, and his salt, if I may dare to say so, almost insipid. Juvenal is of a more vigorous and masculine wit; he gives me as much pleasure as I can bear."[3] Horace's satires are said by most eighteenth-century observers to contain more raillery and Juvenal's more railing, Horace's to philosophize and Juvenal's to castigate, Horace's to laugh at follies from the perspective of an insider and Juvenal's to declaim against crimes from the vantage of alienation. But this contrast represents both authors at their extremes, as many writers recognized, and modern classicists still debate how to read the tone of these satirists. Both exhibit great range, from earthiness to Socratic dialogue in Horace's case, from scatological misogyny (*Satire* VI) to reflective sublimity (*Satire* X) in Juvenal's. One measure of the complexity of their influence is the fact that while Horace became the subject of Pope's important "Imitations" in the 1730s, in these same poems Pope would increasingly proclaim the inadequacy of Horatian "delicacy," as he came to assume a Juvenalian position of internal exile in the face of "Vice Triumphant."

The labels "Horatian" and "Juvenalian" matter less to the modern reader than one's recognition that satiric poetry meant a range of attitudes and topics to eighteenth-century writers and readers, extending from comic sociability to near-tragic isolation. The Horatian stance was by far the more popular, but Juvenal was, as we will see, an important model for Johnson, Charles Churchill, and William Cowper. The success of both Pope's direct imitations of Horace and his other poems in Horace's manner (the group of "Epistles to Several Persons" or "Moral Essays") was so great that after the 1730s it is difficult to separate Horace's influence from Pope's. Thus it may be instructive to turn to an earlier example of the Horatian mode, Edward Young's group of seven satires in Horace's manner, begun in 1725 and collected in 1728 as *Love of Fame. The Universal Passion. In Seven Characteristical Satires.*[4]

Although Young draws the thematic epigraph for his satires from Juvenal – *Tanto major Famae sitis est, quam Virtutis*: "so much greater is the thirst for fame than for virtue" (*Satire* X.140) – he immediately invokes as his model Horace, the "courtly Roman" who was "severely kind" and could "sharply smile prevailing Folly dead" (I.44–6). The word "characteristical" in Young's title does not mean that the poems sum up the age (although Young probably thought they did) but that they are built of type portraits or character sketches.[5] Some of these satiric sketches are psychologically ambitious and probably influenced Pope's practice a few years later in his satiric epistles. Most use fictional, generic names and depict foolish rather than vicious behavior. Here is a portrait of a book collector, "Codrus," more interested in interior decoration than reading. (Epictetus was a Stoic philosopher, Jacob Tonson a leading London book publisher.)

> With what, O Codrus! is thy fancy smit?
> The flower of learning, and the bloom of wit.
> Thy gaudy shelves crimson bindings glow,
> And Epictetus is a perfect beau.
> How fit for thee, bound up in crimson too,
> Gilt, and, like them, devoted to the view!
> Thy books are furniture. Methinks 'tis hard
> That science should be purchased by the yard;
> And Tonson, turn'd upholsterer, send home
> The gilded leather to "fit up" thy room.
>
> (II.57–66)

As is frequently the case in Horace's poems, the satiric "I" himself is not beyond criticism. Young's speaker concedes that he shares the "universal passion." He not only loves fame irrationally but pursues it foolishly:

what wise means to gain it hast thou chose?
Know, Fame and Fortune both are made of prose.
Is thy ambition sweating for a rhyme,
Thou unambitious fool, at this late time?
While I a moment name, a moment's past;
I'm nearer death in this verse than the last:
What, then, is to be done? Be wise with speed;
A fool at forty is a fool indeed.

(II.273–80)

Mary Leapor picks up Young's theme two decades later in *An Epistle to Arte-mesia. On Fame* and deepens the wit of self-implication. "Mira," as Leapor calls herself, smiles at the "Slaves of Fame" around her who seek distinction, while acknowledging that she, too, "presuming on the Bays" (the poet's laurel wreath), "Appears among the Candidates for Praise" (63–4).[6] In this and several other poems, Leapor insists on her right as a woman to write, while creating a comic dialogue that includes herself in the social satire:

Then comes *Sophronia*, like a barb'rous *Turk*:
"You thoughtless Baggage, when d'ye mind your Work?
...
Go, ply your Needle: You might earn your Bread;
Or who must feed you when your Father's dead?"
She sobbing answers, "Sure, I need not come
To you for Lectures; I have store at home.
What can I do?"
          "—Not scribble."
                    "—But I will."
"Then get thee packing—and be aukward still."

(153–4, 157–62)

Leapor's portrait of herself as yet another poet who cannot help but "scribble" endows her with the same sort of compulsiveness ("But I will") that marks those depicted in other comical sketches. But her readiness to include herself in the parade also helps indirectly to heighten her polite credibility among her "barb'rous" neighbors. The poem ends with some of those neighboring women visiting Leapor and asking to read her work in manuscript – for want of something better to do on a rainy day. Again, the speaker who is able to recognize her own comic role automatically assumes more reliability than the characters around her who lack perspective and any capacity for irony.

This Horatian combination of self-deprecation and self-promotion is central to countless formal verse satires in the eighteenth century, and failure to recognize its conventionality has often led later readers to overly earnest responses to the genre. Thus, many Victorian and early twentieth-century readers have expected straightforward autobiography in Pope's *Epistle to Dr. Arbuthnot* or Swift's *Verses on the Death of Dr. Swift*, for example, and have been disappointed by "inconsistency" or "insincerity," rather than taking pleasure in rhetorical inventiveness. Before looking more closely at those most iconic satiric poems, we may get a fuller idea of what following Horace could mean for the creation of a satiric "I" by comparing one of Pope's imitations of Horace with a stricter verse translation. The first passage is the opening of Thomas Creech's translation (1684) of Horace's *Satire* II.i (the first satire of the second book). I have inserted "P." and "T." (for Poet and Trebatius) to make the dialogue easier to follow and compare with Pope's freer version. Here is Creech:

> [P.] Some Fancy I am bitter when I jeer
> Beyond the Rules of Satyr too severe;
> Some that my Verse is dull and flat, and say,
> A Man may write a Thousand such a day.
> What shall I do *Trebatius?*
> [T.]   *Why give o're,*
> *Thy scribling humor check, and write no more*:
> [P.] The Counsel's good, and oh that I could choose,
> But I can't sleep for my unruly Muse:
> [T.] *Why then (for that will lay a rambling Head)*
> *Go always tir'd, or else go drunk to Bed.*
> *Or if you needs must write, go raise thy Fame,*
> *By Caesar's Wars, for that's a noble Theme,*
> *And that will get Thee Wealth and an Esteem.*[7]

Creech translates Horace closely, sometimes in the manner Dryden called *metaphrase*, that is, "turning an author word by word, and line by line, from one language to another," and sometimes in *paraphrase*, by which Dryden means "translation with latitude." Translation with *attitude* might best describe *imitation*, the freest mode; Dryden described it as "where the translator (if now he has not lost that name) assumes the liberty, not only to vary from the words and sense, but to forsake them both as he sees occasion."[8]

Pope's *imitation* of this satire expands, modernizes, and personalizes from the start. Creech rendered Horace's eleven and a half lines in thirteen lines, a feat of economy given the longer Latin line. Pope expands this part to twenty-two lines, finding counterparts (his lawyer friend, William Fortescue, replaces Horace's Trebatius, for example), and broadening the poem's range of "historical particulars."[9] I indicate the essentially new material by bold type, although the distinction between old and new is not always perfect:

P. There are (I scarce can think it, but am told)
There are to whom my Satire seems too bold,
Scarce to wise *Peter* complaisant enough,
And something said of *Chartres* much too rough.
The lines are weak, another's pleas'd to say,
Lord *Fanny* spins a thousand such a day.
Tim'rous by nature, of the Rich in awe,
I come to Council learned in the Law.
You'll give me, like a friend **both sage and free,**
Advice; **and (as you use) without a Fee.**
F. I'd write no more.
P.   Not write? but then I *think*,
And for my Soul I cannot sleep a wink.
I nod in Company, I wake at Night,
Fools rush into my Head, and so I write.
F. **You could not do a worse thing for your Life.**
Why, if the Nights seem tedious—**take a Wife**:
Or rather truly, if your Point be Rest,
Lettuce and Cowslip Wine; *Probatum est.*
But talk with *Celsus*, *Celsus* may advise
Hartshorn, or something that shall close your Eyes.
Or if you needs must write, write CAESAR's praise:
You'll gain **at least a *Knighthood*, or the *Bays*.**

The first Dublin printing footnoted "Lord *Fanny*" as "Lord H—y," that is, Lord John Hervey, the courtier who within weeks would collaborate with Lady Mary Wortley Montagu in attacking Pope and who would reappear as Sporus two years later in *An Epistle to Dr. Arbuthnot.* Many readers would have recognized Peter as Walter Peter, a rapacious money lender, who would later appear as Peter Pounce in Henry Fielding's *Joseph Andrews* (1742), and Chartres as Francis Charteris, a notorious gambler and rapist, who could also be seen leering out of the doorway in the first plate of William Hogarth's *Harlot's Progress* (1732). Not all of the added lines are topical: "Celsus," for example, is not in Horace, but he was a Roman physician. Pope imagines more detailed prescriptions, including sexual intercourse with a wife rather than simply getting tired (Creech) or swimming the Tiber (Horace) for calming the sleepless body. That mock prescription fits the unmarried Pope, as, with varying degrees of irony, do the jokes about being in awe of the rich (Pope had several aristocratic friends all his life), not paying his lawyer (the old friend Fortescue is being paid in verse), and nodding in company during the day (Pope reportedly dozed off once while speaking with the Prince of Wales).[10] While Horace writes simply because he can't sleep at night, Pope writes because "Fools rush into" his mind and inspire satire. Fortescue suggests the practice is unhealthy, even dangerous ("for your life"). The increased specificity in the last line of elevation to "Knighthood" or the "Bays" of the Poet Laureate brings the generalized "rewards" (*praemia*) of Horace or "wealth" and "esteem" of Creech into the corrupt patronage world of Sir Robert Walpole's administration.

In the Horatian formal verse satire Pope finds a means of combining genial self-characterization, ethical conversation, and social engagement. Imitating freely and usually expanding the Horatian originals by half or more, Pope invokes the weight of classical tradition even while writing poems dense with contemporaneity. The titles of each of his several Imitations of Horace and their method of publication, with the Latin original on the verso, keep the act of "translation" steadily in view, while the English – and London – particulars on the recto invite the reader's continual alertness to parallels and departures. This rhetorical position has great potential strength. The poet can persuade both because he is following a revered classical author and because he is not. He is reliable, in other words, as one who senses strongly the force of both tradition and change. Swift found Horace attractive for similar reasons, imitating one of his epistles and two of his satires (as well as three of his odes). One of the satires is the work we have been examining, *Satire* II.i, which Swift imitated more freely and selectively than did Pope, and the other is the first part of *Satire* II.vi, an imitation that Pope later completed. Imitation does not play as large a part in Swift's poetic career as in Pope's, but Horace frequently influences Swift's original poetry, as he of course does Pope's. Arguably, the two most significant Horatian formal verse satires of the eighteenth century are not direct imitations but poems informed by the practice of imitation. These works, in which two great satirists reflect on their work, invite comparison.

Pope's *Epistle to Dr. Arbuthnot* and Swift's *Verses on the Death of Dr. Swift*

These two virtuoso poems are the work of writers who had long been in the public eye and who undertake to set the record straight. Pope characterizes his *Epistle to Dr. Arbuthnot* (1735) as a "Sort of Bill of Complaint, begun many years since, and drawn up by snatches, as the several Occasions offer'd." He insists he "had no thoughts of publishing it, till it pleas'd some Persons of Rank and Fortune ... to attack in a very extraordinary manner, not only my Writings (of which being publick the Publick may judge) but my *Person, Morals,* and *Family*, whereof to those who know me not, a truer Information may be requisite." Swift's *Verses on the Death of Dr. Swift* (1739) appears with no autobiographical preface, only the information in the subtitle that the poem was "Written by Himself, November 1731" and an epigraph announcing that the poem was "Occasioned by reading a Maxim in Rochfoulcault. *Dans l'adversité de nos meilleurs amis nous trouvons quelque chose, qui ne nous deplaist pas.*" Swift first translates these words of Duc François de la Rochefoucauld (1613–80) in prose – "In the Adversity of our best Friends, we find something that doth not displease us" – and then more jauntily in verse:

> "In all Distresses of our Friends
> We first consult our private Ends,
> While Nature kindly bent to ease us,
> Points out some Circumstance to please us."[11]

The first seventy lines of Swift's poem comprise a "proem" in which he illustrates the justness of Rochefoucauld's estimate of human nature. While Pope's poem will argue that his attackers too think only of their "private ends," his epistle posits a norm of disinterested virtue that he, his friend Arbuthnot, his parents, and a few others live up to. Interestingly, the egocentric orientation of La Rochefoucauld, whose *Maximes* were first published in 1665 and translated into English five years later, seems to have been one of the few philosophical questions on which Pope and Swift disagreed. When in 1725, perhaps having already begun *An Essay on Man*, Pope confided to Swift that he was "writing a Set of Maxims in opposition to all Rochefoucaults Principles," Swift replied that La Rochefoucauld has been his "Favorite because I found my whole character in him."[12] He adds that he "will read him again because it is possible I may since have undergone some alterations." Since he writes a few days before his fifty-eighth birthday, presumably Swift speaks playfully of changes of character. In any case, he seems not to have altered six years later, when *Verses on the Death of Dr. Swift* is supposed to have been written, or fourteen years later, when it appeared with La Rochefoucauld leading the way.

The maxim Swift quotes is characteristic of La Rochefoucauld's emphasis on self-love, and other maxims – such as "We have all of us strength enough to bear the misfortunes of other People" and "Self-Love is of all Flatterers the greatest" – influence the *Verses*.[13] We might expect that a poem based on La Rochefoucauld would be more pessimistic than one by a writer who saw the *Maximes'* psychology of self-love as too reductive, but that is not really the effect. Selfishness, pettiness, envy, and malevolence abound in both poems, and enemies to the independence and integrity of the poet-satirists lurk everywhere. These may seem less of a threat in Swift's poem than in Pope's because *Verses on the Death of Dr. Swift* contains more comedy, but in both poems the poet triumphs over his malingers. Part of the joke of Swift's poem is that the poet lives on by dying, but in fact both poems are constructed not only as apologias for their authors' lives but as posthumous monuments. This feature of the poems is underscored by the authors' own footnotes, many of which are written as a historical record for posterity.

We might expect, too, that a poem illustrating egoism might be more of an unbroken monologue than one proceeding from different principles. But nearly two-thirds of the lines in Swift's *Verses* are spoken by other characters. The poem can be divided into five sections:

1. "Proem" pondering La Rochefoucauld's maxim (1–72)
2. Reactions to his illness (73–150, "The time is not remote …")
3. Reactions to his death (151–244, "Behold the fatal day …")
4. Literary reputation a year later (245–98, "One year is past …")
5. "My character impartial" (an auto-eulogy, 299–484, "Suppose me dead …")

Following the argumentative proem, the middle sections (lines 73–298) are stages in a dramatic comedy, moving through imagined responses to Swift's final illness and death to a scene a year later in which the bookseller Bernard Lintot tells a would-be purchaser that Swift's works are now too unfashionable to keep in stock. Then comes a displaced monologue spoken by a supposedly "impartial" speaker who eulogizes Swift for some 178 lines.[14] The counterpart to this section in Pope's *Epistle* is the concluding eighty-six lines, beginning immediately after the portrait of Sporus, cast as the poet's opposite. No one doubts that Pope's grand conclusion is straightforward in purpose, but Swift's has given rise to curious debates about authorial control and ironic intention. The basic problem is reflected in the poem's textual history. Swift sent the work to an English friend, William King, to oversee its publication. King, who consulted with Pope, cut much of Swift's final section, defending his action partly on the ground that the speech "might be considered by the public a little vain, if so much were said by himself of himself."[15] Much displeased with the changes, Swift immediately had his Irish publisher issue a version with the eulogy restored, which is the version now read.

King's judgment of the section as "a little vain" is remarkably understated, unless taken to be ironic. Much modern criticism has taken Swift to be ironic. The tide turned most explicitly in this direction in the early 1960s with an article by Barry Slepian. Slepian argued that King, Pope, and Swift's later editors and commentators had overlooked the appropriateness of a vain conclusion in a poem about vanity. Swift was – ironically – proving the point by including himself in the parade of self-love. More recently, Stanley Fish used this turning point in Swift criticism to argue that literary interpretations are unstable, historically conditioned, and unpredictable. This episode refutes those who might like to think that some interpretive points are self-evident and immovable, Fish claims. Mistaken theorists of "stable" irony (such as Wayne Booth) may need to believe "that there be at least some works of which it can be said that they are indisputably either straightforward or ironic" and have "always been read" as one or the other. But the reception history of Swift's *Verses* shows their naïveté: "Here, however, is a work or part of work that until 1963 was considered ironic by nobody, and since 1963 has been considered ironic by nearly everybody."[16]

Fish overstates the case. Some early readers seem to have found the poem as a whole ironic. William Hazlitt in 1818 pointed to "not only a dry humour" but also "an exquisite tone of irony" in Swift's *Verses* and his imitations of Horace. And many critics since 1963 have either questioned whether Swift meant for the eulogy to be read ironically or what such a reading amounts to. Are we to assume that Swift somehow did *not* seriously regard himself as an honest citizen, good churchman, justified satirist, and defender of Irish liberty? Irony may be one way of explaining how Swift can profess that as a satirist he "lash'd the Vice, but spar'd the Name" (460) when he not only named many names in several of his works but in *this* work, or how he can claim absolute originality in a couplet – "To steal a Hint was never known, / But what he writ was all his own" (317–18) – that echoes one from a seventeenth-century poet he knew well: "To him no Author was unknown, / Yet what he wrote was all his own" (Sir John Denham, "On Mr. Abraham Cowley," lines 30–1). Irony is certainly a better explanation than blind egocentrism or incipient senility, but invoking it as if it somehow undercut or qualified everything has the great drawback of robbing impassioned lines like these of any truth claim:

> "With Princes [he] kept a due Decorum;
> But never stood in Awe before 'em.
> He follow'd David's Lesson just,
> *In princes never put thy trust.*
> And, would you make him truly sower,
> Provoke him with *a slave in Power*:
> The *Irish* Senate if you nam'd,
> With what Impatience he declaim'd!
> Fair Liberty was all his Cry;
> For her he stood prepar'd to die;
> For her he boldly stood alone;
> For her he oft expos'd his own."

(339–50)

One advantage of reading Swift's *Verses* as a satiric *poem* is that we may come to it readier to accept and respond to the ambiguity, complexity, and indeterminacy that characterize many kinds of poems, rather than approaching it as an autobiographical satire that just happens to rhyme.

It is no longer the fashion to treat Pope's *Epistle to Dr. Arbuthnot* as supposedly straight autobiography marred by reprehensible insincerity. Since the 1950s and Maynard Mack's influential essay "The Muse of Satire," students of Pope have generally acknowledged the importance of rhetoric and of distinguishing between Pope and the poem's speaker – or actually speakers. Mack identified three personas assumed in the poem: 1) an *ingénu* or *naif*, 2) a man of plain living or *vir bonus*, and 3) a hero or public defender.[17] While the second and third personas also loom large in Swift's *Verses* (especially in the "impartial" portrait), Pope's poem differs in combining these personas with that of the simple man who can't help but be offended by vice and isn't prudent enough to keep quiet about it.

The *Epistle* also differs from Swift's poem in being a direct response to personal attacks, the most immediate co-authored by Lord Hervey, the poem's Sporus. Much has been written about the vehemence of this climactic character sketch (lines 305–33), some of the most disapproving remarks made by critics who seem not to have read the Hervey–Montagu *Verses Address'd to the Imitator of Horace*. But more to the point here than who struck the first – or lowest – blow is the way the poem's major portraits shape the poem's architecture. Like Swift's *Verses*, the *Epistle Arbuthnot* falls into a five-part structure. Yet unlike Swift, who announces his changes of scene and topic explicitly, Pope moves to a new topic more implicitly and gradually. Finer divisions could be made, but this general framework allows analysis and comparison:

1. Depiction of Pope's present (besieged) situation (1–124)
2. Pope's history (125–230)
3. Present situation of the poet in society (231–60)
4. Pope's ethical artistic program (261–367)
5. Assertion of human over literary values (368–419).

After the first part, which we might consider analogous to Swift's "proem," each section is dominated by a major portrait. The Atticus sketch (193–214), usually taken to represent Joseph Addison, dominates section two. Most of the third part is the portrait of Bufo (231–48), a composite character whose debased patronage epitomizes an unhealthy literary climate. The Sporus portrait (305–33), denouncing attractive vice in high places (through the character of Lord Hervey), shows satire at its most indignant, and it contrasts immediately with the virtuous and more "manly" portraits of Pope himself (334–59) in the fourth section and of his father (388–405) in the fifth section.

The psychological complexity and arrangement of Pope's character sketches lie at the heart of his poetic satire, as they do in his other most popular formal verse satire, the *Epistle to a Lady*. Swift could write strong character sketches, but in *Verses on the Death of Dr. Swift* he favors crudely representative groups rather than emblematic individuals. Instead of individual motivation, Swift's poem gives deliberately broad-brush stereotypes, in harmony with the fast-paced, tumbling tetrameters. In contrast, a close look at Pope's Atticus ("Willing to wound, and yet afraid to strike") or Sporus ("His wit all see-saw between *that* and *this* / … And he himself one vile Antithesis") shows how their psychologies develop through the slower and fuller parallelisms of the heroic couplet.[18]

Swift's use of groups makes possible great dramatic comedy, as in the card-table conversation conducted "in *doleful Dumps*, / 'The Dean is dead (*and what is Trumps?*')", or in the imagined crowd scenes (79–116, 147–64), where nearly every couplet could be spoken by a different "friend." The interchange-ability of reactions tends to reinforce the sense of a collective "they" in contrast with whom the honest satirist is defined ("And then their Tenderness appears / By adding largely to my Years" [105–6]). Of course, Pope also portrays him-self as outnumbered by a nearly overwhelming group, from the mock-heroic cadre of bad authors ready to besiege the poet whether he travels by road or river – "They stop the chariot, they board the barge" (10) – to the accumulat-ing crowd of named attackers who make up the "race that write" (219). The babbling voices contrast ethically with the steadfast voice of the satirist, but at the same time the crowd's boisterous polyphony provides much of the energy of both satires. We can say that the antagonistic "they" of the poems perform three essential services: they provide a plausible motivation for the satirist's impatience, they keep the formal verse satire from becoming an unrelieved sermon, and they constitute the chaotic "other" from which the formal satir-ist's coherent integrity emerges.

Because both of these poems are somewhat autobiographical and because we tend to be somewhat obsessively interested in self-representation, crit-ical attention naturally focuses on the poets' defense of themselves. But it is important to notice that both poems are defenses of satire, not simply defenses of the satirist; or perhaps more accurately, they defend the satirist by show-ing how important satire is. They do so in many ways, such as attacking cor-ruption at high levels (Pope's Hervey and Swift's Walpole both have the king's ear, for example) and insisting upon satire's commitment to truth. Pope makes a pair of resonant distinctions in a single line when he attacks disingenuous misreaders who "with a lust to misapply, / Make Satire a lampoon, and Fiction lye" (301–2). The first distinction is one Dryden and other satirists had insisted upon in arguing that they were attacking more than a single individual.[19] The second, more profound distinction goes back to arguments like Sir Philip Sidney's, in the *Defence of Poesie* (1595), defending poets from the charge of lying on the ground that they do not actually claim to tell the truth: the poet "nothing affirmeth, and therefore never lieth." But Sidney's defense runs the risk of giving the poet immunity at the cost of reducing poems to beautiful fables, and thus may not be very useful for a satiric poet. In the context of this poem, part of the later satiric work in which Pope has "stoop'd to Truth" (341), Pope's discrimination between fiction and lie implies that a good fiction may do more than, in Sidney's terms, present a golden world instead of the brazen one of reality. Pope and Swift, like other writers of formal verse satire, make strong truth claims for poetry's representation of the real world. The world of satire is brazen, though "Truth" is the gold standard in rendering it.

Both Pope and Swift reinforce the truth claims of their satires through extensive footnoting. The modern reader needs these author's notes not only to help make sense of some parts of the poems (where we are often helped, too, by editors' notes) but also to make whole sense of them as poetic satires. Both poets present their poems as true histories of their age, in contrast to the paid, partisan prose everywhere else. Pope footnotes sparely in this poem compared to his practice in *The Dunciad*, but several of his notes are written, like Swift's, as a history for future generations, and they are essential to the claims of truth-telling in his later poetry. Swift's notes especially extend the satire of his *Verses*, a fact often obscured for modern readers, since some of the notes are so extensive that recent editors have cut them altogether or shortened them confusingly.

For example, here is Swift's note on the lines (191–6) where he imagines the reaction of "Bob" to his death:

> Sir Robert Walpole, *Chief Minister of State, treated the* Dean *in* 1726, *with great Distinction, invited him to Dinner at* Chelsea, *with the* Dean's *Friends chosen on Purpose, appointed an Hour to talk with him of* Ireland, *to which* Kingdom *and* People, *the* Dean *found him no great Friend; for he defended* Wood's *Project of Half-Pence, &c. The* Dean *would see him no more, and upon his next Year's return to* England, *Sir* Robert *on an accidental Meeting, only made a civil Compliment, and never invited him again.*

Readers of many editions and anthologies, including the widely-used *Norton Anthology of English Literature*, will learn only that Bob equals Walpole. Readers of the popular *Longman Anthology of British Literature* will fare better but will not find the clause about Wood's coinage project or the words following "see him no more." The first editorial elision omits Swift's reference to the historical episode in Anglo-Irish relations that gave rise to his pamphlets written in the persona of an Irish "drapier" (or cloth merchant), while the second leaves the reader with a stronger impression of Swift's haughtiness than of his desire to document Walpole's cold calculation for the historical record.

These two poems and many lesser formal verse satires exhibit a difficult balance of centrifugal and centripetal tendencies. The centripetal force is everything that helps the poem cohere, in structure, tone, and consistency of imagery. The centrifugal force is the continual pull of poetic satire toward "historical particulars" and toward insisting on poetry's referential duty and scope. For many later eighteenth-century authors of formal verse satire, this balance becomes more difficult to maintain. Another, related equilibrium that becomes more precarious is that of the Horatian speaker confident of satire's place and his own. We turn now to five formal verse satirists who, imaginatively and chronologically, follow Pope.

Formal verse satire after Pope: Samuel Johnson, Mary Jones, Mary Leapor, Charles Churchill, William Cowper

Formal verse satires and other first-person satiric poems continue to be written in the later half of the century, but they begin to show more uncertainty and strain in the decades following the death of Pope and Swift (1744, 1745). Samuel Johnson's two ambitious ventures into poetic satire help characterize significant tensions.

London (1738) and *The Vanity of Human Wishes* (1749), loose imitations of Juvenal's third and tenth satires, suggest the difference between the politically charged verse satire of the earlier period and a more diffuse mode that one of Johnson's modern biographers refers to as "satire *manqué*" (frustrated or failed satire). *London*, published anonymously, was immediately praised by Pope, whose political indignation it shares. Johnson's speaker through most of the poem is a man about to leave London, a corrupt capital now best suited for compliant courtiers, French flatterers, and assorted beneficiaries of "publick crimes" – a place where "in these degen'rate Days" the honest, poor, outspoken satirist does not stand a chance. Juvenal had of course complained about the corruptions of Rome in Johnson's model, and cities tend to fare badly in satire generally. But Johnson took pride in "adapting Juvenal's Sentiments to modern facts and Persons," and he grounds his poem unmistakably in the England

of the 1730s. As the capital of a "cheated" and "sinking" nation, London epitomizes Walpolean corruption. The evils of what the speaker sarcastically calls
"this discerning Age" are systemic but not inevitable. England has not always
had a government at war with its own people:

> A single Jail, in Alfred's golden Reign,
> Could half the Nation's Criminals contain;
> Fair Justice, then, without Constraint ador'd,
> Sustain'd the Ballance, but resign'd the sword;
> No Spies were paid, no *Special Juries* known,
> Blest Age! but ah! how diff'rent from our own![20]

To recall Rosenheim's definition of satire, *London*'s "attack" lands squarely
"upon discernible historic particulars."

The Vanity of Human Wishes, on the other hand, repeatedly goes beyond
its Juvenalian source in elevating the general over the topical, locating unhap-
piness in the human condition rather than in historical conditions. Johnson
immediately generalizes the poem geographically and temporally, stretching
from ancient history to the present and finding all eras pretty much alike. The
poem generalizes linguistically and figuratively as well. Even the definite article is pressed into service to create a sense of indefinite iteration: "the gen'ral
Massacre of Gold" has been occurring throughout human history, "the gaping
Heir" impatient for generations, "the baffled Prince" heading toward "the fatal
Doom" of defeat time after time. These generic agents and events merge readily into the host of personifications who haunt the poem, from "Observation"
in the opening lines, through "Misfortune" and "hissing Infamy," to "celestial
Wisdom" at the end.

Satiric attack in *The Vanity of Human Wishes* broadens into exposition and
eventually consolation as the poem uses historical particulars ultimately to
merge them into abstraction ("Let Hist'ry tell ..."). Johnson departs much
more from Juvenal's tone than he had in *London*. Although *Satire* X is Juvenal's most philosophical poem, it has less of the pensive melancholy that distinguishes Johnson's whole poem and especially its conclusion. The religious
skepticism and scorn of Juvenal become faith and sympathy in Johnson. Juvenal mocks prayer in general: his last lines say roughly, "If you still cannot out-
grow the need to pray, at least ask for something harmless, like a sound mind
in a sound body." By contrast, Johnson concludes in a "supplicating Voice" for
the Christian virtues of faith, hope, and charity; these are the gifts with which
"celestial Wisdom calms the Mind, / And makes the Happiness she does not
find." Whether Johnson's studied withdrawal from the political realm makes
The Vanity of Human Wishes a "failed" satire, a "tragic" satire, or something

else entirely, the poem embodies the tentative brooding, otherworldly personification and uneasy resignation that become conspicuous in many kinds of non-satiric poetry during the middle and later eighteenth century.

Despite this trend toward visionary otherworldliness, poetic satire in a Popean, epistolary, *this*-worldly mode does not suddenly vanish, and some of it is quite good. Two interesting women poets who wrote satire, Mary Jones (1707–78) and Mary Leapor (1722–46), both imitate and respond to Pope in major poems. Jones's *Of Desire. An Epistle to the Honorable Miss Lovelace* (published in her *Miscellanies*, 1750) follows Pope's *Epistle to a Lady*, much as Leapor's *Crumble-Hall* (published in the second volume of her posthumous *Poems*, 1751) follows Pope's value-laden portrait of Timon's villa in his *Epistle to Burlington*. But it is their versions of Pope's apologia, the *Epistle to Dr. Arbuthnot*, and the various apologias by Churchill and Cowper that together give us a broad sense of the shifting grounds of poetic satire in the later decades of the century. The first two poems reflecting on the situation of poetry and satire are Leapor's *An Epistle to Artemesia. On Fame* (1751) and Jones's *An Epistle to Lady Bowyer* (1736 [?], pub. 1750). These deft poems and works such as Churchill's *The Apology* (1761) and Cowper's *Table-Talk* (1782) bear closer comparison than space permits, but a few features are emblematic.

Writing as women *to* women, both Jones and Leapor assume a more private voice in their epistles than does Pope. Pope's addressee, Arbuthnot, is a figure conspicuously identified with national affairs. At every turn, the former royal physician to Queen Anne silently reminds the reader of the distance between the England of 1714 and that of 1735, and his friendship tacitly underscores Pope's assumed role of public diagnostician and healer. Pope is himself a national figure, which is why he can portray himself humorously as a besieged celebrity. Misrepresented and misunderstood, he is nonetheless at the center of the cultural stage.

Leapor writes self-consciously from the wings, not as a poet burdened with fame but as someone wondering what its achievement might mean. She addresses her close friend Elizabeth Freemantle ("Artemesia"), a private woman and thus also on the margins of political society. Mary Jones, who occupied a somewhat higher status, addresses a titled friend, Lady Bowyer, who urges her to publish; but she still writes as a relative outsider who faces obstacles specific to her gender. When her speaker seeks the literary patronage of a lord, she is offered more personal attention. The lord's assistant and, apparently, procurer suggests she leave her poems with him, "And if I find they'll bear my nicer view, / I'll recommend your poetry—and you" (*An Epistle to Lady Bowyer*, 78–9). Jones's protestations of honest independence are thoroughly conventional in formal verse satire; but with the sympathetic female audience implied by Lady Bowyer and her friend Charlot Clayton in view, these protestations take a more decided turn toward domestic privacy:

> ... if sometimes, to smooth the rugged way,
> *Charlot* should smile, or You approve my lay,
> Enough for me. I cannot put my trust
> In lords; smile lies; eat toads, or lick the dust.
> Fortune her favours much too dear may hold:
> An honest heart is worth its weight in *gold*.

(122–7)

Similarly, at the end of *An Epistle to Artemesia*, Leapor retreats from the role of public satirist. When she asks Artemesia "shall I speak or no?" the answer is that "The Muse shall give herself no saucy Airs, / But only bid 'em softly – Read their Pray'rs." Whether the answer comes from Artemesia or the speaker is uncertain (quotation marks are used inconsistently in the original) but perhaps irrelevant. The two female voices in the poem by now agree that the role of public monitor is unavailable.

Interestingly, withdrawal from the public sphere and a corresponding appeal to personal sincerity – norms of private validation that women writers have little choice but to adopt – become increasingly common for male poets. Even Charles Churchill, the most political satiric poet of the latter part of the century and densely topical, dwells as much on his personal mood and melodrama as on the referential accuracy of his poems. Churchill's *The Apology* (1761) interests later readers less for its personal satire of Tobias Smollett than for its statement of general satiric principles, including his professed preference for Dryden over Pope. *The Apology* is actually more reminiscent of several of Pope's Horatian poems than of any single work of Dryden's, but Churchill praises Dryden's "strong invention," "noblest vigour," and "varied force" over Pope's "polished numbers and majestic sound."[21] Churchill vows not to polish his own verse to the point of refining away the "generous roughness of a nervous line," a promise he had little trouble keeping. He equates overly smooth versification with decadent modernity, defanged satire, and the warbling of operatic eunuchs. His opposition of "vigour" to "sound" actually harks back to satire before Dryden, to the angry young Elizabethan satirists of the 1590s such as John Marston and John Donne, who made the harshness of the "satyr" a mark of alienated sincerity.

But Churchill seems to have difficulty deciding on just what grounds to defend his role as a satiric poet. At one point in *The Apology* he casts himself as assuming the "Muse's office" of telling the high truths necessary

> To make pale Vice, abash'd, her head hang down,
> And, trembling, crouch at Virtue's awful frown.

Now arm'd with wrath, she bids eternal shame,
With strictest justice, brand the villain's name …

(318–21)

But near the end of the same poem he defends his literary career as merely his "darling singularity" and his poems as "harmless rhyme." *Night* (1760) projects deeper ambivalence and alienation. Here Churchill sets himself and his friend Robert Lloyd against the tamely conformist values of the "prudent" majority:

Let slaves to business, bodies without soul,
Important blanks in Nature's mighty roll,
Solemnize nonsense in the day's broad glare:
We NIGHT prefer, which heals or hides our care.[22]

The poem mixes social criticism, bohemian bravado, and earnest individualism without quite fusing them. The honest partisans of night will continue to pay court to "wine's gay god" and to women (Churchill and the wife he had married at eighteen would soon separate) even "tho' in our teeth are hurl'd / Those *Hackney Strumpets*, PRUDENCE and the WORLD" (lines 294–5). He then goes on to anatomize both terms. "Prudence" in its modern "perverted" sense is now merely another name for "hypocrisy," and the judgment of "the World" at present means nothing more "Than many fools in the same opinion join'd" (lines 302–3, 357–8).

Satirists have often declared themselves in the minority, trumpeting their independence and casting majority opinion as Fashion, temporary delusion, the mob's fever. But Churchill puts himself in opposition to common sense categorically. His individualistic relativism and self-referentiality are extreme. These qualities render much of his satire ethically and formally incoherent compared to the first-person satires of earlier writers such as Pope, Swift, and Young. But Churchill repays a different kind of reading. Like Laurence Sterne in *Tristram Shandy* (which he admired), Churchill presents a participatory, implicated "I" unable to remain above or detached from the frenetic world he depicts. Like Sterne's Tristram or Yorick, Churchill's speaker is paradoxically authentic because he is unreliable; his whimsical spontaneity and inconsistency signal his integrity. The same conflicts that diffuse many of his satiric attacks also frequently energize his poems. Churchill is unusual in putting uncertainty and ambivalence at the forefront, projecting internal argument into staged debate. Satirists are not given to Hamlet-like indecision, at least not in their personas. So it is striking to see Churchill allude to Hamlet's famous lament that "the native hue of resolution / Is sicklied o'er with the pale cast of thought." In *An Epistle to William Hogarth* (1763) Churchill follows his vehement attack on the aging painter with a debate between the satirist and "Candour," a personification (representing good will), who urges the poet to abandon satire for other modes. Her arguments let Churchill counter that he is too honest *not* to write satire and that the times demand it. But Candour's charge that Churchill's "guilty rage" actually discourages virtue because it "Sicklies our hopes with the pale hue of Fear" is never really refuted (lines 244, 275, 285). With such tensions unresolved the effect is a striking, unstable compound of self-disclosure and exposé, a sort of confessional satire.

William Cowper outlived his former schoolmate Churchill, who died at thirty-three, by some thirty-six years. Cowper admired Churchill's "genius," "vigor," and "dignity of thought" while regretting his haste and carelessness. He characterizes him shrewdly as "Too proud for art, and trusting in mere force." *Table-Talk* (1782), the poem from which this estimate comes, is Cowper's closest approximation of Pope's *Epistle to Arbuthnot*.[23] It lacks Pope's autobiographical framework, but it reflects on the poet's place in the current cultural situation and lays out, with the help of an interlocutor, the speaker's ethical and poetic program. The poem praises Pope directly (lines 646–61), not only his "harmony" but also his ability to give "virtue and morality a grace." Cowper is frequently quoted out of context as complaining that Pope lowered poetry: he "Made poetry a mere mechanic art; / And ev'ry warbler has his tune by heart" (lines 654–5). In fact, Cowper means that Pope's ethical achievement ("In verse well disciplin'd, complete, compact") has by the late eighteenth century devolved to mere facility in many writers: a "servile trick and imitative knack" (line 666).

Clearly Cowper admires Pope's reformative poetry and the "serious mirth" of Pope's fellow Scriblerians John Arbuthnot and Jonathan Swift. In *Table-Talk* he follows the dialogic mode of Pope's Horatian epistles, and he assumes the indignant prophetic voice of the more Juvenalian *Epilogue to the Satires*, in which Pope's figure of Vice Triumphant decrees that "Not to be corrupted is the Shame" and "Nothing is Sacred now but Villany" ("Dialogue I," 160, 170). Cowper's prophetic vision casts the present age as a time

> when a country (one that I could name)
> In prostitution sinks the sense of shame;
> When infamous venality, grown bold,
> Writes on his bosom, *to be let or sold*
> ...
> When av'rice starves (and never hides his face)
> Two or three millions of the human race,
> And not a tongue inquires, how, where, or when ...
>
> (414–17, 422–4)

But *Table-Talk*, like others in the group of long poems it introduces, at once defends and disavows satire. The concluding section of *Table-Talk* expresses a distrust of satire that will surface more completely in other poems of the 1780s: "Satire has long since done his best," and now Religion must take over (lines 728–39). The fifth poem of this group, *Hope*, contains satiric character sketches that match many of Pope's in the *Epistles to Several Persons*, but nearly sixty lines of the next poem, *Charity*, question the usefulness of satire and the motives of satirists and their readers (lines 491–556). True, grants Cowper, the Swiftian satirist claims to be called by virtue and urgency:

> But (I might instance in St. Patrick's dean)
> Too often rails to gratify his spleen.
> Most satirists are indeed a public scourge;
> Their mildest physic is a farrier's purge;
> Their acrid temper turns, as soon as stirr'd,
> The milk of their good purpose all to curd.
>
> (*Charity*, 499–504: a farrier's purge is a laxative administered
> by a horse doctor)

Three years later, in *The Task*, Cowper would ask rhetorically, "what can satire, whether grave or gay? / … What vice has it subdued? whose heart reclaim'd / By rigour, or whom laugh'd into reform?" (II.315–21).

Questions about satire's efficacy were hardly new. Swift had opened the preface to the *Battle of the Books* in 1704 by defining satire as a "sort of glass wherein beholders do generally discover everybody's face but their own," and Pope had closed the second dialogue of the *Epilogue to the Satires* in 1738 by noting that satire "had become as unsafe as it had ineffectual." But later eighteenth-century satirists increasingly question satire's *motives* as well as its use. This questioning intersects with doubts about whether satire and poetry really belong together, doubts that, to our loss, persist today. Byron, who would continue to insist that they did, comes to mind as the great nineteenth-century counter-example. But Byron, as Auden said of Yeats, has "become his admirers," relatively few of whom read him now for his satire. Reading late eighteenth-century satiric poetry proves most rewarding as we learn to look and listen for something in it more ambivalent than either the public confidence assumed by Pope or the self-contained lyric confidences of Romantic poetry.

Chapter 7

Pope as metapoet

Autobiography and self-reflexivity in Pope's early poetry   *115*
The Rape of the Lock as "tertiary epic"   *119*
The early *Dunciad* as epilogue and prologue   *124*
The metapoetics of Pope's later career   *128*

One thumbnail generalization in literary history has it that eighteenth-century poetry is about the World, nineteenth-century poetry about the Poet, and twentieth-century poetry about Poetry. Anyone who has heard or made this claim probably suspects it oversimplifies too vastly to be true, and yet it has a stubborn appeal. If we think, say, of Dryden and Pope, Wordsworth and Keats, and Yeats and Wallace Stevens, we may also think of corresponding shifts of emphasis from poems heavily *referential* (*Absalom and Achitophel, An Essay on Man*) to *autobiographical* (*The Prelude, Ode to a Nightingale*) and to *aesthetic* (the "Byzantium" poems, *Notes toward a Supreme Fiction*).

But the more closely we look at the eighteenth century, and especially at the poetry of Pope, the more this supposedly linear narrative of poetic development curves and twists. Pope's idea of autobiography may not be Jean-Jacques Rousseau's or Wordsworth's, but he is one of the more insistently autobiographical of English poets. Paradoxically, this tendency is most explicit in the poems one expects to be least personal, the several Imitations of Horace (1733–8) he wrote in his forties. But autobiographical moments mark major and minor poems from every stage of Pope's career. Moreover, much of his poetry invites us to read it as metapoetry, that is, as self-reflexive poetry about poetic creation and possibility. In this metapoetic mode Pope arguably influenced mid and late eighteenth-century practice even more than he influenced it stylistically.

While Pope naturally has figured prominently at several points thus far, I have tried to avoid concentrating on him in isolation so that we might attend to broader patterns in the century, even in its first half, which is commonly thought of as the Age of Pope. It is time now to consider one way – only one – that periods are defined, which is less by representative breadth and more

114

by the practice of their greatest artists. Bach and Mozart are hardly "typical" early and late eighteenth-century composers, but studying their music deeply may take us further into some aspects of the century's musical tensions and possibilities than would an exhaustive survey. Gertrude Stein, countering the popular idea that artists somehow dwell in the future, insisted that "No one is ahead of his time." But she then went on to suggest that while major artists are wholly of their times, many of their contemporaries may be "generations behind themselves."[1] Perhaps we can say that the best artists turn out to have been most deeply in their era, as we might say that Hume, for example, was more keenly attuned to the philosophical problems of his age than were more representative and less talented thinkers popularly felt to have refuted him.

Like Hume, Pope displays a precocious intelligence attuned to questions about what knowledge is possible in his discipline. But none of Pope's writings, early or late, suffered the fate of Hume's great *Treatise concerning Human Understanding*, which Hume ruefully said "fell *dead born from the press*."[2] Pope succeeded early and was recognized by mid career as the leading poet of the age. The fact that Pope was both exceptionally gifted and widely emulated – and, inevitably, resisted – makes his achievement and concerns especially important to understanding eighteenth-century poetry. Here I will offer an approach to Pope's work as metapoetry, an approach slightly off-center and perhaps helpful for that reason. The next chapter will then turn to poems by other writers who follow Pope in reflecting on poetry and the poetic imagination.

Autobiography and self-reflexivity in Pope's early poetry

Pope hardly invented poetic self-consciousness. Spenser and Milton took Virgil's poetic career as models for their own, a way of thinking that simultaneously emphasizes continuity with the classical past and the uniqueness of their latter-day situation. This double awareness can be traced back further to Dante, who had made Virgil his personal guide in the *Divine Comedy*. And we might say that Virgil himself displays his consciousness of Homer and other predecessors at every turn. Authorial self-consciousness seems to some extent a perennial as well as period phenomenon. In his elegant *The Burden of the Past and the English Poet*, W. J. Bate acknowledges from the outset that even some writers who were ancient indeed felt "burdened" by having been anticipated. He quotes an Egyptian scribe of 2000 BCE who wrote, "Would I had phrases that are not known, utterances that are strange, in new language that has not been used, free from repetition, not an utterance that has grown stale, which men of old have spoken."[3] But, as Bate argues, a literary-historical self-conscious of a more intense kind comes into view in later periods. The English Civil War was a signal event in literary as well as political thought. The war and the subsequent closing of the theaters and cultural disruptions during the Interregnum (1649–60) made historical reflection inescapable during the Restoration era. Complimenting the young playwright William Congreve, Dryden looks back in 1694 to the Elizabethan and Jacobean writers as great authors indispensable to the modern poet's education but, at the same time, somewhat irrelevant because they belong to a different world. They are, for Dryden, "the Gyant Race, before the Flood."[4]

Pope's most explicit attempt to place himself within a usable literary history is *An Essay on Criticism* (1711), large parts of which are narrative. But he also indicates how self-consciously he takes modern poetry as a central subject of his poems through two often related practices: apt quotation and autobiographical self-assertion. His earliest published poem, "Summer" of *The Pastorals*, quotes Spenser, and *Windsor-Forest* (1713) ends in auto-quotation: by echoing the opening line of his *Pastorals* ("First in these Fields I try the Sylvan strains," with "try" changed to "sung"), Pope calls attention to genre, vocation, and poetic development.[5] The *Temple of Fame* (published in 1715 but written in 1711) is a free adaptation of Chaucer that pays homage while highlighting the distance between medieval and modern senses of history. Pope quotes much of the original in his notes, inviting comparison, as he later would with Horace. The poem ends in poetic autobiography:

> Nor Fame I slight, nor for her favours call;
> She comes unlook'd for, if she comes at all.
> But if the purchase costs so dear a price,
> As soothing folly, or exalting vice:
> Oh! if the Muse must flatter lawless sway,
> And follow still where fortune leads the way;
> Or if no basis bear my rising name,
> But the fal'n ruins of another's fame:
> Then teach me, heav'n! to scorn the guilty bays ...
>
> (513–21)

Such assertions of individual integrity – that virtue matters more to him than poetry – are often associated with Pope's later defense of himself as a satirist, but they actually form part of a larger pattern of nearly compulsive self-reflexivity as much aesthetic as ethical.

When at the end of *Eloisa to Abelard* (1717), after quoting (and footnoting) both Chaucer and Crashaw, Pope enters the poem personally through

Eloisa's imagining "some future Bard" depicting her, the effect is openly melodramatic:

> Such if there be, who loves so long, so well;
> Let him our sad, our tender story tell;
> The well-sung woes will sooth my pensive ghost;
> He best can paint 'em who shall feel 'em most.

But the lines also reflect on the paradoxical likeness and unlikeness of Eloisa's writing (she is composing an epistle to Abelard) and Pope's writing *of* her writing. The "sad similitude" she imagines between herself and her latter-day poet is exactly that, a relation of metaphoric similarity, not sameness. More inclusively, what feels like a spoken dramatic soliloquy is and is not the actual poem; the two things are connected by contrast as much as resemblance. Pope calls attention from the outset to writing as simultaneously less direct than speech and more intimate. In Eloisa's speculative history, "letters" means both epistles and written language generally:

> Heav'n first taught letters for some wretches aid,
> Some banish'd lover, or some captive maid;
> They live, they speak, they breathe what love inspires,
> Warm from the soul, and faithful to its fires ...

(51–4)

Eloisa's is a version of literary history that begins not with epic or drama but with the epistle, more particularly the kind of amatory epistle that, as she speaks, Pope is writing. Another romantic poem of the same year, the *Elegy to the Memory of an Unfortunate Lady*, ends with a surprising autobiographical turn:

> Poets themselves must fall, like those they sung;
> Deaf the prais'd ear, and mute the tuneful tongue.
> Ev'n he, whose soul now melts in mournful lays,
> Shall shortly want the gen'rous tear he pays;
> Then from his closing eyes thy form shall part,
> And the last pang shall tear thee from his heart,
> Life's idle business at one gasp be o'er,
> The Muse forgot, and thou belov'd no more!

Melodrama in both cases has usually been explained by Pope's infatuation at this time with Lady Mary Wortley Montagu, then romantically inaccessible in Turkey and perhaps seen by Pope as "entombed" in a marriage of convenience. But we might look for an artistic reflection as well, on the connection of poetry to mortality. Poets will go on about *im*mortality, as Pope himself had done in

The Rape of the Lock when he promised Belinda that her lock would last forever. But that same poem would as convincingly enshrine mortality through Clarissa's speech: "painted or not painted all shall fade …" The power of poetry comes, these poems of Pope's twenties suggest, through the poignancy of mortality. In Wallace Stevens's words, "Death is the mother of beauty" (*Sunday Morning*, line 63). This truth is not for Pope simply a piece of self-realization or an existential observation but a meditation on poetry, on its power and its limits. He broods during this period on how the arts resist mortality but do not conquer it. After they have done their best, he writes in a poem to the portraitist Charles Jervas, his friend and teacher, painting preserves but a "Form" and poetry but a "Name." When in the Preface to his collected *Works* of 1717 Pope remarked that he was unsure "whether to look upon my self as a man building a monument, or burying the dead," he seems not merely to have been joking.[6]

Pope's autobiographical and metapoetic reflections might interest only Popeans were it not for the connection of these reflections to larger concerns in the period, preoccupations that can generally be thought of as epistemological and aesthetic. The concern with determining of what things and in what manner one can have reliable knowledge leads increasingly in the period to subjectivity, that is, to the idea that knowledge depends on the perceiving subject. Therefore, speech or writing that is grounded in the perspective of an identifiable agent – whether a diarist, narrator in a novel, or the speaker of a poem – may come to be seen as more authentic and, despite its limitations, more interesting and persuasive. I do not mean that writers abandon the goal of neutral objectivity often associated with the "scientific spirit" of the age. Pope himself seems to have attempted a scientifically objective "view from nowhere" in parts of *An Essay on Man*.[7] But the counter-tendency of appealing to individual experience for authenticity surfaces not only in purportedly true first-person accounts such as *Robinson Crusoe* (1719) but also in poetry localized in time and space, such as epistolary poems (which specify a speaker and addressee) and occasional poems (which specify a temporal context). Pope excelled in and reflected on these modes.

The two most sustained metapoems of Pope's early career (to 1717) are the expressly theoretical *An Essay on Criticism* and the implicitly metapoetic *The Rape of the Lock*. In the first of these, as we have seen in Chapter 3, Pope projects himself through a very complex voiceprint. The performance is so complex that I divided it heuristically into three voices. All of these add up to an autobiographical identity that establishes the model early eighteenth-century poet as the practitioner of an art as old as Homer but engaged with particular modern realities. This figure in one sense portrays himself as entering a stream that flows from the Ancients, but in another he appears as separated from them, for all his piety, by even more floods than Dryden had imagined. One of these is the very recent flood dividing Dryden's own era – the Restoration's "fat Age of Pleasure, Wealth, and Ease" in Pope's historical account (*Essay on Criticism*, line 534) – from the more culturally ambitious Age of Queen Anne. In both the concluding part of *Windsor-Forest* and *An Essay on Criticism*, Pope suggests that the present is the beginning of a new era of greater responsibility, including a more self-conscious approach to the arts.

The Rape of the Lock as "tertiary epic"

The distinction between "primary" and "secondary" epic put forward by C. S. Lewis in *A Preface to Paradise Lost* (1942) differentiates oral from written epic. It replaces a less satisfactory distinction between "primitive" and "artificial" epic for the good reason, according to Lewis, that no epics are really primitive and all poetry is in some sense artificial. Authors of written epics, such as the *Aeneid*, *The Faerie Queen*, or *Paradise Lost*, are all aware of two great primary epics of Greece, the *Iliad* and the *Odyssey*, and pattern their works to some extent upon them. So, the secondary epics are secondary in the sense of being later and necessarily displaying a consciousness of having been preceded (unlike *Beowulf*), not because they need be inferior. Self-awareness is cumulative. As Virgil is everywhere conscious of Homer, Spenser and Milton are everywhere conscious of Virgil (as well as Dante and other European writers). Occasionally one even hears the term "tertiary epic" applied to the poems of Spenser or Milton because those works are based so firmly on earlier primary *and* secondary epics. But I will use the term more narrowly here to refer to the mock-epic, a poem which imitates epic features, beginning with its style, not necessarily to critique those features but inevitably to reflect and comment on them. Not surprisingly, the best poet to adopt the mode and the one most engaged in epic practice and reflection – Pope was at this time immersed in translating and commenting on Homer – wrote the great tertiary epic in English poetry.

That would not be the case had Pope been content to leave well enough alone. *The Rape of the Lock* (conventionally dated 1714 but only fully completed in 1717) first appeared as *The Rape of the Locke* in the 1712 collection published by Bernard Lintot, *Miscellaneous Poems and Translations. By Several Hands*. It was a poem of two cantos and only 334 lines, about 40 percent of the five-canto poem's eventual length. The original poem was popular and admired, and when Pope told Addison that he was thinking of enlarging it, Addison reasonably enough counseled him against tinkering with a fine thing. Pope ignored the advice, and would later say that revising the poem to incorporate the "machin-ery" of the sylphs was "one of the greatest proofs of judgement of anything I ever did."[8] It is also an act of composition that will repay careful study by anyone interested in the development of poetic genius. Comparing the two versions has become easier in recent years, with the inclusion of *The Rape of the Locke* in some widely available editions.[9] I strongly recommend reading the first ver-sion before reading (or re-reading) the complete poem. For one thing, doing so will make the poem's story line clearer, since the addition of the sylphs nearly swamps the primary narrative. But more significantly, comparing the two lets readers experience the growth of an extremely clever mock-epic into a poem of imaginative brilliance and self-reflexive depth.

A modern reader can approximate the experience of reading the 1712 text by reading only these lines the first time through:

I.1–18
II.1–46
III.1–24, 105–34, 147–8, 153–78
IV.1–10, 93–140, 143–74
V.1–6, 37–52, 57–88, 97–130, 133–50

These lines contain the basic action: Belinda goes to Hampton Court with her friends, they gossip, they have coffee, the Baron prays for success, snips the lock, refuses to return it, war ensues, and the lock ascends to the sky. Moving from this reading to the completed poem, a reader encounters seven distinct new scenes, including some of the poem's most powerful moments:

1. Ariel's "background" speech to the sleeping Belinda (I.19–124)
2. Belinda at the dressing table, assisted by Betty and sylphs (I.121–48)
3. The voyage up the Thames by Belinda, friends, and sylphs (II.47–72)
4. Ariel's speech assigning the sylphs their duties and threatening punish-ment for dereliction (II.73–136)
5. The card game (III.33–100)
6. The Cave of Spleen (IV.11–92)
7. Clarissa's speech (V.15–34)

All of these episodes call attention in different ways to *poeisis*, the making of the poem itself and of poetic imagining more generally. They all draw out and vastly elaborate the implications of two moments in the original poem. The first of these occurs in the final battle over the lock when the narrator relates that two of the men were killed: "One dy'd in metaphor, and one in song" (V.60).[10] The comic force of the line derives from literalizing the figurative, and it reminds the reader that *everything* in the poem is taking place *in* metaphor and song. The second is the poet's protestation that Belinda's lock ascended to the heavens even if unobserved by the participants: "But trust the Muse—she saw it upward rise, / Tho' mark'd by none but quick poetic eyes" (II.168–9 in 1712 version, now V.123–4). In the finished poem, however, it will turn out that the poet's eyes are not the only ones to see the lock's ascent: "The *Sylphs* behold it kindling as it flies, / And pleas'd pursue its progress thro' the skies" (131–2). This added couplet associating the sylphs and the poet expresses in miniature a larger pattern in which the sylphs represent poetic imagination.

The sylphs are never really causal agents in the poem's action, which was already complete without them. In this capacity, or incapacity, they may remind us of W. H. Auden's remark that "poetry makes nothing happen" (*In Memory of W. B. Yeats*, line 36). But they in effect make most of the poetry happen, figuring centrally in the poem's richest descriptive and imagistic passages. Pope uses the sylphs to create an unseen world containing the "real" facts of psychology and perception. These realities are invisible to all but the sylphs and the poet. When Ariel tells the dreaming Belinda that guardian sylphs protect virgins from seduction, "Tho' *Honour* is the Word with Men below," or that the behavior of young women that "blind" mortals call "Levity" actually occurs because "the *Sylphs* contrive it all" (I.77–8, 103–4), Pope is making a joke about coquettes but also proposing the sylphs as the poetic solution to a mystery. The sylphs turn the empty abstractions of prosaic explanation (Honor caused X, Levity led to Y) into visible beauty. Thus, the sylphs assist in "arming" the epic heroine at the dressing table, making her more beautiful than her maid could have done. But since they are invisible, "*Betty's* prais'd for Labours not her own." Praised by all except the poet, that is, and the enlightened reader, now allowed to see through "quick poetic eyes."

Quickened vision of this kind is nowhere more remarkable in *The Rape of the Lock* than in the first major addition to the second canto, the description of the boat making its way up the Thames to Hampton Court: "But now secure the painted Vessel glides, / The Sun-beams trembling on the floating Tydes …" (II.47–8). Pope uses the sylphs, the "Denizens of Air," to paint the nearly unpaintable atmosphere:

> The lucid squadrons round the sails repair:
> Soft o'er the shrouds aerial whispers breathe,
> That seem'd but zephyrs to the train beneath.
>
> (II.56–8)

Pope employs the same formula here as for "Honour," "Levity," and Belinda's transformation: what *seems* the effect of merely natural causes is really evidence of the presence of the sylphs. Of course, any place where we might imagine a sign reading "Sylphs at Work" we might substitute for it one reading "Poet at Work." Such signs grow larger as the description deepens:

> Some to the sun their insect-wings unfold,
> Waft on the breeze, or sink in clouds of gold.
> Transparent forms, too fine for mortal sight,
> Their fluid bodies half dissolv'd in light,
> Loose to the wind their airy garments flew,
> Thin glitt'ring textures of the filmy dew …
>
> (II.59–64)

Pope's study of painting during these years seems to have intensified his already keen visual sensitivity and his interest in the complementary capacities of poetry and painting. By the end of this rich passage the lines not only paint the scene but paint the painting of it:

> … Dipp'd in the richest tincture of the skies,
> Where light disports in ever-mingling dyes,
> While ev'ry beam new transient colours flings,
> Colours that change whene'er they wave their wings.
>
> (II.65–8)

Painting and optical metaphors remain important, as we will see in a moment, for the rest of Pope's career.

The climactic four-line passage in the 1712 *The Rape of the Locke* that narrates how the Baron came to "divide" Belinda's lock from the rest of her hair becomes in 1714 an eight-line reflection on how cultural changes divide Pope's world from Milton's. Pope originally described the Baron's "rape" of Belinda's lock in two couplets:

> He first expands the glitt'ring *Forfex* wide
> T'inclose the Lock; then joins it, to divide;
> One fatal stroke the sacred Hair does sever
> From the fair Head, for ever, and for ever![11]

In 1714 these couplets, somewhat revised, are separated by four new lines:

> The Peer now spreads the glitt'ring *Forfex* wide
> T'inclose the Lock; now joins it, to divide;
> **Ev'n then, before the fatal engine clos'd,**
> **A wretched Sylph too fondly interpos'd;**
> **Fate urg'd the shears, and cut the Sylph in twain,**
> **(But airy substance soon unites again) …**
> The meeting Points the sacred Hair dissever
> From the fair Head, for ever, and for ever!
>
> (III.147–54)

Pope of course did not advertise the new lines in bold type, but he did call attention to the addition with a footnote, to line 152: "See Milton, *lib*. 6." This reference to the war in heaven in Book VI of *Paradise Lost* announces the poem's position as post-Miltonic and definitively tertiary. Milton had modeled the war of good and bad angels on Greek and Roman epic, but he had an improbability to deal with that his predecessors did not face in depicting heroic combat, namely the fact that angels are immortal. So, when Michael deals Satan what would among mortals have been a fatal wound, Milton writes "But th' etherial substance closed, / Not long divisible" (VI.330–1). A bit later, Satan underscores the fact, as he encourages his troops:

> we find this our empyreal form
> Incapable of mortal injury,
> Imperishable, and though pierced with wound
> Soon closing and by native vigor healed.

> (VI.433–6)

Pope's addition to the pivotal action scene of his poem is itself "interpos'd" as comically as the sylph's body is inserted between the beginning and end of the act of cutting. The conventional wisdom about the mock-epic says that it does not mock the epic genre but rather the relatively trivial actors and actions that it treats in incongruously high language. The point seems worth keeping in mind especially in the case of Pope, whose reverence for Homer is profound. But Pope does suggest in these few lines that there is something inescapably comic and anachronistic in the most significant recent attempt to sustain the epic. Just as his remark on Milton's language (see p. 75 above) suggests that Milton just barely succeeded and is probably not to be imitated by later writers, so this comic allusion reflects on the distance between Milton's "strange out-of-the-world things" and Pope's consciously modern poetic world.

Pope renders that world both comically and metapoetically by allowing representations to function as if they were objects. Thus, the humor of the card game in Canto III derives only secondarily from the epic language in which Pope narrates; the more basic joke resides in the fact that the representations of Kings, Queens, and Knaves (Jacks) on playing cards behave as if human ("The Knave of Diamonds tries his wily arts ..." [III.87]), behavior readers are better able to see because the diminutive sylphs surrounding the scene help magnify the cards. The inversion of signifiers and signifieds plays out many times but most infamously in Belinda's apparent wish that the Baron had taken her chastity rather than the symbol of it, that he had "been content to seize / Hairs less in sight, or any hairs but these!"[12] The "quick poetic" vision associated with the sylphs magnifies inward as well as outward scenes and thus presents psychology made visible; these parts of the poem comprise a self-conscious display of poetry's ability to "show" the conscious mind and even the unconscious. The sylphs can see which "Ideas crowd the vacant Brain" of young women, and they can pursue these images into the

> moving Toyshop of their heart;
> Where Wigs with Wigs, with Sword-knots Sword-knots strive,
> Beaus banish Beaus, and Coaches Coaches drive.
>
> (I.83, 100–2)

And of course just before the fatal theft of Belinda's lock, Ariel "watch'd th' Ideas rising in her mind," and found "An earthly Lover lurking in her heart" (III.142–4).

I have emphasized Pope's use of the sylphs as instruments of poetic vision and reflection. They are ways of letting us look outward to see light particles or inward to see "ideas" and to reflect on just how poetry can make such imagery possible. In stressing the metapoetic dimension of *The Rape of the Lock* I do not want to lose sight of the real woman behind Belinda, Arabella Fermor, and her social world, or to suggest that the poem is not satiric and that its more obvious subjects are not important to Pope and to our experience of the poem. But the poem is part of another story as well, the narrative of Pope's continuing exploration and experimentation as a poet. Pushing into new territory, *The Rape of the Lock* self-consciously displays visual reach and adroitness much as *An Essay on Criticism* had displayed vocal complexity and aural mastery. Both of these poems look back on the poetic tradition while calling attention to their *post*-ness and raising the expectations for a distinctly modern poetry.

The early *Dunciad* as epilogue and prologue

Pope spent most of the decade after the publication of his *Works* in 1717 completing his translations of Homer and his edition of Shakespeare. Then in 1728 he published, anonymously, *The Dunciad*, a three-book mock-epic about bad writers (the poem's "dunces") and corrupted contemporary culture ("dulness"). The poem appeared with virtually no annotation and with many blanks or asterisks standing for proper names. In the next year Pope published an elaborate mock-scholarly edition of the poem, *The Dunciad, Variorum. With the Prolegomena of Scriblerus.* Much later, in 1742, Pope published what is now essentially the fourth book of the poem with the title *The New Dunciad: As it was Found in the Year 1741.* Finally, in 1743, the year before Pope's death, the full poem was published, with Colley Cibber rather than Lewis Theobald as the "hero." That is the version usually read – or excerpted – today. (Anthologists tend to favor parts of Book IV.) In this section, however, I will focus on *The Dunciad Variorum* of 1729 as the transitional work between Pope's early career and the major phase of "ethick epistles" in the 1730s.

For our purposes Pope's *Dunciad* is less interesting as satire or personal retaliation than as a self-conscious analysis and demonstration of the modern poetic situation. Approaching the poem this way is not meant to ignore the elements more commonly emphasized but simply to give a broader picture of Pope's project. Readers who want to get a sense of the personal satire need only spend a while reading in the footnotes by Pope and the additional ones by modern editors. And readers who are still unpersuaded that Pope was a man more sinned against than sinning, for all his pugnacity, might peruse *Pamphlet Attacks on Alexander Pope, 1711–1744*, a 360-page book that is largely an annotated *list* of works critical of Pope, many of them violently personal.[13] Pope quotes many of these attacks in his notes and prefatory material as justification for what he insists are counterattacks. Later critics willing to see the poem as general satire rather than merely protracted retaliation sometimes give the impression that the poem is "saved" from mere topicality by the addition in 1743 of Book IV, parts of which are more categorical and philosophical than most of the three-book poem. But it is striking how much of the earlier poem is already about a culture rather than a mere host of individuals. Perhaps another way of saying this is that Pope makes the case that the cast of particular dunces add up to something unified that might be called Dulness.

The metapoetic nature of *The Dunciad Variorum* fairly jumps off the page. The text looks like nothing in the history of English poetry before it. (Or since, excepting a few deliberate imitations of Pope in the twentieth century.)[14] Even after the reader passes through several prefaces and pieces of scholarly apparatus, the text of the poem itself is nearly swamped in commentary. Two lines of verse appear on each of the first two pages, with the rest given over to footnotes. This disproportion is part of the "Scriblerian" joke and satire directed at heavy-handed commentators on ancient texts like Lewis Theobald or Richard Bentley. Page three of the main body of the text gives a good idea of the presentation of the 1729 poem. Immediately notable is the mere fact that it has taken three pages to get to the fifth line of the poem. Much of the page is devoted not only to explanatory notes but to quotations from the classical and other works that Pope's lines imitate. Not just the poem's subject matter, then, but every aspect of its appearance advertises its self-awareness – not coincidentally, a quality the dunces conspicuously lack.

The poem takes self-referentiality further than had the tertiary epic *The Rape of the Lock*. If secondary epic acknowledges its literariness, and tertiary epic its relative lateness in the literary tradition, *The Dunciad* projects its even more advanced textuality at every turn, one entirely dependent on printing. The work is unimaginable without the burgeoning publishing industry, not simply because the flood of books constitutes much of Pope's target but because *The Dunciad* could no more exist apart from its technology than could Swift's great prose satire, *A Tale of a Tub* (1704). When we read a primary or secondary epic today in a printed book we may feel that the original work in a sense lies elsewhere, that we are reading a reproduced version of manuscript (which may in the case of primary epic itself be the reproduction of oral performances). Print seems largely accidental. The same is roughly true with *The Rape of the Lock*, although authorial footnotes complicate the experience somewhat by highlighting the poem's bookishness. But as soon as we begin *The Dunciad* we enter a work that seems "always already" printed. It becomes impossible to imagine a manuscript that would in any way be the "original."

That the poem is so embedded in print highlights its place in a current of historical change. The topicality of the poem is never in doubt, given its plethora of writers' names and its "plot" based on an annual Lord Mayor's Day procession through specified streets of the London of the 1720s. But the poem becomes historical in a more general way in the third book, much of which consists of a chronological survey of Dulness through the ages. The ghost of Elkanah Settle shares with his "son" Cibber a grand vision (based partly on the *Aeneid* and *Paradise Lost*, especially Book XI) of the "past triumphs of the empire of Dulness, then the present, and lastly the future." For Settle the progress is triumphant, but the reader of course experiences his encomium of Dulness as mock-encomium. (Like Swift, Pope greatly admired Erasmus, the author of *The Praise of Folly*, 1511.) Through Settle's speech Pope projects a poignant counter-vision of the fragility of human enlightenment:

> "How little, mark! That portion of the ball,
> Where, faint at best, the beams of Science fall.
> Soon as they dawn, from Hyperborean skies,
> Embody'd dark, what clouds of Vandals rise!"[15]

The depredations of military conquest, tyrannical rule, religious warfare, and fundamentalism, all lead up to the cultural corruption of the present. Pope presents this picture in phrasing now usually encountered as part of Book IV of the 1743 *Dunciad* but which is part of the poem's vision from the beginning:

> Thus at her felt approach, and secret might,
> Art after Art goes out, and all is Night.
> See sculking Truth in her old cavern lye,

Secur'd by mountains of heap'd casuistry:
Philosophy, that touch'd the Heavens before,
Shrinks to her hidden cause, and is no more:
See Physic beg the Stagyrite's defence!
And Metaphysic call for aid on Sence!
See Mystery to Mathematics fly!
In vain! they gaze, turn giddy, rave, and die.
Thy hand, great Anarch! lets the curtain fall;
And Universal Darkness buries All.

(III.345–56)

Many satires, perhaps most, are about their own necessity. The satirist describes the state of affairs that demands exposure, the vices or follies that, in Juvenal's claim, make it "difficult *not* to write satire." Many of Pope's footnotes testify to this effect, but *The Dunciad* argues for more than necessity. *The Dunciad* is a poem about its own possibility. It is a poem that describes the historical conditions that make such a historical poem viable. By characterizing the poem as historical I do not mean to assume Pope's objectivity but to describe his project. Even in the 1729 version Pope claimed that the poem's prophecy is actually historiography:

> As Prophecy hath ever been one of the chief provinces of Poesy, our poet here foretells from what we feel, what we are to fear; and in the style of other Prophets, hath used the future tense for the preterit: since what he says shall be, is already to be seen, in the writings of some even of our most adored authors, in Divinity, Philosophy, Physics, Metaphysics, &c … (III.337n)

This claim is in part conventional satiric rhetoric: we live in bad times and these general complaints really *do* apply accurately to particular individuals among us. But the statement also helps advance the poem's continual reflection on the relation of poetic images to general propositions. The poem's author appears to "read" his culture as his poem asks to be read, with a continual alertness to the cultural significance of individual instances. The *Dunciad*'s implied reader is someone who can move easily from the riot of particularity, crowd scenes, minute topicality, monstrous scatology, and carnivalesque inversion of Books I and II to a higher sense of historical pattern and poetic coherence.

Pope's view of the history of the West was largely in place as early as *An Essay on Criticism*. The *Dunciad Variorum*'s vision of the destruction of Classical achievements by early Christian zeal – "'Lo Rome herself, proud mistress now no more / Of arts, but thund'ring against Heathen lore …'" (III.93–104) – had been articulated in 1711:

> *Learning* and *Rome* alike in Empire grew,
> And *Arts* still *follow'd* where her *Eagles flew*;
> From the same Foes, at last, both felt their Doom,
> And the same Age saw *Learning* fall, and *Rome*.
> With *Tyranny*, then *Superstition* join'd,
> As that the *Body*, this enslav'd the *Mind*;
> Much was *Believ'd*, but little *understood*,
> And to be *dull* was constru'd to be *good*;
> A *second* Deluge Learning thus o'er-run,
> And the *Monks* finish'd what the *Goths* begun.
>
> (*An Essay on Criticism*, 683–92)

Pope's view of cultural history is common in the period, but less so is his tragi-comic version in which the Renaissance recovery from "Gothic" darkness turns out to be short-lived.

The *Dunciad* of 1728–9 reprises most of Pope's major poetry up to this point in his career. It is of course a darker version of Pope's great success in the mock-epic, *The Rape of the Lock*. Its historiographic sweep and its focus on poetic practice connect it to Pope's other triumph in metapoetry, *An Essay on Criticism*. The *Dunciad* is in large part *An Essay on Criticism* in reverse, a showcase of how not to write poetry and how not to read it. Negative examples abound, especially in Book I, with its images of monstrous creativity, and in Book II, with its loud poets who nonetheless put everyone to sleep, nurtured by critics and publishers who instinctively favor bathos. Book III, with its prophetic vision, connects the *Dunciad* to Pope's unironically prophetic *The Messiah* and the concluding section of *Windsor-Forest*, two early poems that celebrate a new reign and a new era. Finally, the *Dunciad* looks back self-consciously to Pope's *Temple of Fame*: the later poem consciously inverts Pope's youthful dream vision to create his "Temple of Infamy."[16]

The metapoetics of Pope's later career

As suggested by its incorporation in the second volume of collected *Works* that Pope published in 1735, the *Dunciad* of 1728–9 is as much the prologue to his later poetry as a conclusion to his earlier work. Part of the acute self-referentiality of the *Dunciad* is its documentary insistence on fact. Of course, Pope's notes often go beyond objectivity, or fall short of it, but they point continually to a verifiable world of particulars from which the poem itself has been made. This feature of the *Dunciad* emerges in several poems of the 1730s as self-conscious appeals to a poetry of "things" rather than "sounds," of "Nature's light" rather than "Wit's false mirror," of the "heart" rather than "fancy." These oppositions all come from the closing lines of *An Essay on Man*, completed in 1734, and Pope would amplify them the next year in the *Epistle to Dr. Arbuthnot*. There the mature poet looks back on his earlier poems and announces that he has since left "pure Description" behind for "Sense," departing "Fancy's Maze" for "Truth" (148, 340–1).

Such statements are not merely thematic assertions about the importance of the subject or the veracity of the author. They are also announcements of a new *poetic* understanding or contract with the reader, in which austerity and accuracy will matter more than fictional enchantment. The *Essay on Man* immediately puts this claim forward in metapoetic terms. First comes Pope's prefatory staging of the question of why he is treating the topic "in verse, and even rhyme," a question he answers disarmingly and somewhat disingenuously by claiming that he could keep the *Essay* shorter in poetic form and that maxims make more of an impression in rhyme ("The Design").[17] The claim makes the poem sound closer to prose than it is, as anyone discovers who tries to paraphrase closely ten lines together. But in making the claim Pope also calls attention, as he had in the *Dunciad*, to the way poetry is being made out of what might seem hopelessly prosaic and unpromising materials.

The opening verse paragraph of *An Essay on Man* highlights the poem's post-Miltonic position. To enter the work as *meta*poem we need only recall that its opening paragraph ends with the promise to "Laugh where we must, be candid where we can; / But vindicate the ways of God to Man" (15–16). These lines of course echo Milton's mission to "justify the ways of God to Man," but they do so in a very different tone of voice. Pope follows Milton in writing a theodicy, a word which literally means "God justice" and is usually applied to works like these which address the problem of evil (essentially, the question of why, if God is both good and all-powerful, evil exists). Pope's theodicy will veer from Milton's by relying on secular philosophical argument rather than biblical narrative, but it differs almost as radically in proceeding by way of shared observation and conversation rather than soliloquy.

The "we" who engage to laugh when necessary and be candid (that is, generous) when possible are the poet and his friend, Henry St. John, Viscount Bolingbroke. Pope's address to Bolingbroke here and at the end of the poem reminds us that *An Essay on Man* first appeared as "Ethic Epistles" – and that we are in a world of poetic discourse altogether different than Milton's. Milton memorably grounds the authority of his vision in his isolation. Cut off from others by historical circumstance and by his blindness, the poet of *Paradise Lost* may be inspired by the Holy Spirit. The poetic mode of *An Essay on Man* is instead rooted in conversation and empirical observation. "What can we reason, but from what we know?" Pope asks, and in the next couplet shows that knowing means seeing: "Of Man what see we, but his station here, / From which to reason, or to which refer?" (I.18–20). The poem's conclusion again insists on worldly conversation as the poem's guiding principle. As Pope compliments Bolingbroke, he reflects on his own practice throughout *An Essay on Man*: "Form'd by thy converse, happily to steer / From grave to gay, from lively to severe ..." (IV.379–80). If the lines describe Pope's relation to Bolingbroke they also model the reader's relation to Pope, and they set the expectations of the "Ethic Epistles" and Horatian satires to which Pope would devote most of his remaining years.

We know from Pope's letters and conversation that he thought of his poetry of the early 1730s as part of a new, unified project, a grand ethical work for which *An Essay on Man* would merely be a sort of Prelude. But even without this testimony, the poems themselves evince an acute self-consciousness about the relation of the poems to each other and about undertaking a new kind of poetry. They do so through cross reference, echo, and direct auto-quotation. A good example is the *Epistle to Bathurst*, which appeared in 1733, before three of the four parts of *An Essay on Man* had come out but which was written to follow from it. Several of Pope's editors note that these lines (161–4) from the *Epistle to Bathurst* –

> Hear then the truth: "'Tis Heav'n each Passion sends
> "And diff'rent men directs to diff'rent ends.
> "Extremes in Nature equal good produce,
> Extremes in Man concur to gen'ral use"

– paraphrase and quote two couplets from *An Essay on Man* (cf. II.165–6, 205–6). But Pope quotes himself even more fully in this epistle. Another couplet Pope soon put in quotation marks, "The ruling Passion, be it what it will, / The ruling Passion conquers Reason still" (155–6), usually goes unidentified as Pope quoting himself because it does not appear elsewhere in modern editions of his work. But the couplet appeared in the first few editions of *An Essay on Man*, until Pope deleted it.[18] These textual and intertextual niceties concern us here simply for the glimpse they give of the depth of Pope's preoccupation with psychology in this cluster of works and the web of intertextuality connecting them.

The theory of the "ruling passion" that Pope sketches out in *An Essay on Man* and in the *Epistle to Bathurst* develops more fully in the *Epistle to Cobham*, the poem Pope in 1735 placed just after *An Essay on Man* and before the rest of the "Epistles to Several Persons," sometimes also called the "Moral Essays." From the time the poems appeared to the present many have wondered whether the theory is much of one (Pope seems to have thought of it as a "hypothesis"),[19] whether it explains very much, and whether Pope's own character sketches really depend on it. In general terms, the ruling passion is for Pope a way of specifying an underlying, often compulsive motivation. We might think of it as midway between traditional "humour" theory, based on physiology, and current ideas of the unconscious. But more important than the theory itself is what it tells us about Pope's idea of what the modern poetry of his time should be, namely epistemological and psychological. Pope intensified a "theoretical turn" that had begun to emerge in Dryden's criticism and the many theories of the passions published in France and England in the late seventeenth century. Dryden argued in 1677 that the best poets, those able to "sound the depth of all the passions," are those who have "philosophy" enough to find the "springs of human nature" that are "not so easily discovered by every superficial judge."[20]

The subtitle of the *Epistle to Cobham* soon became "Of the *Knowledge* of the Characters of Men" (my italics), emphasizing that the poem is not just about psychological character but about how to read – and write – character. Understanding the true basis of behavior, Pope argues in the *Epistle to Cobham*, requires more than untutored observation because "Not always *Actions* show the man."[21] The point seems obvious enough as a truth about the world, but the statement has more resonance as a truth about poetry. The metapoetic implication is that traditional poetic modes such as epic and drama – "action poems," so to speak – will no longer give the level of self-consciousness and analysis that modern poetry must undertake. Identifying the inadequacies of one set of observers after another – cloistered scholars, worldly wits, and "sage" historians – Pope implies in these epistles that what it now takes to make sense of human conduct is the quickness of a psychologically informed poetry. Increasingly in the century, when poets use poetry to think about poetry, they begin to cast their art as grounded less in the representation of action than in states of consciousness. The expectation rises that the most serious poetry portraying human nature will be overtly philosophical and psychological.

Before turning to how Pope's metapoetic concerns connect to those of other eighteenth-century poets, it is worth returning to the fact of his pre-eminence. While the word "genius" may not in itself be very helpful, neither is ignoring the fact of Pope's extraordinary brilliance and imaginative fertility. Less mysterious but no less extraordinary are his dedication and discipline. That Pope was the first poet to make his living as a poet, independent of patronage or of the stage, many have noted, beginning with Pope himself. It is less often remarked just how rare such an achievement is in any period, and of course Pope himself could not have managed the feat without his profitable translations of Homer, as he also noted. His lifelong attention and unflagging hard

Chapter 8

Metapoetry beyond Pope

The vocation of invocation: melancholy, contemplation,
celebration   *133*
Collins, Gray, and modern ambition   *139*
Smart's *Song* and Cowper's *Task* as metapoems   *143*

Since Pope had the richest poetic career in the eighteenth century, it is not surprising to find the deepest and most sustained metapoetic reflection in his work. But such metapoetic self-consciousness appears in many other writers as well, and focusing on it allows us to see the active tensions in a range of eighteenth-century poetry. Working from within the poetry, rather than assuming a "background" of pre-existent ideas that are then versified, should give us more meaningful ways of reading much of the period's poetry. Eighteenth-century poems are of course about many things other than poetry; indeed, rarely in literary history has poetry's purview been wider. Yet poet after poet writes with self-conscious reflection on two metapoetic topics that are theoretically distinguishable but frequently overlap: the nature of poetic vocation and the role of poetry. We sometimes assume that poetry became its own preoccupation only in the modern era, but metapoetic themes abound in eighteenth-century poetry.

The vocation of invocation: melancholy, contemplation, celebration

When Thomas Gray says of the poet within his *Elegy Written in a Country Churchyard* that "Melancholy mark'd him for her own," he epitomizes an association between the poet and solemnity that had begun to appear earlier in poems by writers such as Anne Finch and Thomas Parnell and that would continue throughout the century. Milton explicitly linked the poet and melancholy in *Il Penseroso* (16), but *Il Penseroso* is a somewhat playful poem, paired with a counter-argument, *L'Allegro*, in which the poet chooses Mirth over Melancholy. *Il Penseroso* had many imitators in the 1740s and after, but the suggestion that the poet chooses or is chosen by melancholy shows an influence much broader than Milton's. Renaissance emblem books and other conventional representations associated melancholy with solitude and *reading*; having a character walk on stage alone carrying a book was enough to indicate his melancholy frame of mind. What becomes stronger in the eighteenth century is the association of melancholy and *writing*.

Anne Finch is too complex a poet to be reduced to melancholy musing. A good complete edition of her wide-ranging work is still needed; her more than 200 poems (only about 80 of which appeared in 1713) include sprightly epigrams, playful epistles, and humorous fables, as well as meditative and religious poetry.[1] But several of her most deeply self-reflexive poems foreground melancholy as the motive for writing poetry. Among the best known of her works today, *To the Nightingale* characterizes poetry as consolation for injury:

> Poets, wild as thee, were born,
> Pleasing best when unconfin'd,
> When to Please is least design'd,
> Soothing but their Cares to rest;
> Cares do still their Thoughts molest,
> And still th' unhappy Poet's Breast,
> Like thine, when best he sings, is plac'd against a Thorn.

In *The Spleen* Finch includes herself in the ambitious survey of the dominion of depression over people of all stations and professions. ("Spleen" in the eighteenth century could mean everything from a bad mood to serious depression, Finch's use.) Significantly, she portrays herself not simply as a woman given to depression –

> O'er me alas! thou dost too much prevail:
>   I feel thy Force, whilst I against thee rail;
> I feel my Verse decay, and my crampt Numbers fail.
> Thro' thy black Jaundice I all Objects see,
>   As Dark, and Terrible as Thee …

– but also as a poet whose writing often *depends on* melancholy dejection:

> My Lines decry'd, and my Employment thought
> An useless Folly, or presumptuous Fault:
>   Whilst in the *Muses* Paths I stray,
> Whilst in their Groves, and by their secret Springs
> My Hand delights to trace unusual Things,
> And deviates from the known, and common way …

Finch apostrophizes depression, her "old, inveterate foe," in a more directly personal poem, *Ardelia to Melancholy*, after attempts to escape melancholy through diversions other than poetry have proved insufficient:

> These failing, I invoked a Muse,
> And poetry would often use
> To guard me from thy tyrant power;
> And to fly the every hour
> New fancies then I choose.
> Alas, in vain ...[2]

Finch's consciousness of her poetic vocation as something apart from the familiar social sphere is not always gloomy, reminding us that the connotations of melancholy include pensiveness and introspection. *The Petition for an Absolute Retreat* pursues a pleasant fantasy of "transport" beyond the world of "wild Ambition" to "Contemplations of the Mind." *A Nocturnal Reverie*, one of her best-known poems, achieves meditative withdrawal partly through quietly sustained syntax, as we saw in Chapter 2. More conspicuously, the poem is founded on the poet's double withdrawal from company and from her own sense of sight. Out of sight – both unseen and unseeing – the poet can hear and answer a call to imagine her sphere more contemplatively than others.

Thomas Parnell, another poet whose breadth of achievement has not been sufficiently recognized, wrote metapoetry of several sorts. His first published poem, *An Essay on the Different Stiles of Poetry* (1713), is a sort of allegorized survey of the elements and powers of poetry. In his tour, the speaker looks on devices such as metaphor, simile, personification, narration, and poetic description:

> Here bold *Description* paints the Walls within,
> Her Pencil touches, and the *World* is seen:
> The Fields look beauteous in their flow'ry Pride,
> The Mountains rear aloft, the Vales subside ...

Sometimes Parnell demonstrates as he surveys:

> There *Repetitions* one another meet,
> Expressly strong, or languishingly sweet,
> And raise the sort of Sentiment they please,
> And urge the sort of Sentiment they raise.[3]

This sort of poetic self-consciousness is close to the technical sections of his friend Pope's *An Essay on Criticism*; but in several other poems Parnell's reflections on poetry are concerned less with poetry's rhetoric than with the poet's call.

The speaker of *A Hymn to Contentment* wanders into a wood to seek the "Lovely lasting *Peace* of *Mind*."[4] He knows he will not find her in ambition, adventure, or even ordinary retreat, having learned "That *Solitude*'s a Nurse of Woe" (24). But he is able to see and hear her through prayer-like invocation:

> Lovely lasting *Peace* appear;
> This World it self, if thou art here,
> Is once again with *Eden* bless'd,
> And Man contains it in his Breast.

> (33–6)

Invocation grows into vocation as Peace tells the poet to find grace through religion. Modern readers may attribute this directive to conventional piety, but the exchange becomes poetically revealing because of its effect on the speaker. He resolves not only to become more religious personally but also to accept his calling as a modern prophetic poet, a singer of "heav'nly Vision, Praise, and Pray'r" (54). More particularly, he will praise the "great SOURCE of NATURE" by celebrating the beauties of creation:

> All of these, and all I see,
> Wou'd be sung, and sung by me:
> They speak their Maker as they can,
> But want and ask the Tongue of Man.

> (71–4)

Parnell declares his poetic vocation in more biblical terms in *Piety: Or, The Vision*, published posthumously. Convinced that his dream vision results from angelic intervention, the poet resolves to

> mount the roving wind's expanded wing,
> and seek the sacred hill, and light to sing;
> ('Tis known in Jewry well) I'll make my lays,
> Obedient to thy summons, sound with praise.[5]

The most extreme acceptance of the role of religious visionary will come in the second half of the century in the poetry of Christopher Smart, but before we turn to Smart's *Song to David* (1762), let us explore the idea of pensive withdrawal leading to the poet's devotion in some of the poetry of the 1730s, 1740s, and 1750s. James Thomson in *Autumn*, which completed *The Seasons* in 1730, orchestrates a visionary encounter resembling that in Parnell's *A Hymn to Contentment*. Instead of the female Peace, a male figure of "PHILOSOPHIC MELANCHOLY" visits the poet, urging him to higher poetic ground:

O'er all the Soul his sacred Influence breathes!
Inflames Imagination; thro the Breast
Infuses every Tenderness; and far
Beyond dim Earth exalts the swelling Thought.[6]

Simply by his presence Philosophical Melancholy inspires poetic activity:

Ten thousand thousand fleet Ideas, such
As never mingled with the vulgar Dream,
Crowd fast into the Mind's creative Eye.

(1014–16)

The power of such pensiveness moves the poet to declare himself its follower, in lines that appeared in the first edition of *Winter* before eventually settling in *Autumn*:

Oh! bear me then to vast embowering shades,
To twilight groves, and visionary vales;
To weeping grottos, and prophetic glooms;
Where angel forms athwart the solemn dusk,
Tremendous sweep, or seem to sweep along;
And voices more than human, through the void
Deep sounding, seize the enthusiastic ear.

(1030–6)

Given Thomson's deism and sociability, he soon has second thoughts about becoming a votary of gothic gloom and grottos. Thomson's speaker alternates between a poetic self grounded in melancholy solitude and one of patriotic cheerfulness. Several of the younger poets coming of age in the 1740s would be less equivocal about identifying the poet's calling with separation from the "madding crowd" of Gray's *Elegy* and declaring an affinity for Philosophical Melancholy.

Thomas Warton's *The Pleasures of Melancholy* (1747) suggests how a rising generation of writers sought to escape Pope's influence by defining the poet's identity in melancholic terms. Warton acknowledges Pope's "happiest art" but prefers Spenser's "wildly-warbled song." The idea that Spenser, of all poets, was less artful than Pope is of course a willful fiction. Warton seems to have subject matter in mind more than style, preferring the shadowy solitude of Spenser's scene (Warton remembers Spenser selectively) to the sunlight of Pope's. He is more touched by seeing

deserted Una wander wide
Thro' wasteful solitudes, and lurid heaths,
Weary, forlorn, than when the fated Fair

> Upon the bosom bright of silver Thames
> Launches in all the lustre of Brocade,
> Amid the splendors of the laughing Sun.[7]

Warton's true poet is part of – and writes for – a melancholy elite:

> Few know that elegance of soul refin'd,
> Whose soft sensation feels a quicker joy
> From Melancholy's scenes, than the dull pride
> Of tasteless splendor and magnificence
> Can e'er afford.
>
> (92–6)

Thomas's older brother, Joseph, creates a less "Gothic" scene in *The Enthusiast: or, The Lover of Nature. A Poem* (1744), but he likewise associates the poet's vocation with a propensity for "midnight-walks" and solitude. Freed from the world of "smoaky cities," "commerce," and "luxury," the poet could attend fully to virtue and beauty.[8]

Thus far we have seen the poet characterized through negation. The poet is *not* the man or woman of the world, *not* fit for the daytime bustle of business or politics or even for most social intercourse. At the extreme, the poet in Gray's *Elegy* seems not only alienated from both the rich and the poor by his sensitivity but also too frail to survive into full adulthood. Yet even these instances privilege the poet's vocation. William Collins, the most promising of all the mid-century poets (he had written the bulk of his work by the age of twenty-four), renders the poet's calling deeply if hesitantly visionary, most famously so in the *Ode on the Poetical Character*. That demanding poem is best approached by considering moments of vocational declaration in the three poems Collins placed just before it in his *Odes on Several Descriptive and Allegoric Subjects* (1746): *Ode to Pity*, *Ode to Fear*, and *Ode to Simplicity*.

Collins speaks of – and to – Pity, Fear, and Simplicity, calling them both inspirations *for* and subjects *of* poetry, reflecting on how these qualities have animated great works in the past and then implying how he is qualified, by his ardor and understanding, to employ them in the present. For Pity he constructs a shrine and asks only to live as her votary. In this passage, the "shell" is a lute, and thus symbolizes poetry:

> There let me oft, retir'd by Day,
> In Dreams of Passion melt away,
>   Allow'd with Thee to dwell:
> There waste the mournful Lamp of Night,
> Till, Virgin, Thou again delight
>   To hear a *British* Shell![9]

Pity is one Aristotelian requisite of tragedy, and thus of the tragedian. Addressing Fear, the other requisite, Collins asks, in exchange for lifelong commitment, merely for a single experience of the intensity she regularly gave to Shakespeare:

> Teach me but once like Him to feel:
> His *Cypress Wreath* my Mead decree,
> And I, O *Fear*, will dwell with *Thee*.
>
> (Ode to Fear, lines 69–71)

Interestingly, Collins asks for Shakespeare's sensitivity, rather than, say, his verbal facility. The presumption that from profound feeling the rest will follow resonates with ideas of genius emerging at the time. William Duff in *An Essay on Original Genius* (1767), for example, would distinguish between the ordinary person and the poetic genius on the basis of susceptibility to feeling. The ordinary observer misses much, Duff writes, but a "Poet ... who is possessed of original Genius, *feels* in the strongest manner every impression made upon the mind, by the influence of external objects on the senses, or by reflection on those ideas which are treasured up in the repository of the memory, and is consequently qualified to express the *vivacity* and strength of his own feelings."[10]

In his third ode, addressed to Simplicity, Collins makes a rather complex pledge. Other poets may ask for genius or epic grandeur, but

> I only seek to find thy temp'rate vale,
>   Where oft my Reed might sound
>   To Maids and Shepherds round,
> And all thy Sons, O *Nature*, learn my Tale.
>
> (Ode to Simplicity, lines 51–4)

This vocational utterance is typical of Collins's odes in combining modesty and ambition. He asks Simplicity (or artlessness) for success only in the "temperate" poetic registers. (The "reed" means the shepherd's flute of pastoral poetry.) But at the same time he boldly envisions an audience of "all" of Nature's sons, which is to say all who are fit to hear the voice of poetry.

Collins, Gray, and modern ambition

Collins's *Ode on the Poetical Character* is arguably the most difficult English lyric poem published before the nineteenth century and one of the most difficult of any era. In it Collins takes on the subject of such demanding later works as Coleridge's *Kubla Khan*, Yeats's two Byzantium poems or many of Wallace

Stevens's meditations: the source and power of poetic imagination itself. Collins approaches the subject obliquely, beginning with an extended simile alluding to Spenser's *Faerie Queen*. Just as the belt ("girdle") properly belonging to the chaste Florimel cannot be worn by an unchosen claimant, poetic genius devolves upon only a few. But given the poem's difficulty, a brief overview and paraphrase may be in order before proceeding further.

The *Ode on the Poetical Character* has three elaborate sections: the strophe, mesode, and antistrophe. Strophe and antistrophe literally mean turn and counter-turn, and these sections follow identical metrical patterns; the middle mesode separating them consists (in this case) of thirty-two lines in tetrameter couplets. Anna Laetitia Barbauld understandably called these audacious lines (23–54) a "strange and by no means reverential fiction concerning the Divine Being."[11] A minimalist paraphrase might run thus:

> *Legends say the band was woven when God the Creator, long loved by Fancy, retired with her alone and put her on his throne; then Fancy sang and the youth of morn (Apollo) and his subject life were born. The dangerous passions took no part in weaving the belt, but Wonder, Truth, the shadowy tribes of mind, and the benign powers all did. Where is the poet who can avow his own ambition and imagine this hallowed work meant for him?*

The reference to Apollo, the "Youth of Morn," suggests at once the sun and poetry, both closely associated with the primal act of divine creation. What modern poet could imagine Creation itself as his destined theme? This question concludes the mesode, and the antistrophe answers it. Again, a prosaic "translation" might be this:

> *High on a wild cliff, steep, gloomy, guarded by holy genii, lies an Eden like Milton's. I see the oak under which Milton slept at night receiving heavenly inspiration and on which the ancient (prophetic) trumpet was hung. Often moving toward this Miltonic scene and away from Waller's milder poetry, I vow to follow Milton and do so with trembling feet. But in vain: one mortal alone has known such bliss, and Heaven and Fancy have now destroyed the inspiring bowers or hidden them from every future view.*

This paraphrase loses (among much else) the optimistic implication of the ode's conclusion. While the bowers that inspired Milton may be gone, Collins has in fact just recreated them in imagination along with what they inspired, the Edenic sublimity of *Paradise Lost*. Far from admitting defeat or being one of the "doomed poets of an Age of Sensibility,"[12] Collins triumphantly suggests two truths. First, he has just seen both Spenser's beautiful bowers and Milton's Eden, which are – as of the last words of his ode – closed to "every *future* view."

Second, the English epic line of Spenser and Milton has just been incorporated into lyric poetry. The epic may be inaccessible, but the sublime lyric is coming into its own.

Gray's two great odes published in 1757, *The Bard* and *The Progress of Poesy*, enact a similar exaltation of the lyric mode. The latter poem makes lyric not only the highest of the arts but, astonishingly, heaven's highest gift to man. After cataloguing "what ills await" humanity –

> Labour, and Penury, the racks of Pain,
> Disease, and Sorrow's weeping train,
> And Death, sad refuge from the storms of Fate!

– Gray takes on nothing less than the Problem of Evil, as Milton had in *Paradise Lost* and Pope in *An Essay on Man*:

> The fond complaint, my Song, disprove,
> And justify the laws of Jove.[13]

In this self-proclaimed *lyric* theodicy, "song" will "justify" our human situation not by story or argument but simply by existing. The gift of poetry compensates for human ills, just as the spectacular sunrise – poeticized in the figure of Hyperion – counterbalances the specters of night. (Gray underscores this point in a note added in 1768 as giving "life and luster to all it touches" and "enriching" all that is "otherwise dry and barren.")[14] The close association of Hyperion with Apollo, thus with poetry, fuses the image of returning sunlight with the idea of the return of poetry, a recurrent sunrise in human affairs:

> Say, has he giv'n in vain the heav'nly Muse?
> Night, and all her sickly dews,
> Her Spectres wan and Birds of boding cry,
> He gives to range the dreary sky:
> Till down the eastern cliffs afar
> Hyperion's march they spy, and glittering shafts of war.
>
> (48–53)

Unlike *The Bard*, this poem does not ventriloquize an earlier poet – at least not directly. The poem's opening line – "Awake, Aolian lyre, awake" – invokes both Pindar and David, as Gray would note in 1768. Still, the poem speaks in the voice of the modern poet who relays the history of poetry up through the English greats, Shakespeare, Milton, and Dryden – he whose "long-resounding" lines are praised in the stanza just before this passage:

> Hark, his hands the lyre explore!
> Bright-eyed Fancy hovering o'er

Scatters from her pictur'd urn
Thoughts, that breath[e], and words, that burn.
But ah! 'tis heard no more—

(107–11)

Dryden's lines, animated by "Bright-eyed Fancy," may breathe and burn, but
who comes next in the great lyric line? Gray's final stanza first asks a question –
"Oh! Lyre divine, what daring Spirit / Wakes thee now?" – then answers in a
voice that moves quickly from deference:

tho he inherit
Nor the pride, nor ample pinion,
That the Theban Eagle bear
Sailing with supreme dominion
Through the azure deep of air

to self-assertion:

Yet oft before his infant eyes would run
Such forms as glitter in the Muse's ray
With orient hues, unborrow'd of the sun:—

to defiance:

Yet shall he mount and keep his distant way
Beyond the limits of a vulgar fate,
Beneath the Good how far—but far above the Great.

(111–23)

The answer comes, as it did in Collins's *Ode on the Poetical Character*, in a mixture of personal diffidence and vocational determination. The clear answer to
the question posed to the lyre – "what daring Spirit / Wakes thee now?" – is
the speaker himself. Gray does not profess inferiority to the English Dryden
but only to Theban Pindar. The turn to Dryden, following upon the lines on
Shakespeare and Milton in the preceding sections, returns the poem to where
it began, as a poem about the power of lyric poetry. (Gray first had in mind
calling the poem "The Power of Poetry" but had been anticipated.) And on this
lyric ground he yields nothing to any English poet.

The real vindication of his claim would be (and I think is) the success of the
poem he is now completing. But oddly Gray professes to vindicate it by recalling that his "infant eyes" saw forms "unborrow'd of the sun." The word "infant"
need not mean a baby; it could refer to a child, or a beginner, or even, as it does
in Blackstone's *Commentary on the Laws of England* of 1765, a minor. For Gray,
the Latinate, etymological meaning would have been important: *infans* means

one not yet speaking. Gray's young poet-self had poetic visions while still a mute, inglorious Dryden. But he differentiates himself from Dryden in a subtle but powerful way. Dryden's "bright-eyed" and "pictur'd" poetry belongs to a world of sunlit *representation*. Gray's youthful self is a visionary who saw forms that had no original in the empirical world, forms brilliant ("orient") beyond sunlight, a *revelation* to the soul of the seer. "Unborrowed of the sun" may recall Mark Akenside's invocation of Beauty, in *The Pleasures of Imagination* (1744), as "thou, better sun."[15] Gray had complained at the time of Akenside's "Hutchinson-jargon" – referring to Francis Hutcheson, author of *An Inquiry into the Original of Our Ideas of Beauty and Virtue* (1725) – and he probably does not use the word "forms" (119) in a Platonic sense. But the speaker's privileged vision does seem to promise transcendental access to a reality higher than that perceived by Fancy, attractively "bright-eyed" but ultimately sight-dependent rather than visionary.

Smart's *Song* and Cowper's *Task* as metapoems

While Collins and other mid-century poets such as Joseph Warton and Mark Akenside assume the role of chosen votary and priest in their odes to abstractions, much as Keats would later in his odes to Psyche and Melancholy, and Gray takes on the mantle of bardic prophet, it is Christopher Smart who takes the role of celebrant and prophet more literally, or at least more biblically. In *Jubilate Agno* ("Rejoice in the Lamb"), an often oracular manuscript not published until the twentieth century, Smart writes, "For by the grace of God I am the Reviver of ADORATION amongst ENGLISH-MEN" (B332).[16] The line could stand as an epigraph for his more intelligible *A Song to David*, where the word "ADORATION" rings through stanza after stanza of that powerfully structured work acquiring, as we will see in Chapter 10, the motivating force of a personification. Here, I want to attend briefly to the metapoetic aspect of *A Song to David* to suggest that, for all his idiosyncrasies, Smart participates in the later eighteenth century's increasing poetic self-consciousness. Smart might have written about David as a king and warrior but chooses to celebrate him primarily as a poet, as the author of psalms rather than as military commander. The poetic apotheosis of David as a lyric poet necessarily makes Smart's lyric poem self-reflexive. *A Song to David* describes creation so encyclopedically and with such gusto – from the vast "clustering spheres" down to the "quick peculiar quince" – that one might forget it is a poem of praise that makes its primary subject the *poetry* of praise. Like Collins, Gray, and other contemporaries, Smart writes at once about his personal vocation as a poet and about the vocation of poetry itself. Reading his poetry with an alertness to its metapoetic preoccupations highlights its connections to our comparatively secular literary moment. Smart's religious faith seems to have been implicit; his faith in religious poetry's social function seems to require continuing confirmation.

The most serious religious poet of the two decades following Smart is William Cowper. But Cowper probably has been or will be encountered by most readers of this book through his great poem *The Task*, a much more secular work than his hymns, certainly, or than some of the satires considered in Chapter 6. Religion informs *The Task* throughout, however, both as a discursive topic (Cowper deplores religious laxity in practice and doctrine) and as a metapoetic concern, relating to how the poet's identity and the function of poetry are imagined. As Cowper approaches the poem's conclusion, in which he anticipates an apocalypse of harmony and regeneration, he modestly pulls back from the role of poetic prophet:

> Sweet is the harp of prophecy: too sweet
> Not to be wrong'd by a mere mortal touch;
> Nor can the wonders it records be sung
> To meaner music, and not suffer loss.[17]

Immediately, however, he retreats from this retreat, in self-referential lines that resonate with earlier sections of the poem:

> But when a poet, or when one like me,
> Happy to rove among poetic flowers,
> Though poor in skill to rear them, lights at last
> On some fair theme, some theme divinely fair,
> Such is the impulse and the spur he feels
> To give it praise proportioned to its worth,
> That not to attempt it, arduous as he deems
> The labour, were a task more arduous still.

(VI.751–8)

The Task had begun, famously, as a poem about poetic labor, with the joke – and enabling premise – of the poet's having been given the improbable commission to write a poem in blank verse about a sofa. He steadily treads a long but clear path from the first book, "The Sofa," to the poetic vocation of the conclusion. At several key points along the way, Cowper articulates the calling of poetry. "There is a pleasure in poetic pains / Which only poets know," he announces in Book II, and then glosses the claim in this remarkable long sentence of psychological analysis:

> The shifts and turns,
> The expedients and inventions multiform
> To which the mind resorts, in chase of terms
> Though apt, yet coy, and difficult to win,—
> To arrest the fleeting images that fill
> The mirror of the mind, and hold them fast,
> And force them sit, till he has pencil'd off
> A faithful likeness of the forms he views;
> Then to dispose his copies with such art
> That each may find its most propitious light,
> And shine by situation, hardly less
> Than by the labour and the skill it cost,
> Are occupations of the poet's mind
> So pleasing, and that steal away the thought
> With such address, from themes of sad import,
> That lost in his own musings, happy man!
> He feels the anxieties of life, denied
> Their wonted entertainment, all retire.

(II.286–303)

We have brushed against the connection between poetic composition and authorial composure earlier in the idea of poetry as relief from melancholy; but Cowper in a sense makes the composition of his poem his main subject. This foregrounding becomes most conspicuous in the fourth book, "The Winter Evening," a large part of which concerns reading the newspapers. More than any poem since *The Dunciad*, and giving more emphasis than Pope does to the *moment* of writing, this part of *The Task* invites the reader to watch the conversion of facts into poetry. Disparate news items and advertisements of the day's paper enter the poem as bits of information and as glimpses into the poet's evolving consciousness. Cowper departs from Locke, who had equated thinking and consciousness, as he celebrates reverie and its relation to creativity.

> I am conscious, and confess
> Fearless, a soul that does not always think.
> Me oft has fancy ludicrous and wild
> Sooth'd with a waking dream of houses, towers,
> Trees, churches, and strange visages express'd
> In the red cinders, while with poring eye
> I gazed, myself creating what I saw.

(IV.285–91)

We considered this passage at more length earlier (see pp. 79–80) in discussing Cowper's use of blank verse. Here I hope to have quoted enough to convey the psychological texture and subtlety of a poem that suffers in aphoristic representation. These lines impressed Jane Austen (as did Cowper's poetry generally), who quotes the phrase "myself creating what I saw" while Mr. Knightley considers his suspicion of a relationship between Frank Churchill and Jane Fairfax (*Emma*, ch. 41), and of course the passage impressed Coleridge, who adapts much of it to his purposes in *Frost at Midnight*. For Cowper, this "indolent vacuity of thought" refreshes the understanding and "restores me to myself" (IV.297–307). The interplay between external stimuli – here a late eighteenth-century version of information overload – and internal fantasy composes the poem, and the poet.[18]

Many more parts of *The Task* call attention to the process and psychology of composition, and in fact its "Arguments" (lists of contents for each book) advertise the poem's combination of design and whimsicality, continually reminding the reader of authorial spontaneity. Here, for example, is the "Argument" of "The Garden" (Book 3):

> *Self-recollection and reproof.—Address to domestic happiness.—Some account of myself.—The vanity of many of their pursuits who are reputed wise.—Justification of my censures.—Divine illumination necessary to the most expert philosopher—The question, What is truth? answered by other questions.—Domestic happiness addressed again.—Few lovers of the country.—My tame hare.—Occupations of a retired gentleman in his garden.—Pruning.—Framing.—Greenhouse. Sowing of flower-seeds.— The country preferable to the town even in the winter.—Reasons why it is deserted at that season.—Ruinous effects of gaming and of expensive improvement.—Book concludes with an apostrophe to the metropolis.*

One can imagine some practical function for these arguments; a reader wanting to reread the lines on the poet's hare would know roughly where to look, for example. But on a larger scale, the jumbled lists with their Shandean dashes emphasize the poet's creative ability to range deftly from autobiography to metaphysics, from greenhouse cucumbers to national morality.

But the deepest if briefest moment of metapoetry occurs in Book 5 when, in the midst of a conventional assertion of revelation's superiority to philosophy, Cowper implies a connection between poetry and the divine. The loud voice of reason is inadequate to his higher task – the sofa having been left long behind – of bringing about human liberty, a mission which depends on grace:

> The still small voice is wanted. He must speak
> Whose word leaps forth at once to its effect,
> Who calls for things that are not, and they come.

(V.685–7)

Literally and doctrinally, the voice is God's. Metaphorically, it is the voice of poetry at its purest, resembling Revelation because performative speech-acts bring into being what they name. The moment, one of the period's most powerful, is akin to the conclusion of the *Dunciad*, whose performative words imaginatively end at once the poem and the poem's subject, and akin to the end of Smart's *Song to David*, in which both Smart's song and David's are, by creative fiat, "DETERMINED, DARED, and DONE."

Part III

Vision

Chapter 9

Reading visions

The first part of this book explored how poems have to be produced aurally if we are to hear their voices. In this part we will consider some strategies for producing poems imaginatively – in the root sense of *imaging* – to experience their visions. If a poem is a script for hearing, it is also a script for seeing. While this is true for all poems, eighteenth-century poetry may present some special imaginative challenges for modern readers. Why so?

We might start with two qualities of much eighteenth-century poetry: an appetite for abstraction and a preference for imagistic restraint. Abstraction often takes the form of personification, what we would call the personification of abstract ideas. But that way of putting it may be something of a retrospective distortion, one that assumes a fully formed abstract concept exists first and is only then given a figurative personhood. The relation between conceiving and "picturing," however, may well have been more reciprocal. The popularity of personification will require fuller attention in the next chapter, but here we can grasp the visual challenge it may present readers who lack the associations that were more common in the eighteenth century. We can see the distance between then and now very dramatically by looking to a nicely documented instance of eighteenth-century reader-response criticism of a passage from James Thomson's *The Seasons* (1726–46). These three lines from James Thomson's *Summer* will not now strike most readers as visually rich, perhaps hardly visual at all:

> O Vale of Bliss! O softly-swelling Hills!
> On which the *Power of Cultivation* lies,
> And joys to see the Wonders of his Toil.[1]

But eighteenth-century readers seem to have been more alert to personification than most of us today. Their familiarity with illustrated emblem books, classical statuary, painting, popular allegory such as John Bunyan's *Pilgrim's Progress* (1678), or poems such as Edmund Spenser's *Faerie Queen* (1590–6) made readers of the period remarkably ready to fill in imagistic details with minimal encouragement. Commenting on these lines of Thomson's, a contributor to the *British Magazine* in the 1760s did not find "Cultivation" an inertly abstract noun but a full-length personification:

> We cannot conceive a more beautiful image than that of the Genius of Agriculture, distinguished by the implements of his art, imbrowned with labour, glowing with health, crowned with a garland of foliage, flowers, and fruit, lying stretched at his ease on the brow of a gently swelling hill, and contemplating with pleasure the happy effects of his own industry.[2]

If we meet them halfway, some fleeting personifications become potentially forceful. Swift evokes the psychological fine line between admiration and jealousy in this couplet from *Verses on the Death of Dr. Swift* in this manner:

> Her End when Emulation misses
> She turns to Envy, Stings, and Hisses.[3]

Swift's concision, like Pope's, often makes more demands on the reader than does the work of other writers. Here, in *The Authors of the Town, a Satire*, published in 1725, a few years before Swift's *Verses*, is Richard Savage elaborating the same distinction between Envy and Emulation:

> Artists on Artists scoul with jealous Eyes,
> And Envy Emulation's place supplies.
> With *Envy*'s Influence the dark Bosom's fraught,
> But *Emulation* brightens ev'ry Thought!
> Pale *Envy* pines, if Excellence aspires,
> And most she slanders what she most admires;
> Charm'd *Emulation* can, with Transport, gaze,
> Yet wou'd outsoar the Worth, she loves to praise.[4]

Another kind of submerged or nearly obscured imagery results not from abstraction or personification but from a kind of concise understatement, a self-imposed economy and restraint. This phenomenon is easier to illustrate than to describe categorically. A powerful instance occurs in *The Vanity of Human Wishes* when Johnson describes the retreat of Xerxes, King of Persia, after his disastrous defeat at Salamis. Once, mad with pride, Xerxes had ordered his sailors to whip the sea for not obeying him; now, he flees for his life:

> Th' insulted Sea with humbler Thoughts he gains,
> A single Skiff to speed his Flight remains;
> Th' incumber'd Oar scarce leaves the dreaded Coast
> Through purple Billows and a floating Host.[5]

Teaching Johnson's poem, I find that most readers emerge from these lines with a confused or at best vague idea of Xerxes' situation. Johnson has a very clear idea of it, and he concentrates most of that idea (image) in two words that may not at first do much for us: "incumber'd" and "purple." In the eighteenth century "purple" could mean simply brightly colored or it could carry our meaning of bluish red (the first meaning in Johnson's *Dictionary of the English Language*), but it also meant the specific color of venous blood. So Johnson's waves, normally gray, are running red with blood. More graphically – and tactilely – they are so crowded with corpses that the oars of the living are *encumbered* by the dead, a grimly understated modifier. Once grasped, the image of rowing through dead bodies grows not only vivid but nightmarish, as in Ingmar Bergman's 1968 film *Shame*. Perhaps it is just tinged, too, with the ironic recollection of another meaning of "purple" that surrounds the desperate Xerxes: purple was once the color reserved for emperors.

In this case the imagery abounds once we read carefully. In others, poets deliberately pare imagery down to a few generalized examples, allowing a turn from descriptive detail to more inward psychology. We can see this phenomenon at work if we return to Gray's *Sonnet on the Death of Richard West*, the poem Wordsworth wanted to reduce to five lines. This time, let us concentrate more on vision than voice, thinking about just how Gray "sets" this poem that notes the arrival of spring and the speaker's detachment from the season. Gray did not invent the subject; many poets before T. S. Eliot realized that April could be particularly cruel. The strategy and emphasis of Gray's poem stand out if we compare it to a Renaissance sonnet about a similar disparity between the season's renewal and the speaker's sadness, the Earl of Surrey's *The Soote Season*, published in 1557. ("Soote" means sweet; in line 4 "turtle" is turtledove and "make" is mate; in line 11 "minges" means remembers, and in line 12 "bale" means harm.)

> The soote season, that bud and blome furth bringes,
> With grene hath clad the hill and eke the vale;
> The nightingale with fethers new she singes;
> The turtle to her make hath tolde her tale.
> Somer is come, for euery spray nowe springes;
> The hart hath hong his olde hed on the pale;
> The buck in brake his winter cote he flings;
> The fishes flote with newe repaired scale;
> The adder all her sloughe away she slinges;
> The swift swallow pursueth the flyes smale;
> The busy bee her honye now she minges;
> Winter is worne that was the flowers bale.
>   And thus I see among these pleasant thinges
>   Eche care decayes, and yet my sorow springes.[6]

Surrey's nearly Chaucerian catalogue of spring's changes teems with physicality, leading up to the abrupt reversal of the final couplet. Eighteenth-century readers would have found Surrey, whom Pope calls "one of the first refiners of the English poetry," appreciably more modern stylistically than Chaucer.[7] But his vision belongs to an older order of things. Gray's natural setting, in contrast to Surrey's catalogue, centers on merely three objects: the morning sunlight, the fields, and the birds – not nightingales, turtledoves, and swallows, as for Surrey, but simply birds:

> In vain to me the smiling Mornings shine,
> And redd'ning Phoebus lifts his golden fire:
> The birds in vain their amorous descant join;
> Or cheerful fields resume their green attire:
> These ears, alas! for other notes repine,
> A different object do these eyes require.
> My lonely anguish melts no heart but mine;
> And in my breast the imperfect joys expire.
> Yet Morning smiles the busy race to chear,
> And new-born pleasure brings to happier men.
> The fields to all their wonted tribute bear:
> To warm their little loves the birds complain:
> I fruitless mourn to him, that cannot hear,
> And weep the more, because I weep in vain.

Surrey's poem strikes most readers as more sensuous than Gray's, but it is not more experiential. Instead of emerging contextually out of *an* experience, Surrey's details are stereotypic; these things happen *every* spring, not just from a particular vantage or at a particular moment. Rather, Surrey's poem is more sensuous owing to its abundance and detail, a dozen lines devoted to a catalogue of springtime activity. Gray, on the other hand, chooses selectivity, repetition, and symmetry over accumulation. The first and last phrase of Gray's sonnet is "in vain," and other items mirror each other within this frame: *Mornings* and the *Morning* in lines 1 and 9, *birds* in lines 3 and 12, *fields* in lines 4 and 11.

This symmetrical concentration forces attention inward, toward the season of the speaker's mind in counterpoint with the season of the year. But the scene itself is more substantial than it might at first seem to us. The description of the virile sun (Phoebus) as both *redd'ning* and *golden* (2) superimposes an image of the fully risen sun on the red sunrise. The statement that the fields *resume their green attire* (4) may not automatically bring an image to mind for the modern reader, the verb *resume* seeming abstract and the direct object *attire* feeling somewhat artificial. But for Gray and eighteenth-century readers *resume* would mean "put on, or take to oneself," and *attire* had been used often enough to mean verdure that it need not feel like a far-fetched clothing metaphor – or even a metaphor at all. When Milton in the late seventeenth century observed that "Earth in her rich attire / Consummate lovely smil'd" (*Paradise Lost*, VII.501) the word had just come into literal botanical usage, usually referring to the floral leaves of a plant. Gray's "*green* attire" is thus quite specific and perhaps slightly metaphorical, describing plants in early spring when their only "flowers" are their leaves.

Birds, as a higher-level general noun, will prove more difficult to imagine than Surrey's nightingales, doves, and swallows; but Gray seems to have a broader phenomenon in mind: not the discrete characteristics of several birds but the pervasive sound of birdsong and the collective fact – all the birds are mating – signaled by it. This "amorous" concert seems all the more distant from the speaker's isolation precisely because nature's imperative *is* collective. The word *tribute* may not allow for much visualization today, when it usually means compliments rather than tangible gifts, but it conveys the sense of an offering being given recurrently and universally. Or nearly so: the field bears its tribute of fruits and pleasures to all creatures but one, the pained and *fruitless* speaker.

The sort of generalized display that carries Gray's melancholy wit in this sonnet is common enough in the period that we should reflect on just what sort of readerly readiness it assumes. As we have just seen, it requires close attention to diction. Today we often associate the Latinate diction that tends to accompany generalization with pomposity, "scientific" social writing, and (understandably) Orwellian political vagueness. But when we look to the etymology and history of a poem's words we often find them precise *for the relevant level of generalization*. The fact that eighteenth-century poets sometimes prefer generalized objects – such as birds rather than several species of birds, fields rather than *that* field in such-and-such locale – is something we should try to understand rather than deplore or explain away too easily. We do need to keep in mind that many poets did indeed write about particular locales and that some catalogued the local flora and fauna with considerable particularity. But when they do not, we should be careful about concluding that "neoclassical dogma" encouraged abstract concepts over perception and sense experience. It is often assumed that Samuel Johnson promulgated such dogma in chapter 10 of *Rasselas*, speaking for all and speaking categorically:

> The business of a poet, said Imlac, is to examine, not the individual, but the species; to remark general properties and large appearances: he does not number the streaks of the tulip, or describe the different shades in

> the verdure of the forest. He is to exhibit in his portraits of nature such
> prominent and striking features, as recall the original to every mind;
> and must neglect the minuter discriminations, which one may have
> remarked, and another have neglected, for those characteristicks which
> are alike obvious to vigilance and carelessness.

Yet the context of this statement shows that Johnson wants to keep in view
the difference between experiential *generalization* and disembodied *abstraction*.[8] We can grasp this distinction in eighteenth-century terms by thinking of
the difference between the second and third parts of *Gulliver's Travels*. In his
second voyage Gulliver encounters Swift's ideal ruler, the King of Brobding-
nag, whose practicality does not preclude prudential generalizations. In deliberate contrast, the political elite encountered in the third voyage, the abstracted
Laputans, have grown so detached from experience as to require "flappers" to
bring them back to their senses. In *Rasselas*, Imlac the Poet does usually speak
for Johnson, but when he goes on from his statement about selective and generalized imagery in poetry to a more transcendental claim that the poet "must
write as the interpreter of nature, and legislator of mankind" and even feel
himself "superiour to time and place," he has clearly gone too far. Young Rasselas momentarily becomes the teacher here, interrupting Imlac's "enthusiastic
fit" to remind him that by his account "no human being can ever be a poet"
(*Rasselas*, chapter 10 and opening paragraphs of chapter 11).

Johnson's ironic phrases seem to anticipate the unironic transcendental-
ism of Shelley's *Defense of Poetry* (1821): "A Poet participates in the eternal,
the infinite and the one; as far as relates to his conceptions time and place
and number are not." For Johnson and most of his contemporaries the idea of
human beings composing poetry superior to time and place would be hubris-
tic and delusory. Some kinds of poetry are more conspicuously tied to time
and place than others: occasional poetry, including satire, often makes a virtue
of topicality, and locodescriptive poetry makes a virtue of being rooted in a
place. But even poems as given to generalization as Johnson's *Vanity of Human
Wishes* or Pope's *An Essay on Man* situate themselves within a world of human
history.

So we need not learn to "see" disembodied abstraction or bloodless universality in the period's poetry but imagery often generalized, understated, or
conveyed in words whose physicality may require recovery. Gray's "attire" is an
example of the last, and we will encounter more instances of subtle generalization when we explore eighteenth-century nature poetry. But first we need to
turn to personification, an important kind of generalizing imagery common in
the period that poses uncommon challenges today.

Chapter 10

Personification

Recovering personification   *157*
Personification herself?   *164*
The knowledge of personification   *169*

This chapter aims to help the twenty-first-century reader respond alertly and sympathetically to personification, a prominent feature of eighteenth-century poetry sometimes met with impatience. The first section attempts to recover how personification operated for the period's poets and readers. The second reexamines the use of gender in creating personifications as significant, not simply conventional, figures; and the third looks at personification as a way of knowing and interpreting the world, not merely decorating it.

Recovering personification

Many modern readers automatically sympathize with Wordsworth's renunciation of most personification in the Preface of 1800 to *Lyrical Ballads*:

> The Reader will find that personifications of abstract ideas rarely occur in these volumes; and, I hope, are utterly rejected as an ordinary device to elevate the style, and raise it above prose. I have proposed to myself to imitate, and, as far as is possible, to adopt the very language of men; and assuredly such personifications do not make any natural or regular part of that language … I have wished to keep my Reader in the company of flesh and blood, persuaded that by so doing I shall interest him.[1]

But to read a lot of eighteenth-century poetry profitably we also need to respond sympathetically to passages like these from two of the period's best-known poems. In the first, Johnson refers to Charles X of Sweden:

> O'er Love, o'er Fear, [he] extends his wide Domain,
> Unconquer'd Lord of Pleasure and of Pain;
> No Joys to him pacific Scepters yield,

War sounds the Trump, he rushes to the Field …

—*The Vanity of Human Wishes* (1749), 196–9

In the second, Gray writes of the rural people buried in a country church-yard:

But Knowledge to their eyes her ample page
Rich with the spoils of time did ne'er unroll;
Chill Penury repressed their noble rage,
And froze the genial current of the soul.

—*Elegy Written in a Country Churchyard* (1751), 49–52

Unless we imagine "War," "Fear," "Knowledge," and "Penury" as possible real-ities, even as potential agents, passages like these will seem lifeless. They need not.

Wordsworth views the personification of abstract ideas as artificial in the worst sense, a "device to elevate the style," related to the "poetic diction" that he believed marred 9/14ths of Gray's *Sonnet on the Death of Richard West*. Why should contemporary readers not reject such artifice and remain instead with Wordsworth in the "company of flesh and blood"? Why take poetic personifi-cation seriously?

One fairly tautological answer is "Because it's there," *there* being every-where in the period. And why bother with a body of poetry that relies so heavily on personification? Because personifications do not lie outside the "company of flesh and blood" but within it, within us. No mere ghostly dec-orations, personifications express ways of thinking about the world that we all use more than we realize and often with powerful effect. These practices may have much to tell us about how we organize our experience, and studying them critically may help us think more deeply about current habits of thought and discourse.

Our own uses of personification range from speaking to our cars and computers as if they were human, often with comic exasperation, to solemn political phrasing with potential life-and-death consequences. A twenty-first-century example of the latter has been the attempt to put a single face on a host of social and military actions by grouping them together as a "War on Terror." The phrase is worth pondering as an illustration of how personifications work cognitively as well as emotionally. While most English speakers would regard "war on terror" as synonymous with "war on terror*ists*," it in fact differs sig-nificantly by suggesting something at once less definite and more personal. It conjures a subliminal personification, Terror, or we might say Terror himself, since politicians using the phrase in one sentence have regularly spoken in the next of combating "the enemy" and of the need to defeat "him." In this light, they personalize *Terror* as some*one* who can be fought; but, since Terror is still an abstraction and a "mass" noun, "he" also appears potentially limitless and omnipresent. On the other hand, *terrorists* – a plural, "count" noun – could conceivably be numbered and placed concretely. (Mass nouns can not normally take the plural, while count nouns regularly do: "food" is a mass noun, "plum" a count noun). The imaginative and ethical implications of one word choice over another can be profound. In this case, whether one sees a danger as limitless (a mass) or limited (enumerable) will have much to do with what one regards as a rational and proportional response.

Eighteenth-century uses of personification range similarly from the incidental and comic to the geopolitical. Before rushing to judgment concerning the appropriateness of this figure by eighteenth-century poets we need to consider just what it is and how to identify it. We cannot rely on capitalization to signal personification. As we have seen, some printers regularly capitalized all nouns, especially early in the century. Later, this practice waned, and in any case an author or publisher might or might not consistently capitalize personifications. Definitions of personification differ slightly at the edges, but if we take it to be "endowing nonhuman objects, abstractions, or creatures with life and human characteristics,"[2] we have to look not for typography but for attributes such as the ability to hear or speak, behave like a person, or have gender. Thus in the lines from Gray above it is not the capitalization of "Knowledge" that signals personification but gender and agency, the fact that *she withholds* "her ample page" from the uneducated. If Johnson's "War" can blow a trumpet, it (he) is personified. And so are London ("thou freckled fair") and England ("with all thy faults, I love thee still") if they can hear William Cowper address them. Pronouns, verbs, syntax, and context all mark personification more reliably than capitalization.

Eighteenth-century readers and theorists recognized a range of personifications, unlike Wordsworth and many modern critics. Wordsworth reluctantly approved of using personification rarely, as a "figure of speech occasionally prompted by passion," and modern criticism often follows him. Romanticists in our day sometimes write as if only apostrophe – preferably uttered at moments of "uncanny" intensity when poets are really addressing themselves – counted as personification. Even some thoughtful latter-day defenses of eighteenth-century personification tend to take "sublime" odes as the truly significant instances, prizing visionary moments when the poet seems possessed or when the personification grows intensely pictorial. Later we will turn to some great moments of this sort, especially in the odes of Collins and Gray. But poets frequently use personification in quieter ways that are no less important in understanding the period's imagination.

While we may be inclined to dismiss personifications as "merely conventional," for an eighteenth-century reader their very conventionality might be what helped release their active potential. In other words, an acquaintance with paintings, prints, statues, emblem books, and earlier literary works representing virtues, vices, and other abstractions would make a reader more alert to fill in possible details imaginatively. Thus in these lines from the *Ode to Adversity* Gray depends on his readers' familiarity with this parade of figures:

> Wisdom in sable garb arrayed,
> Immersed in rapturous thought profound,
> And Melancholy, silent maid
> With leaden eye that loves the ground,
> Still on thy solemn steps attend:
> Warm Charity, the general friend,
> With Justice to herself severe,
> And Pity, dropping soft the sadly-pleasing tear.

(25–32)

Although eighteenth-century theorists sometimes anticipate Wordsworth in connecting personification to "passion," they also recognize less exalted, more discursive uses of the figure. Lord Kames, Joseph Priestley, and Hugh Blair, for example, all distinguish between personifications that are temporarily delusory and those that are overtly fictive. For Priestley, a "real" rather than "ideal" personification is the product of temporary delusion (a "real" belief), as when King Lear talks to the winds. An "ideal" personification elsewhere in Shakespeare might be Enobarbus's description of the winds as "love-sick" for Cleopatra's barge. (Kames's parallel terms for "real" and "ideal" personifications are "passionate" and "descriptive," respectively.)[3]

The shrewd and barometric Blair, whose *Lectures on Rhetoric and Belles Lettres* (1783) would school generations of students, celebrates personification as the "life and soul" of poetry, because poetry pleases largely by allowing us "to find ourselves always in the midst of our fellows; and to see every thing thinking, feeling and acting, as we ourselves do." Personification "introduces us into society with all nature, and interests us, even in inanimate objects, by forming a connection between them and us, through that sensibility which ascribes it to them." Blair regards personification more exactly even than Kames or Priestley, preferring to discriminate *three* degrees of it: "The first is, when some of the properties or qualities of living creatures are ascribed to inanimate objects: the second, when those inanimate objects are introduced as acting like such as have life; and the third, when they are represented either as speaking to us, or as listening to what we say to them." The first occurs so commonly in ordinary language – even in non-verbal behavior, as when we kick the object we stumbled over – that some might question whether it is personification at all: a raging storm, for example, or the thirsty earth. The second degree, although somewhat more conspicuous, might illustrate "works of cool reasoning" as well as poetry. Blair gives an example from Cicero, where the orator imagines the Roman laws "reaching forth their hand to give us a sword for putting one to death." Only Blair's third degree of personification involves apostrophe or ventriloquism, the devices that tend to preoccupy modern critics. But Blair's designating it merely *one* version of the figure suggests the narrowness of our current focus.

Blair's first degree of personification, which we might call animation ("some of the properties or qualities of living creatures are ascribed to inanimate objects"), may require no more than a simple adjective. When James Thomson, in the first edition of *Winter* (1726) included among the sailor's perils "Unlist'ning Hunger" and "fainting Weariness" (line 353) he created two personifications in a single line. Hunger is not something but someone, capable of listening or not listening, just as Weariness is someone capable of fainting. Four years later, when Thomson revised the first phrase to "Heart-gnawing Hunger," he eliminated one personification, for most readers at least. "Gnawing" may be an action, but a "gnawing pain" is such a familiar metaphor that it requires no imagined agent to be intelligible.[4] These boundaries often blur, as the rhetorical theorists acknowledge. Kames questions whether the wind sweetly kissing the trees in *The Merchant of Venice* (V.i) and the "ambitious" ocean swelling in *Julius Caesar* (I.vi) constitute true "persons." He settles on a pragmatic conclusion: "it must depend upon the reader, whether they be examples of personification, or a figure of speech merely: a sprightly imagination will advance them to the former class, with a plain reader they will remain in the latter" (336–7).

We can see all three degrees of personification at work in this passage from Cowper's *The Task* in which he laments the loss of rigor in schools and universities, where formerly

> There dwelt a sage call'd Discipline. His head
> Not yet by time completely silver'd o'er,
> Bespoke him past the bounds of freakish youth,
> But strong for service still, and unimpair'd.
> His eye was meek and gentle, and a smile
> Play'd on his lips, and in his speech was heard
> Paternal sweetness, dignity, and love.

(II.702–8)

"Discipline" is 1) animate, 2) a deliberate agent, and 3) a fellow speaker. Although modern readers often concentrate attention on those personifications spoken to (apostrophe) and perhaps speaking, the mere fact of agency – purposeful action – may be most significant. Let us try to approach this possibility by looking further at examples of mild personification.

To see subdued rather than sublime personification, we need look no further than Gray's *Elegy*, a poem central in every sense to the period. Many of the personifications of ideas cluster in the quatrains leading up to the lines on Knowledge and Penury quoted earlier:

> Let not Ambition mock their useful toil,
> Their homely joys and destiny obscure;
> Nor Grandeur hear, with a disdainful smile,
> The short and simple annals of the poor.
> ...
> Nor you, ye Proud, impute to these the fault,
> If Memory o'er their tomb no trophies raise,
> Where through the long-drawn aisle and fretted vault
> The pealing anthem swells the note of praise.
>
> Can storied urn or animated bust
> Back to its mansion call the fleeting breath?
> Can Honour's voice provoke the silent dust,
> Or Flattery soothe the dull cold ear of Death?
>
> (29–32, 37–44)

To the company in these lines of Ambition (29), Grandeur (31), Memory (38), Honour (43), Flattery, Death (44) we can add several personifications later in the poem (some capitalized, some not): mercy (68), shame (70), luxury, pride (71), Forgetfulness (85), nature (91), Contemplation (95), Science (119), Melancholy (120), Misery (123). Perhaps none of these count as "passionate" or "real" in Kames's and Priestley's terms, or reach Blair's third degree of intensity, unlike various personifications in Gray's odes. Ambition and Grandeur might just barely qualify, since they speak and listen: "Let not Ambition mock ... Nor Grandeur hear ..." (29–33). But most rise to the level of "descriptive" or "ideal" personifications, since, to use Blair's criteria again, they either have "some of the qualities" of animate beings or act animately, typically through verbs indicating deliberate action. "Science *frowned* not" on the poet, and "Melancholy *marked* him for her own" (119–20).

Some others are more ambiguous. When Gray speculates that some kindred spirit might be "*led*" by Contemplation (95) to inquire after the poet, is Contemplation no more than a quality? Or is she (?) to be imagined as a matronly relative of Melancholy, beckoning with outstretched arm? (I will say more of the gender of various personifications in a moment.) In imagining a villager unable to "*shut* the gates of mercy on mankind" do we see only a faint metaphor or yet another female behind closing doors? Are Luxury and Pride more personified for sharing an altar ("To quench the blushes of ingenuous shame, / Or heap the shrine of Luxury and Pride" [70–1]) than shame for blushing, or are those blushes enacted not by a personification but by hypothetical flesh-and-blood blushers? Would there be a difference between the poem's concluding report that the poet "gave to *Misery* all he had, a tear" and an alternative pronouncement that he gave what little he could to *the miserable*?

It depends. It depends partly, as Kames would say, on the sprightliness of the reader's imagination. It also depends – as Kames and most other eighteenth-century critics would not feel the need to say – on the reader's iconographic repertoire. The reader who found Thomson's figure of Cultivation so compelling was accustomed to emblematic personifications and to pictured as well as literary allegories and "temples." We need to recognize that personification exists in hints as well as in elaboration, something latter-day critics looking for pictorial detail tend to ignore. At the same time, one need not go quite as far as Donald Davie, who maintains that personification results "to some extent" when any abstraction governs an active verb.[5] If I write that "conscience compels me to apologize for yesterday's rudeness," I may sound pretentious as well as sheepish, but *conscience* seems no more personified than *rudeness*. To report, however, that "conscience beat me up last night until I resolved to apologize" is to start to sound somewhat "poetic," as we say, which in this case means to begin to personify. The difference is not simply that "beat" is a *more* active verb than "compelled" or even that it is more visually suggestive, but rather that it suggests an *agent* performing an *intentional* action.

What difference does it make whether we come to eighteenth-century poems ready to meet the personifications halfway? First, our enjoyment increases if we see them as something more vivid than abstractions posing for an under-developed photograph. Second, we come closer to the probable experience of eighteenth-century readers. And third, we more fully apprehend the poem's statements and pleasures at once. The personifications in Gray's *Elegy* do not decorate a thesis. The poem is largely about the relation of rural obscurity to opportunity and power, asking "What mute inglorious Milton" might lie buried in the churchyard. It asks who can act independently and efficaciously, who are the nation's potent actors, and who are its buried potential. The poem's personifications, as shadowy figures existing on the border *between* description and action, embody the poem's meditation on problems of agency, autonomy, responsibility, and human capacity. To read hurriedly over the personifications as mere conventions would not only be to have "had the experience but missed the meaning," as T. S. Eliot says in *Dry Salvages*, but to miss both.

I will delve more into the meaning – that is, the cognitive work of personification – later in this chapter. Grasping that work requires first taking seriously a dimension of personification often thought to be merely incidental, its gender.

Personification herself?

One particular version of the view that underestimates personification as conventional is the so-called "grammatical theory" of personification. In general terms, it claims that since most personifications derive from abstract nouns in Greek, Latin, or later European languages that have grammatical gender, they become male or female in English simply because of their origins. Female personifications preponderate because abstract nouns are commonly grammatically feminine in these languages. So we should not make too much of the gender of Truth (*veritas*, f.), Liberty (*libertas*, f.), or any other "celestial maid" we encounter in poetic groves. How well this theory explains earlier literature remains in question, but it does not take us very far into the reality of eighteenth-century English poetry. Unlike most European languages, English does not have grammatical gender. English has only "natural" gender, which means that nouns for things and ideas are neuter and will normally take the pronoun "it." Eighteenth-century theorists begin to take note of this fact (preceded of course by the poets). Thus, as soon as an *English* poet speaks of Truth and "her" beauty or Time and "his" menace we are in the presence of personification, even without any further elaboration.

The gender of personifications like Liberty or Time seems obvious or inescapably conventional, but if feminist criticism of the last several decades teaches that little about gender is "self-evident," closer attention to eighteenth-century writing teaches that convention is less fixed than conventional wisdom might have it. In perhaps the period's most sustained attempt at a "philosophical" explanation of gender assignment, James Harris argued that while linguistic history determines some English personifications (an early version of the "grammatical theory"), many others are more "natural." In such cases, Harris believes, external reality, not language, determines the gender of the personification: "we may imagine a more subtle kind of reasoning, a reasoning which discerns even in *things without Sex* a distant analogy to that great natural distinction, *which* (according to *Milton*) *animates the World*." Harris devotes several pages of *Hermes: or, a Philosophical Inquiry concerning Lan-*

guage and Universal Grammar (1751) to explicating this supposedly natural divide and the force of inherited convention. Both efforts reveal interesting unacknowledged tensions in the use of personification.[6]

Harris begins, none too surprisingly, by equating male with activity and female with passivity.[7] Those substantives have been considered masculine – again, "naturally," not merely grammatically – that appeared "conspicuous for the Attributes of imparting or communicating; or which were by nature active, strong, and efficacious, and that indiscriminately whether to good or to bad; or which had claim to Eminence, either laudable or otherwise." Feminine substantives, on the other hand, were notable for the "Attributes either of receiving, of containing, or of producing and bringing forth; or which had more of the passive in their nature, than of the active; or which had respect to such Excesses, as were rather Feminine, than Masculine." Thus, the sun is masculine "from communicating Light" and from the "efficacy of his Rays," while the moon is feminine "from being the receptacle only of another's light, and from shining with Rays more delicate and soft." A ship is feminine because it/she is "so eminently a *Receiver* and *Container*," as is a city or a country, while Time is masculine due to "*his mighty Efficacy upon everything around us.*" Sometimes Harris's linguistic "logic" needs elaboration. For example, while the ocean might seem to be as much a receiver and container as is a city or country, and thus to be a likely female, "its *deep Voice* and *boisterous Nature* have, in spight of these reasons, prevailed to make it *Male*." Harris acknowledges that it is "not so easy to explain" the femininity of the Furies – certainly a strong and "efficacious" set – still, he theorizes, it is because "female Passions of all kinds were considered as susceptible of greater excess, than male Passions … that the *Furies* were to be represented, as things superlatively outrageous."

Harris, like many of the poets, has both a Platonic predilection for finding unchanging essences and a historian's interest in cultural practice. Convinced that personifications typically embody both, he points at once to the logic of things and to convention when opining on the appropriate gender of Death. It will invariably be masculine. If Time is masculine for its "mighty efficacy," Death's "irresistible Power" demands that it too be masculinized, as in *Paradise Lost*. Moreover, in personifying Death as male, Milton had the same "*Sanction of national Opinion*" as the ancient poets had for their deities. "Even the Vulgar with us," Harris concludes, "are so accustomed to this notion, that a FEMALE DEATH they would treat as ridiculous." Indeed, most of the representations of Death are of a male, usually wielding a dart or a scythe, and Milton himself had certainly added to the weight of "national opinion" in Harris's day since the figures of Death and Sin from Book II of *Paradise Lost* were widely known and illustrated, most recently by Hogarth in *Satan, Sin, and Death* (c. 1735–8). But it is an interesting index of the tension inscribed in eighteenth-century poetic personification that Harris was wrong about even a figure so well established and culturally determined as Death. Two poems published just a few years before *Hermes*, Robert Blair's *The Grave* (1743) and Gray's *Ode on a Distant Prospect of Eton College* (1742, pub. 1747), do in fact feature a female Death. Gray parades a host of personified ills awaiting the schoolboys in later years, among whom walks a conspicuously feminized Death:

> Lo, in the vale of years beneath
> A grisly troop are seen,
> The painful family of Death,
> More hideous than their Queen ...

(81–4)

Blair puts Death and Christ in opposition:

> *Death* disarm'd
> Loses her Fellness quite: All Thanks to him
> Who scourg'd the Venom out.

(710–12)

Despite Harris's confidence in the weight of custom, Blair's popular "grave-yard" poem presented a female Time as well:

> Sepulchral Columns wrestle but in vain
> With all-subduing Time: Her cank'ring Hand
> With calm deliberate Malice wasteth them ...[8]

(200–2)

These may be extreme cases, but they point toward more pervasive gender instability in the personification of the many figures much less constrained by convention, from Ambition to Youth. While feminine gender predominates and seems to be the "default setting" in the coinage of new personifications, eighteenth-century poetry affords many examples of abstract ideas figured as feminine in one poem and masculine in another, occasionally even in the work of the same poet. This gender instability may surprise us less when we notice that even physical entities such as the seasons waver in their identities. All four seasons are masculine in Spenser's *Mutability Cantos*, but only Winter remains invariably male (so far as I can tell) in later poetry. Autumn is generally male prior to Keats's great ode, but James Grainger envisioned a "laughing Autumn, plump and blithe" who has "sprung with the dawn, and whet her scythe."[9] Spring is overwhelmingly female for eighteenth-century poets, including William Collins in *Ode, Written in the Beginning of the Year 1746* –

> When Spring, with dewy fingers cold,
> Returns to deck their hallowed mould,
>   She there shall dress a sweeter sod
>   Than Fancy's feet have ever trod …

– but in another of Collins's own odes "Spring shall pour his show'rs, as oft he wont" (*Ode to Evening*, line 41). In the next lines Collins's Summer is of indeterminate gender ("Summer loves to sport / Beneath thy lingering light"), but masculine for Thomson (and in William Kent's frontispiece) and female for other writers such as William Cowper and William Stevenson.[10]

We might expect personifications to be constrained by mythology or strong literary precedent. But sometimes the tradition is ambiguous. Love appears as a female in Thomson's *Spring* and male in Finch's *Reputation*, for example, presumably because the personification can look back to either Aphrodite/Venus or Eros/Amor. Yet even when the tradition would seem to be unequivocal, poetic practice can vary. Chaos is female in Thomas Cooke's 1728 translation of Hesiod's *Theogony* (the Greek word is neuter) as is common in poems of the period, but "he" is male in James Beattie's *Ode to Peace*, and Henry Baker has Chaos reclaiming "his former right."[11] Strong medieval and Renaissance traditions, as well as grammar, enshrined Melancholy and Philosophy as females. Accordingly, Pope's Melancholy "round her throws / A death-like silence" in *Eloisa to Abelard* (lines 165–6), and Collins speaks entirely conventionally when he hopes to join Philosophy and "her votive train."[12] But Thomson can still create a new figure of Philosophic Melancholy and be inspired by "his" approach (*Autumn*, 1004–16).

If precedented figures vary, then all the more can those personifications with little or no iconographic identity. Knowledge is male in Book VI (line 96) of Cowper's *The Task* but, as we have seen, female in Gray's *Elegy*. Learning, another male figure in Book VI of *The Task* (line 87), is female not only in Thomson's *Autumn* (lines 895–7) but elsewhere in *The Task* itself (III.248–9). Learning is also male in, for example, Pope's *Prologue to Sophonisba* and James Cawthorn's *Wit and Learning: An Allegory* but female in Johnson's *Prologue Spoken by Garrick* and in Mary Masters' *The Female Triumph*, which equates her with Minerva.[13] Charles Churchill personifies Satire as female in *The Ghost*, as does John Brown in his verse *Essay on Satire*; but Cowper refers to Satire as having "long since done his best" and being more blamable "than those he brands."[14]

What are we to make of this array of curiosities and contradictions? The most important point is that context and connotation exert differentiating pressure. Blair presumably personified Death as female to underscore "her" weakness in relation to the male Christ as Redeemer. If, in the same poem, Cowper personifies Learning first as female and then as male, the imaginative contexts must differ. Comparing the two passages in *The Task*, one finds that in the first Learning as a female is associated with an idealized Philosophy and science, all of whom are subordinate to God:

> Philosophy, baptiz'd
> …
> Has eyes indeed; and viewing all *she* sees
> As meant to indicate a God to man,
> Gives *him* his praise, and forfeits not her own.
> Learning has borne such fruit in other days
> On all her branches …

(III.243, 245–9)

But in the later passage, where Learning is male, along with Knowledge and even Wisdom, Cowper seems to have in mind something more personal than European intellectual culture, something like the (representative) Learned Man rather than (universal) Learning. No male Other is present this time to dominate these qualities. Here, Cowper writes, the composed heart

> May give an useful lesson to the head,
> And learning grow wiser without his books.
> Knowledge and wisdom, far from being one,
> Have oft-times no connexion. Knowledge dwells
> In heads replete with thoughts of other men;
> Wisdom in minds attentive to their own.
> …
> Knowledge is proud that he has learn'd so much;
> Wisdom is humble that he knows no more.

(VI.86–91, 96–7)

Simple abstractions at the start of the passage, Knowledge and Wisdom materialize by the end to join Learning as full personifications.

In another imaginative context the small fraternity Cowper creates could easily be a small sorority. Surveying the body of eighteenth-century poetry carefully reveals more variable and creative uses of gender than discussions of personification usually suggest. Even these relatively incidental personifications indicate that the most productive readings will be those in which we assume little and attend contextually to the imaginative work performed by personification. We will now turn to the figure's cognitive work.

The knowledge of personification

Viewing personification cognitively means looking at it as a way of knowing and of communicating knowledge. This approach avoids two post-Romantic errors: on the one hand, dismissing personification as merely decorative, mechanical, or conventional, and, on the other, defining *real* personifications – the only kind to be taken seriously – as dramas of intrapersonal voices in the poet's head or confrontations with a non-human Other, as when Keats's urn or Shelley's Mountain speaks. This latter bias privileges internal conflict, passionate apostrophe, and sublime prosopopoeia (literally, putting a face on something and in Roman rhetoric usually thought of as figurative ventriloquism). A less evaluative and more down-to-earth approach to personification may better allow us to accommodate the range of personifications that eighteenth-century rhetoricians postulate and poets in fact use. In this light, poetic personification becomes interesting as a shared response to some fundamental intellectual problems in the period.

One of these is the cognitive status of poetry itself, that is, its relation to public truth generally or to philosophy more specifically. Personification helps to distance poetry from outworn mythology and to pull it closer to modern intellectual discourse. Eighteenth-century poets tend to see philosophy more as poetry's potential ally than antagonist but of course they recognize that they are different modes. Personification offers a way to bring an art dependent on sensuous particularity into a more harmonious relationship with a discourse of universals. The most conspicuous way of "philosophizing" is to subsume a great many (historical) particulars or sub-characteristics under a personified abstraction, such as Liberty, or Fame, or "Dulness," revealing the particulars' significance as parts of a larger whole.

Closely related to this effort is a cultural response to the problem of abstraction. Many personifications are responses, I believe, to the period's philosophical questions about whether abstract ideas are in fact *possible*. This lively debate begins with Berkeley's response to Locke early in the century. It deepens with Hume's broader skepticism in the middle years, and animates the "common-sense" defensive reactions to Hume by Thomas Reid and others in the later decades of the century. Bishop Berkeley, that still under-recognized champion of imagination, rejected Locke's contention that we can hold in mind ideas of things that are devoid of sensuous particularity. Poetic personifications, both casual and elaborate, thus attempt to transcend particularity while still retaining *some* sense of concreteness –through syntax at least, and often through gender, even when not pictorial.

Hume plays a crucial role in relation to another intellectual preoccupation of the period: the status of causation and thus more generally the understanding of agency. It does not seem mere coincidence that causation and abstraction become conspicuous problems at the same time. Hume's insistence that causation is a "contingent" or empirical relation rather than a "necessary" one is fundamentally similar to his critique of abstract ideas. To the general reader of poetry, thinking of causality as a contingent rather than necessary relation may at first sound like semantic fine-tuning. But it means our conviction that one thing causes another comes from repeated observation, not logical necessity. However convinced I am that the sun will rise tomorrow, only physical experience, not some metaphysical Truth about the fabric of the universe, underwrites my conviction. In the same way, our understanding of abstract ideas derives only from reiterated experience, not from some transcendent reality beyond experience. Having seen enough triangles or birds or people, I can form ideas of these entities which I learn to use, and take, categorically.

These continue to be important ideas, and not just for philosophers. In our time the question of abstraction and the perception of causation have been of great interest to cognitive psychologists. The first is usually discussed as category formation. Since the mid 1970s, the "prototype" view of category formation has become widely accepted.[15] According to this theory, we base our categories for most things not on abstract properties, definitions, or statistical averages, but on mental prototypes – essentially ideas, in Locke's sense of mental images. These form a kind of center of our categories, and we make decisions about other possible members of the category in terms of their proximity to the prototype. Asked to think of a generalized bird, Americans or Europeans are likelier to imagine a wren or a lark than a penguin, for a generic chair an armchair before a beanbag chair, and so on. Cognitive psychologists have shown no interest in Berkeley, but I think he might have been interested in them. The issue at stake is whether general ideas are abstract or imagistic, and Berkeley, Hume, and many cognitive psychologists (including neuropsychologists) are on the same, imagistic side. (Contemporary philosopher Jerry Fodor makes an interesting claim for Hume's *Treatise of Human Nature* [1739–40] as "the foundational document of cognitive science.")[16]

The problems of causation and agency merit attention because they will give us the most concrete sense both of the intellectual historical climate in which personification flourished and of what emerges when we approach it cognitively. In *More than Cool Reason* (1989), George Lakoff and Mark Turner treat personifications as versions of the conceptual metaphor "events are actions" (that is, events are thought of as if they are actions).[17] What work does this conceptual metaphor perform? Unlike events, actions do not just happen; they are caused by *intending* agents. This distinction is not peculiarly modern; something of the sort figures in most systems of ethics, including Aristotle's. But Joseph Butler formulated it in terms closest to those of Lakoff and Turner in the "Dissertation upon the Nature of Virtue" that he appended to *The Analogy of Religion* (1736). For Bishop Butler, "actions, as distinguished from events," result from "will and design, which constitute the very nature of actions as such." Intention is crucial; in fact, it is properly speaking "Part of the Action itself."[18] Looked at this way, many personifications, whether "serious" or not, are revealing instances of human meaning-making, quests for intelligibility. The events portrayed and explained through personification may be large-scale states of affairs or the behavior of individuals, for the personal parallel to the general distinction drawn earlier between events and actions is the distinction between *behavior* and (intentional) *action*. At the simple extremes, I *act* if I decide to leave a room because it grows too warm; I *behave* if, for the same reason, I perspire.

This treatment of agency is not philosophically exact, but it follows a fairly common distinction between action and behavior: action assumes voluntary movement or decision, intentionality, plans, the relevancy of inner states and evaluations, even evaluations of evaluations. Behavior, on the other hand, may be observed entirely externally, indeed is usually regarded as most strictly purely behavior when we limit ourselves to external, preferably measurable movement or changes. It was the proclaimed subject of behaviorist psychology in the mid twentieth century.

The academic tide turned decisively with Ulric Neisser's *Cognitive Psychology* (1967). While not all cognitive psychology is congenial to literary study, the fact that it allows the study of intentional action, not merely involuntary behavior, brings it closer to the kinds of ethical and aesthetic concerns likely to emerge in the study of literature. Its inquiry into learning as something other than conditioning, into perception, memory, inner states, desires, plans, mental representations, schemas, and scripts, have much to offer students of reading and imagination.

The Lakoff-Turner account offers a good starting point because it makes no qualitative assumptions: no personification is regarded as better, more real, less merely rhetorical, more serious, than another. Rather, all turn on the same cognitive step of regarding events as actions. The distinction remains philosophically imprecise, but we can make do, again, with a rough distinction between a change in a state of affairs that is attributable to an intending agent, usually human, and things that "just happen." It depends of course on who does the attributing. A tree branch falling to the ground is an event, unless it is seen, say, as thrown down by Boreas or, intentionally, by the tree itself. Lightning used to be the prerogative of Zeus, but for most readers of this book it probably just happens.

In an age, however, when the gods are dead, God distant, and animism unavailable, the desire to see one's world as the result of intentions, as made up more of actions than events, becomes harder to gratify. Most eighteenth-century writers continued to regard themselves as Christians and believed in divine providence, according to which things happen because God wills them. But increasingly Providence becomes the general background for explanation, a first or final cause to be acknowledged, rather than something invoked to account for most particular events. This familiar story of Enlightenment secularization and the spread of scientific understanding is oversimplified but roughly encapsulated in the historical view of a contemporary "eliminative materialist" such as Paul Churchland. In the primitive past, "the behavior of most of the elements of nature," writes Churchland, was "understood in intentional terms. The wind could know anger, the moon jealousy, the river generosity, the sea fury, and so forth. These were not metaphors ... Despite its sterility, this animistic approach to nature has dominated our history, and it is only in the last two or three thousand years that we have restricted folk psychology's literal interpretation to the domain of the higher animals."[19] In this narrative, intellectual progress means that less and less of what happens in the world can be explained credibly as the result of intention. As philosopher of science Robert N. McCauley puts it, the "history of science has been marked by increasing restriction of the range of phenomena for which agent causality constitutes an appropriate explanation."[20] Zeus has stopped throwing thunderbolts, and so too, for many eighteenth-century poets and readers, has the Judeo-Christian God.

But narratives of progress can often ignore twists and conflicts. Historian Stephen Toulmin complicates and particularizes the story of changing explanations in a way that helps us understand some of the tensions in late seventeenth- and eighteenth-century European consciousness. Part of the "modern world view" or great "division of Nature from Humanity" that Toulmin sees as emerging around the middle of the seventeenth century is the conception of matter as wholly inert. Matter is one thing, life another. Ideas of "thinking matter" or "living machines" (a machine with a soul, say) became unacceptable, and thus "vital" and "goal-directed" activity could less easily be explained in material terms. According to Toulmin, the result is a large historical irony:

> Today, scientists reject "vitalist" or "mentalist" appeals to *immaterial* agencies to explain life and thought as hangovers from the Middle Ages. Yet, far from those two positions being medieval relics, they were forced on seventeenth and eighteenth-century science for the first time, by the need to fill gaps left by the accepted definition of "matter" and "machines"; and, as such, they were purely modern novelties.[21]

In short, various developments in philosophy and science had the double effect of appearing to make explanation easier and harder at the same time: easier by doing without appeals to mysterious agents, harder by calling the traditional vocabulary of explanation into question.

In the rest of this chapter, then, I will try to show that our encounters with many personifications in eighteenth-century poetry may be richer if we think of them as causal explanations, figurative attempts to make events legible by turning them into actions. Toulmin's account suggests that one reason the desire for such legibility might have grown particularly strong during the period is uncertainty about whether to think of causes as material or immaterial entities. A useful feature of personifications is their ambiguous or equivocal ontological status. How or where do they exist? Somewhere between fact and conscious fiction, somewhat spiritual but not literal ghosts, they are liminally objective/subjective creatures, borderline figures seeming at once to live "out there" and in the mind. Two stanzas from Christopher Smart's *A Morning Piece, or An Hymn for the Hay-Makers* (1752) suggest the condition and modernity of some eighteenth-century personifications:

> Brisk chaunticleer his mattins had begun,
>   And broke the silence of the night,
> And thrice he call'd aloud the tardy sun,
>   And thrice he hail'd the dawn's ambiguous light;
> Back to their graves the *fear-begotten* phantoms run.
>
> (lines 1–5, my emphasis)

The phantoms are at once fear-begotten and visible. Not quite embodied abstractions themselves, they prepare the ground for two personifications who are embodied:

> Strong Labour got up with his pipe in his mouth,
> He stoutly strode over the dale,
> He lent new perfumes to the breath of the south,
> On his back hung his wallet and flail.
> Behind him came Health from her cottage of thatch,
> Where never physician had lifted the latch …
>
> (6–11)

Labour and Health are not exactly an individual man and woman, but they are also not exactly *un*individualized. Clearly, on one level, the lines depict robust male and female *workers* going to their tasks. But the lines would represent a different reality if Smart used the plural in that way. The lines would also represent something different had he particularized, say, Robert and Joan. To return to the cognitive theory of category formation outlined earlier, Smart instead seems to be giving the reader an implicit representation of a group or class *through prototypes*.

A Morning Piece, or An Hymn for the Hay-Makers is a celebration, not an argumentative poem, but even here the faintly picturesque personifications move toward interpretation and explanation. Labour and Health embody not only a group but also a view of a group, a view that includes the idea that the rural poor are healthier and generally more virtuous than the rich. This idea presents the existing social order as essentially benign (not being rich has its compensations). In such a world, the three Graces of classical myth can reappear in a parade of rural stability:

> First the vestal Virtue, known
> By her adamantine zone;
> Next to her in rosy pride,
> Sweet Society the bride;
> Last Honesty, full seemly drest
> In her cleanly home-spun vest.

(16–21)

Presiding over the poem, "pious Gratitude" sings "Her morning hymn to heav'n," which could be another name for the work itself. Recognizing that the personifications in this poem help Smart say that all is well with the world, where farm laborers have so much to be grateful for, is not to cast him as a paternalistic villain. The poem is, indeed, a hymn *for* haymakers, not by them. But as this example shows, personifications embody both perceptions and conceptions – a double role that allows them to function poetically as both images and interpretations.

I have been arguing that personification provides a way of addressing period questions about the nature of causes. Why else might poets feel the need to render events more legible by figuring them as actions? Heightened attention to problems of agency and free will lends a further motive. The tension between free will and determinism is one personifications themselves embody when treated as motivating forces or causes. Very generally, the anxieties about agency and free will are primarily individual or personal in the early part of the century and become more cultural or collective in the later years. We can think of the earlier focus as primarily psychological and the second as largely sociological. The first kind of anxiety is represented by Locke's difficulty in *The Essay Concerning Human Understanding* in treating free will. In the first edition of his great work (1690) Locke gave a short, fairly straightforward account of the will choosing the greater good. Within four years he greatly elaborated the account, giving a diminished role to rational, contemplative, judgment and now casting action primarily as a response to "uneasiness." Most of the time, we seem to act not to fulfill a rational intention but to reduce discomfort (*Essay*, Book II, ch. 21). Like any of his contemporaries, Locke needs to posit free will to remain religiously orthodox and ethically coherent, but at the same time his account of voluntary action begins to sound like a description of behavior.

Cultural determinism – less concerned with the constitution of individuals than with the constitution of society – begins to flicker in the Scottish Enlightenment in writing about what is increasingly called "civil society." Cultural determinism might be represented by Adam Smith's "invisible hand" – first articulated not in *The Wealth of Nations* (1776) but seventeen years earlier in *The Theory of Moral Sentiments* (1759). There, the Invisible Hand is a kind of secularized providential force that leads people to do what they did not intend. Nature "imposes on us" by deluding us into thinking that our industry and acquisitiveness will make us happier than they possibly could:

> this deception ... rouses and keeps in constant motion the industry of mankind. It ... first prompted them to cultivate the ground ... build houses ... found cities and commonwealths, and ... invent and improve all the sciences and arts, which ennoble and embellish human life ... The rich ... are led by an invisible hand to make nearly the same distribution of the necessaries of life, which would have been made, had the earth been divided into equal portions among all its inhabitants, and thus without intending it, without knowing it, advance the interest of the society ...[22]

Under Smith's optimistic tone lies a vision as deterministic as the harshest contemporary sociobiology: our motivation springs not from the desire to maximize happiness but from a secret imperative to maximize production and reproduction. Economic optimism keeps the expression of social determinism muted in Smith, but the idea that we do not truly understand the imperatives of our most social deeds suggests a severe limit on our agency. These eighteenth-century versions of cultural determinism raise the same fear that any determinism raises, namely that what one thought was "action" is merely behavior.

The connection of these intellectual problems – causes as material or immaterial and determinism whether individual or social – crystallizes beautifully
in the comedy of Pope's *The Rape of the Lock* and the figures of the sylphs,
those tiny, airy creatures, *nearly* immaterial in their ethereal natures, who
partly work to "explain" the actions of the poem's human characters. Here is
Ariel's account of how young women preserve their chastity despite strong
temptations:

> What guards the purity of melting Maids,
> In courtly Balls, and midnight Masquerades
> …
> When kind occasion prompts their warm desires,
> When music softens, and when dancing fires?
> Tis but their *Sylph*, the wise Celestials know,
> Tho' *Honour* is the word with Men below.

(Canto I, lines 71–2, 75–8)

It is a mock-explanation, as we saw in Chapter 7, but the poem plays with
the idea that the abstraction Honour, although conventionally invoked as a
cause, may at bottom be no less mysterious than the invisible sylphs. The poem
raises questions, lightly to be sure, about what moves material beings into
action, about whether the humans in the poem act freely, about what causal
explanation really amounts to (especially when an abstraction is invoked), and
whether poetry is particularly well suited to such explanation.

Without being too heavy-handed about it, we can see poets later in the century often in a position similar to Ariel's: they explicate visible events in terms
of invisible agents, or rather agents who would normally be invisible to the
reader. Such accounts range from witty just-so stories to teleological histories
to ardent prophecy. An example of playful explanation occurs in *Love, Death,
and Reputation*, a poetic fable by Anne Finch that explains why reputations
are precarious:

> *Reputation, Love,* and *Death,*
> (The Last all Bones, the First all Breath,
> The Midd'st compos'd of restless Fire)
> From each other wou'd Retire;
> Thro' the World resolv'd to stray,
> Every One a several Way …[23]

Finch would personify more earnestly in other poems, such as *The Spleen* and
Upon the Hurricane. But she, Swift, Parnell, and countless other eighteenth-
century authors enjoyed this sport of playful explanation through personifications in action.

At the other end of the spectrum, where personification focuses ardent revelation, lie most of the odes of Collins and much of Smart's *Song to David*. In these two stanzas Adoration acts as the motivating force of all things:

LIII

Rich almonds colour to the prime
For ADORATION; tendrils climb,
  And fruit-trees pledge their gems;
And Ivis with her gorgeous vest
Builds for her eggs her cunning nest,
  And bell-flowers bow their stems …

LIX

Now labour his reward receives,
For ADORATION counts his sheaves
  To peace, her bounteous prince;
The nectarine his strong tint imbibes,
And apples of ten thousand tribes,
  And quick peculiar quince.[24]

In Ariel's terms, one might imagine Smart saying, "'Tis Adoration, though Nature (or Labor or Peace) is the name with men below." Later in the century, poet and critic John Donaldson attributes the motive for personification to a double need to seek life and to admire it. In *Elements of Beauty* (1780) Donaldson concludes that "Man is an image admiring his own likeness: and such is his inclination to admire every thing that has life, that what is wanting in nature he frequently supplies from fancy; and when disposed to admiration, he enlivens every thing, that he may still find more occasion to admire" (p. 47).[25] Donaldson's admiration is Smart's adoration.

As the frequency of personification increases in the second half of the eighteenth century, new kinds of personifications begin to emerge. In keeping with the shift I have outlined, from concern over the possibility of *individual* determinism to greater concern over the possibility of *cultural* determinism, some important personifications begin to function as a kind of proto-social theory. The next chapter will look more closely at these cultural personifications and other poetic representations of society.

Chapter 11

Prophecy and prospects of society

Personification and "society"   *179*
Elizabeth Tollet and William Wordsworth on Westminster
Bridge   *181*
Commerce, Liberty, Dulness, and other goddesses   *184*
Villages of the whole: Goldsmith, Gray, Crabbe   *189*
Social redemption and negative sociology (Pope, Thomson, Thomas
Warton, Macpherson, Chatterton)   *193*

Many eighteenth-century poems are not only social but also sociological. This claim requires illustration, and specification. Modern sociologists would not be convinced by this chapter that their discipline begins with eighteenth-century poets rather than nineteenth-century historians and philosophers, and lovers of poetry may not feel their pulses quicken at the thought of poetic sociology, a phrase that sounds oxymoronic. To any social scientists who have happened upon this chapter and to students of poetry, let me say at once that I do not make scientific claims for Pope, Goldsmith, or other poets of the century. Instead, what follows will focus on eighteenth-century poets' distinctive fascination with the "prospect of society" as a subject for poetry. This phrase comes from the subtitle of Goldsmith's poem *The Traveller* (1764), but it could be the subtitle or title of his more famous poem, *The Deserted Village* (1770) – and of many other works, ranging from major poems such as Pope's *Windsor-Forest* (1714) and the third epistle of *An Essay on Man* ("Of the State of Man with respect to Society"), Thomson's *Castle of Indolence* (1748), Crabbe's *The Village* (1783), and Cowper's *The Task* (1785) to long-forgotten works such as Thomson's *Liberty* (1735–6) or Richard Glover's *London* (1739). It seems emblematic of the period's openness to sociological poetry that Bernard Mandeville's early foray into political economy, *The Fable of the Bees* (1714), began life as a poem (*The Grumbling Hive; or, Knaves Turn'd Honest*, 1705).

Personification and "society"

Probably the most famous eighteenth-century poem embodying social theory, Goldsmith's *The Deserted Village* (1770), features Commerce, Trade, and Wealth merging into Depopulation and controlling the lives of the few remaining villagers. I will return to this work but want to note here the fated contest that Goldsmith stages between the chaste "fair Auburn" (the speaker's native village) and the decadent "Land by luxury betrayed." Neither Auburn nor the "rural virtues" can win out against the combined force of Luxury and "the Tyrant's hand," a kind of malevolent counterpart to Adam Smith's "invisible hand," about which more in a moment as well.

One of Goldsmith's essays in the short-lived weekly paper *The Bee* (1759), "A City Night-Piece," seems to come close to embodying a central precondition for modern sociological thought: a new, less personal definition of "society." As he describes the poorest of the homeless poor huddled on the London streets, Goldsmith reflects that "the world seems to have disclaimed them; society turns its back upon their distress, and has given them up to nakedness and hunger."[1] A section of Cowper's *The Task* endows "society" with a similar agency. In Cowper's nostalgic moralizing about "once simple" country folk now being corrupted by taverns, we can see his perception of "society" as a distinct and secular entity:

> 'Tis here they learn
> The road that leads from competence and peace
> To indigence and rapine; till at last
> Society, grown weary of the load,
> Shakes her encumber'd lap, and casts them out.[2]

Through most of its history, "society" meant "company" – as when one might prefer solitude to society, or Milton's Adam finds "fit society" in Eve. Even the more technical-sounding phrase "civil society" in the first part of the century tended to mean either "polite company" or legal governance. Goldsmith's and Cowper's usage suggests something more than the law and less voluntary than select company. The word is shifting toward a recognizably modern perception of society as having an agency of its own. As Raymond Williams says in *Keywords*, the word would come to mean "a system of common life," where the "laws of society are not so much laws for getting on with other people but more abstract and more impersonal laws which *determine* social institutions" (my italics).[3] The idea of determination emerges in Goldsmith's and Cowper's personified "Society," which embodies a vague perception of forces larger – and less yielding – than individuals.

Curiously, the phrase "social science" seems to make its entry into poetry in the middle decades of the eighteenth century, when it appears in poems by William Collins and Mark Akenside. In *The Manners. An Ode* (1746), Collins refers to Manners or the study of human actions directly (rather than from books) in this way: "Thou Heaven, whate'er of great we boast, / Hast blest this social science most." In Akenside's *The Remonstrance of Shakespeare* (pub. 1772, probably written in the 1760s), Shakespeare rises from the dead to tell British playgoers that he wrote on the side of freedom, virtue, and glory, and that they, a century and a half later, should be doing even better, "now that England spurns her Gothic chain, / And equal laws and social science reign."[4]

Neither Collins nor Akenside mean by "social science" just what we do, but Akenside's phrase seems at least distantly related, suggesting an enlightened advance in "scientific" understanding of a realm that functions independently of, or on another level than, private life. The idea of an advance in understanding society grows simultaneously with the idea that society itself advances. Until society can be imagined as capable of change, it can hardly be imagined at all. But as it gradually becomes possible in the century to speak of the "present state of society," and to imagine the present as a "stage" on the way to some other stage, "society" as an entity comes into being. The passages from Akenside and Collins point toward the way some personifications in eighteenth-century poetry function in social description and explanation: they work as a way of registering and to some extent analyzing "forces" operating in the culture that are more powerful than individuals.[5] Among these sorts of personifications loom Empire, Liberty, and Luxury, closely followed by forces such as Commerce, Industry, Science, and of course Virtue and Vice, portrayed in countless poems as rising or falling, and as the "invisible hands" causing or directing events in the recent past, present, and often future.

As we saw in the preceding chapter, the "invisible hand" that Adam Smith first imagined in *The Theory of Moral Sentiments* (1759) causes individual members of society to contribute to the good of society in ways they did not intend. The idea was not wholly new. Bernard Mandeville's popular, if scandalous, pronouncement in *The Fable of the Bees* that "private vices" lead to "public benefits" had a major influence on Smith's thought. Stronger in Smith is the idea of social agency, that is, agency shifted from individuals to society, which is supported by a kind of secularized Providence. The force that deludes people into pursuing wealth in quest of individual happiness does actually work in Smith's view to make a great *collective* difference, namely modern culture.

Something similar had been developing in Pope's poetry of the 1730s (echoes of which occur frequently in Smith's writings) around his concept of the "ruling passion." Pope develops the idea both individually and socially. At the level of individual psychology, as in the *Epistle to Cobham* and *Epistle to a Lady*, Pope's ruling passion becomes a dominant motive or behavioral tendency: one person's actions are best understood as manifestations of his greed, another's by her love of power, his thirst for fame, her love of pleasure, and so on. But when Pope takes a broader view of society as a whole, the varied ruling passions become Providence's way of assuring that different individuals do the world's many kinds of work. The motives that lead some to hoard wealth, for example, and some to spend it, are implanted by

> That Pow'r who bids the Ocean ebb and flow,
> Bids seed-time, harvest, equal course maintain,
> Thro' reconcil'd extremes of drought and rain,
> Builds Life on death, on Change duration founds,
> And gives th' eternal wheels to know their rounds.
>
> (*Epistle to Bathurst* [1733], 166–70)

Pope returns to the idea a few years later, attributing the harmonious functioning of society to "that Directing Pow'r, / Who forms the Genius in the natal Hour." This phrasing perhaps sounds too close to determinism for comfort, prompting Pope to add immediately, "That God of Nature, who, within us still, / Inclines our Action, not constrains our Will."[6]

Neither Pope nor Smith would have wanted to appear to deny free will, but the modern social thought that emerges in the French and Scottish Enlightenments tends to involve at least some degree of determinism. Seen through these new lenses, individuals increasingly seem products of something beyond their personal control, such as the climate of their nation, the "stage" of society they are born into, or the form of government under which they live. And personification offers one way of figuring such determining forces before the discourse of "social science" emerges. I will turn to several poems built on social personifications shortly. Before doing so, I will juxtapose two poems that help illustrate the imaginative importance of the idea that one's present society is *a* society.

Elizabeth Tollet and William Wordsworth on Westminster Bridge

Wordsworth's *Composed upon Westminster Bridge, September 3, 1802* (pub. 1807) may be found in countless anthologies but I quote it here for convenience:

> Earth has not anything to shew more fair:
> Dull would he be of soul who could pass by
> A sight so touching in its majesty:
> This City now doth, like a garment, wear
> The beauty of the morning; silent, bare,
> Ships, towers, domes, theatres, and temples lie
> Open unto the fields, and to the sky;
> All bright and glittering in the smokeless air.
> Never did sun more beautifully steep
> In his first splendour valley, rock, or hill;
> Ne'er saw I, never felt, a calm so deep!
> The river glideth at his own sweet will:
> Dear God! the very houses seem asleep;
> And all that mighty heart is lying still!

Tollet's poem of the same length, *On the Prospect from Westminster Bridge, March 1750*, is not easy to find and is quoted here out of necessity:

> CAESAR! renown'd in Science as in War,
> Look down a while from thy maternal Star:
> See! to the Skies what sacred Domes ascend,
> What ample Arches o'er the River bend;
> What Vills above in rural Prospect lye,
> Beneath a Street that intercepts the Eye,
> Where happy Commerce glads the wealthy Streams,
> And floating Castles ride. Is this the *Thames*?
> The Scene where brave *Cassibelan* of Yore
> Repuls'd thy Legions on a savage Shore?
> *Britain* 'tis true was hard to overcome,
> Or by the Arms, or by the Arts of *Rome*,
> Yet we allow thee Ruler of the Sphere;
> And last of all resign thy *Julian* Year.[7]

Considering these poems together raises emblematic differences, formal and thematic, between eighteenth-century and Romantic poetry. Although each poem is fourteen lines long, Tollet does not seem to be writing a sonnet; her seven couplets might have been six or eight had she a little more or a little less to observe. Very few sonnets had been written for over a century in 1750, and the form would not enjoy a real revival for a few more decades. By the time of Wordsworth's poem the sonnet's return was well underway; Wordsworth's sonnet is one of hundreds he would write, several of them in London in September, 1802. The occasion of Tollet's poem is public – the opening of the first Westminster Bridge across the Thames – while Wordsworth's occasion is autobiographical, specifying the morning of his visit to the bridge. In a note added later, Wordsworth would specify further that the sonnet was "written on the roof of a coach on my way to France." Tollet's occasion is in fact doubly historical, rather than biographical, as she contemplates the convergence of two topics of 1750: the bridge's completion and the fact that in England the Gregorian calendar has still not displaced the Julian calendar (named for Julius Caesar), as it would two years later. Wordsworth's occasion, on the other hand, turns out to be doubly personal: the poem records not only the time of a particular visit to the spot but also, putatively, of the poem's composition.

As we might expect, Tollet's poem celebrates the human achievement of the bridge itself and the prosperity evident in the built environment: "happy Commerce glads the wealthy Streams." Tollet's lines pose the human constructions against the backdrop of the natural scene, and most of what she points out is new. The first thing the Caesar of 1750 would see are modern churches, many of them built in the reign of Queen Anne (1702–14) and shortly after. "Domes" in eighteenth-century usage are notable buildings of any shape, not necessarily domed; thus, Tollet's "sacred domes" would stand out against the sky because of their tall steeples. The bridge's large and handsome "arches" stand out against the water, and the "Vills" (or villas) that have sprung up recently in an era of commercial expansion also emerge visually in the "rural" background, while new boats substantial enough to look like "floating Castles" contrast with the ancient Thames.

Wordsworth finds the prospect beautiful almost *despite* its ships and buildings, or rather because these structures of human activity are uncharacteristically silent, reduced to a landscape, of a piece for the moment with fields and sky. In dawn's first light these equal the splendor of "valley, rock, or hill," a comparison that ennobles them for Wordsworth but that could only have seemed bizarre or bathetic in Tollet's celebration of the streets, commercial waterway, and human energy of Georgian London.

Both poems move from description to reflection a little more than halfway through. In Tollet's poem the turn comes in the middle of line 8, with "Is this the Thames?", a question half-rhetorical and half imputed to the resurrected Julius Caesar. In Wordsworth, the turn launches the sestet, which shifts from the present moment to this moment's place in the whole of the poet's life: "Never did sun more beautifully steep …" For Tollet, the interesting timescale is vastly historical, millennial, not biographical. Compared to Tollet, Wordsworth's autobiographical perspective can seem somewhat claustrophobic: a whole lifetime, yes, but then *only* a lifetime. Tollet's invocation of Caesar and Cassibelan (also Cassivellaunus: Tollet takes the form of the name used by Shakespeare in *Cymbeline*) frames the Thames in a context of over 1800 years.

Cassibelan was a British chieftain at the time of Julius Caesar's failed invasions of England, in 55 and 54 BCE. The expansive double exposure of ancient and contemporary London resembles in its daring that of Joseph Conrad's narrator Marlow who, at the beginning of *Heart of Darkness* (1899), looks at the Thames and imagines how savage it would have seemed to a Roman soldier "who first came here, nineteen hundred years ago – the other day." Tollet and most of her contemporaries have not yet reached the gloomy historical relativism that would prompt Marlow's ironic reflection, "And this also has been one of the dark places of the earth," implying that in some sense it still may be; on the contrary, Tollet celebrates the bright light of metropolitan modernity. But historical irony of a gentler sort emerges in the poem's wit: while Caesar himself could not conquer England, the Julian calendar bearing his name still holds sway over the English. The act authorizing England's belated conversion to the Gregorian calendar would take effect in 1752, but in March of 1750, the part of Western Europe farthest from Caesar's reach during his life still follows his temporal lead.

I have lingered on Tollet's poem for two reasons: it deserves to be better known and it embodies neatly a self-conscious sense of being part of a modern society, a society visible to the naked eye because of recent changes all around. London, which grew from a city of just over half a million at the start of the century to over a million at the end, was becoming not only an increasingly powerful capital of England but also the largest and arguably most important city in Europe. By Wordsworth's time, these changes could engender melancholy, but through most of the century poets tend to see London's growth as epitomizing the energetic emergence of modern society, for good and ill.

Commerce, Liberty, Dulness, and other goddesses

Not all celebrations of London and the country for which it stands open as easily to modern readers as Tollet's *On the Prospect from Westminster Bridge*. Nationalistic panegyric only rarely enlists the best poets or outlasts its age. It is Johnson's satiric *London* (1738), not Richard Glover's enthusiastic *London: or, The Progress of Commerce* (1739), that is still with us. Pope's cultural vision of the progress of dullness, *The Dunciad, in Four Books* (1743), lives while the five books of James Thomson's progress poem *Liberty* (1736) resist resuscitation. But it is worth pausing over these failed poems long enough to understand the basic framework for more complex "prospects of society." Uncomplicated by irony, Glover's *London* and Thomson's *Liberty* show straightforwardly how prospects, personification, and prophecy tend to go together. In the poetry of natural description, a "prospect" is a pleasing vista of the present. But in the poetry of social description, prospects frequently reach into the future. The fourth part of *Liberty* had already brought Liberty's progress from antiquity to Thomson's London, and the fifth part, Thomson announces, "concludes with a prospect of future times, given by the Goddess of Liberty: this described by the author, as it passes in vision before him." In this vision, Britain's future is determined by Liberty, who will – aided by Justice, Mercy, and "social Freedom" – triumph over Corruption. As Glover explains in his preface, the controlling goddess of his vision, Commerce, "is suppos'd on our invitation to choose England for her chief abode, more particularly London, our principal emporium, as well as capital city."[8] Like many in 1739, Glover wants to keep that emporium bustling through a more aggressive defense of British trade routes. By the end of *London: or, The Progress of Commerce*, he envisions a Britain presiding over other nations by means of its armed "gigantic Terrour" and presided over itself by Liberty, Security, and Fame.

These fantasies of control shape both celebratory and critical prospects of society in eighteenth-century poetry. In the latter, personified forces such as Luxury, Vice, or Dulness lead the country irresistibly to ruin. But not only the pessimistic visions (to which we will return) can succeed poetically. The same imaginative premise manifested in Thomson's dusty *Liberty* – a personified abstraction moves through history and geography to arrive in modern Britain – informs William Collins's brilliant *Ode to Liberty*. Collins succeeds in celebration where Thomson fails partly because his poem runs 144 lines long rather than 3,378. More important, Collins manages to bring to the subject in lyric form a visionary mythopoesis. Myth-making informs each of the four parts of Collins's ode – strophe, epode, antistrophe, and second epode – before the poem concludes with a prophetic sketch of Liberty in an imminent future joining with another personification, Concord (peace), to "rule the West."

The national piety of this conventional apocalypse does little to explain the power of the *Ode to Liberty*, which resides rather in the stages of mythopoesis it employs. Collins introduces Liberty at once as elusive and fragile: elusive because of her mysterious origin, putatively in Sparta, and fragile because the destruction she suffered early in her career in Rome presumably could occur again. A daring synecdoche embodies this vision, as Collins evokes the Fall of Rome through a single symbolic act. Collins frames this arresting symbol in paralipsis, the rhetorical device of saying what one says one won't (as in, "I will not mention the many rumors of my opponent's domestic difficulties"). The poet does not wish to raise the "mindful Tears" of his muse Liberty (or Freedom) by recalling her darkest hour; but of course he *does* want to remind the reader:

> No, *Freedom*, no, I will not tell
> How *Rome*, before thy weeping face,
> With heaviest Sound, a Giant-statue, fell,
> Push'd by a wild and artless Race
> From off its wide ambitious Base,
> When Time his Northern Sons of Spoil awoke,
>   And all the blended Work of Strength and Grace,
>   With many a rude repeated Stroke
> And many a barb'rous Yell, to thousand Fragments broke.
>
> (17–25)

The rapacious destruction of Liberty-as-statue will eventually be balanced by the poetic reconstruction of Liberty's shrine near the end of the ode.

The metaphoric rape of Liberty sets in motion a series of visionary moments, complex enough to call for a brief summary of them prior to commentary. The first epode (lines 26–62) sketches the "progress" of Liberty selectively from the Italian Renaissance to contemporary Britain. The antistrophe (63–88) also ends in modern England but gets there by imagined geology rather than history. Collins elaborates a tradition that England was originally part of the Continent, until a cataclysmic earthquake occurred, and a "wide wild Storm ev'n Nature's self confounding" (74) created what is now the English Channel:

> This pillared earth so firm and wide,
> By winds and inward labours torn,
> In thunders dread was pushed aside,
>   And down the shouldering billows borne.
>
> (76–9)

The providential violence effects a "blest Divorce" that allows Liberty, the poet reminds her, to choose Britain as "thy lov'd, thy last Abode" (88). The word "last" could – and at least partly does – mean "latest" rather than final. But it is a word, as we have seen in the "Ode on the Poetical Character," that Collins likes to have both ways. The idea that "Westward the course of empire takes its way" was well established, and, while sojourning in Rhode Island in the early 1730s, the philosopher George Berkeley had given it a transatlantic updating in *Verses on the Prospect of planting Arts and Learning in America*. The second epode comprises three events: 1) the vision and destruction of an ancient shrine of Liberty that once existed at England's "Navel" and now exists as a "Model" somewhere beyond the sunset (89–113); 2) the poem's imaginative recreation of Liberty's shrine – "Ev'n now ... it seems to rise!" – (114–28); and 3) the prophecy that Liberty will merge with Concord, fully reign in Britain, and receive fitting tribute (129–44) as other nations proclaim, "O how supremely art thou blest, / Thou, Lady, Thou shalt rule the West!"

Like most of Collins's odes, the *Ode to Liberty* explores the role of the poet, and Collins's position ranges between diffidence and daring. He begins by insisting that his subject's daunting magnitude requires a Greek lyric poet reborn, some "New Alcaeus, Fancy-blest" (7), and ends by asserting his own privileged position as Liberty's shrine takes shape "before his favor'd Eyes" (117). More emphatic in this poem is the poet's role in relation to Society as a unified force. In Collins's vision, Concord really functions to give Liberty a "social Form" (132). In other words, the poem imaginatively reconciles peace and Liberty and then gives Liberty control of society – a paradoxical relationship, since Liberty partly means freedom from control. The poem thus creates what it strains to envision: a society under its own "rule."

Britain's imagined political apotheosis in the eyes of the rest of the world concludes many eighteenth-century "progress" or "prospect" poems, examples of what a recent critic has called "anthems of empire."[9] Without ignoring the "aggressive nationalism" or imperialist rationales in many of these poems, we can see a shared imaginative element, as I suggested earlier, in optimistic and pessimistic poems alike: their depiction of a social world ruled and unified by personified forces. In fact, society seems increasingly to *be* these forces. We find this social vision in both its bright and dark lights within the work of Pope, its extremes marked by his first "prospect of society," *Windsor-Forest* (1713), and his last, the final version of *The Dunciad* (1743). At the close of *Windsor-Forest*, Pope's Father Thames himself envisions a dominant Britain in turn ruled by Peace herself:

> Oh stretch thy reign, fair Peace! from shore to shore,
> Till Conquest cease, and slav'ry be no more;
> Till the freed *Indians* in their native groves
> Reap their own fruits, and woo their sable Loves
> …
> Exil'd by thee from earth to deepest hell,
> In brazen bonds shall barb'rous Discord dwell:
> Gigantic Pride, pale Terror, gloomy Care,
> And mad Ambition, shall attend her there:
> There purple Vengeance bath'd in gore retires,
> Her weapons blunted, and extinct her fires …
>
> (407–10, 413–18)

In the fourth book of *The Dunciad* the goddess Peace becomes the goddess Dulness, whose pervasive mental sleep signals the end of an age rather than a beginning. The "fires" going "extinct" are the lights of culture flickering out to make way for her reign:

> Thus at her felt approach, and secret might,
> *Art* after *Art* goes out, and all is Night
> …
> In vain! they gaze, turn giddy, rave, and die.
> *Religion* blushing veils her sacred fires,
> And unawares *Morality* expires.
> Nor *public* Flame, nor *private*, dares to shine;
> Nor *human* Spark is left, nor Glimpse *divine*!
> Lo! thy dread Empire, Chaos! is restor'd;
> Light dies before thy uncreating word …

(IV.639–40, 648–54)

I quoted part of this ending in its 1729 form earlier (pp. 126–7). In the expanded version, two new emphases heighten the self-consciously ironic continuity between *Windsor-Forest* and *The Dunciad*. First, the added lines on Religion and Morality (649–52) intensify the imagery of fires, flames, and sparks; where before Discord was chained and the flames of tyranny smoldered, here Discord governs while flames of culture die out. Second, the new lines make more explicit the relation of the individual to society, as "public" and "private" character are parts of the same cultural whole – a whole now represented by the "resistless" influence of Dulness.

Pope's supposition that as children of Dulness the dunces have no individual agency with which to resist her "sway" is on one level simply an insulting joke: Pope satirizes them precisely as individuals acting badly (many by having attacked Pope in print). Yet readers of *The Dunciad* tend to find the individuals nearly irrelevant. Something more than comic disdain fuels Pope's claim that "the *Poem was not made for these Authors, but these Authors for the Poem*."[10] The attention devoted in Book IV to the formative power of social institutions, especially the "whole Course of Modern Education" (Pope's note to line 501), creates a perspective in which individuals seem less real than the culture of which they are symptoms. Many of them, as Pope's revisions and notes testify, are readily replaceable. Dulness, shadowy and shapeless as she is, carries more ontological weight in *The Dunciad* than does even its ostensible hero, Colley Cibber.

The figure of Dulness presiding over the final *Dunciad* as the consolidating force of contemporary society had been taking shape in Pope's imagination through the 1730s. In the *Epistle to Bathurst* (1733) the unitary force is Corruption, in a prophecy ironically attributed to the greedy Sir John Blunt, director of the South Sea Company:

> "At length, *Corruption*, like a gen'ral flood,
> (So long by watchful Ministers withstood)
> Shall deluge all; and *Av'rice* creeping on
> Spread like a low-born mist, and blot the *Sun* …"
>
> (137–40)

Pope's *Epilogue to the Satires. Dialogue I* (originally published as *One Thousand Seven Hundred and Thirty Eight*) personifies the underlying societal dynamic as Vice, whose triumph anticipates the "all-composing" power of Dulness:

> In golden Chains the willing World she draws,
> And hers the Gospel is, and hers the Laws:
> Mounts the Tribunal, lifts her scarlet head,
> And sees pale Virtue carted in her stead!
> …
> Our Youth, all liv'ry'd o'er with foreign Gold,
> Before her dance; behind her crawl the Old!
>
> (147–50, 155–6)

As I argued in the preceding chapter, personification can be used to envision potentially countable individuals as a collective mass. The "gen'ral flood" of Corruption, the "willing World" of Vice, and the "vast involuntary throng" of Dulness (IV.82) are all images of a society that seems to have grown larger than the total of its parts.

Villages of the whole: Goldsmith, Gray, Crabbe

Pessimistic prophecy of a more melancholy sort dominates the social vision of Goldsmith's *The Deserted Village*. At the close of the poem, Luxury and the depopulation Goldsmith attributes to it drive away all other competing forces, as the speaker sees the "rural virtues" –

> Contented toil, and hospitable care,
> And kind connubial tenderness …
> And piety, with wishes plac'd above,
> And steady loyalty, and faithful love.
> And thou, sweet Poetry

– all "leave the land."[11] The stark inclusion of Poetry in this exodus implies visionary lament for more than the village of Auburn or even for village life generally.

As has long been recognized, traditional pastoral poetry speaks to and about the metropolitan elite rather than to or about shepherds. Similarly, many of the village poems of the middle and later eighteenth century can usefully be read as less about the countryside than about the country. Local village life offers a way of thinking about the national village. Goldsmith's *The Traveller, or, a Prospect of Society. A Poem* anticipates his *Deserted Village* in using the condition of the village as an index of the condition of England. *The Traveller* is sociological because it is about societie*s* – plural – as it compares countries to each other and relates temperaments, manners, and modes of government to one another. As I argued earlier, even rudimentary sociological thinking depends on the ability to imagine alternatives to one's own society, and Goldsmith does. British society of course fares well in the traveler's comparison of Italy, Switzerland, Holland, and France to his home, because Britain's "Freedom" fosters full human self-realization:

> I see the lords of human kind pass by,
> Intent on high designs, a thoughtful band,
> By forms unfashion'd, fresh from Nature's hand;
> Fierce in a native hardiness of soul,
> True to imagin'd right, above controul,
> While even the peasant boasts these rights to scan,
> And learns to venerate himself as man.[12]

But Goldsmith follows these seven stirring lines with six times as many on Britain's societal problems. Chief among these he imagines the "decay" of the natural social ties of duty, love, and honor and their replacement by the "fictitious bonds" of wealth and law. The growing power of money points toward a possible future in which the country becomes "one sink of level avarice." The growing power of law, closely related, already degrades the commonweal because, starkly, "Laws grind the poor and rich men rule the law" (lines 349–51, 359, 386). Village life concretizes all of these ills for Goldsmith. The "fields where scattered hamlets rose" have now been appropriated for estates of the wealthy, and the inhabitants of the "smiling long-frequented village" have become emigrants (403–4). "Have we not seen," the traveler asks rhetorically

> at pleasure's lordly call,
> The smiling long-frequented village fall;
> Beheld the duteous son, the sire decayed,
> The modest matron, and the blushing maid,
> Forc'd from their homes, a melancholy train,
> To traverse climes beyond the western main;
> Where wild Oswego spreads her swamps around,
> And Niagara stuns with thund'ring sound?

(405–12)

The poem's social critique is muted somewhat by the concluding lines that Goldsmith accepted as a contribution from Samuel Johnson:

> How small, of all that human hearts endure,
> That part which laws or kings can cause or cure.
> Still to ourselves in every place consigned,
> Our own felicity we make or find …

(429–32)

The lines are impressive, but they pull *The Traveller* away from its keen analysis of power and toward the somber resignation of *The Vanity of Human Wishes*. We have to read past, or through, this sort of melancholy universalizing to appreciate the societal focus of *The Traveller* and *The Deserted Village*. Gray's *Elegy Written in a Country Churchyard* embodies an even stronger tension between social vision and sententious utterance.

I mean "sententious" in its older, non-pejorative sense of inclining toward maxims, which in turn usually incline toward generality. Most commentary on Gray's *Elegy* from the eighteenth century through much of the twentieth has pointed to the poem's timeless universality. Johnson, who had little patience for Gray's odes, praised the *Elegy* as a work that "abounds with images which find a mirrour in every mind, and with sentiments to which every bosom returns an echo." In particular, the lines on the desire to be memorialized after death as the "voice of nature" within us all (lines 77–92) Johnson declared original in the best sense: "I have never seen the notions in any other place; yet he that reads them here persuades himself that he has always felt them. Had Gray written often thus it had been vain to blame, and useless to praise him."[13] Similar responses by readers of many kinds help explain the poem's extraordinary canonical status and – not always the same thing – its popularity. However, we need not diminish the poem's beauty by reading it with an eye toward its rootedness in Gray's society. William Empson in 1950 put the case for historical particularity in the *Elegy* most baldly by stating that the famous quatrain on gems and flowers going unappreciated "means … that eighteenth-century society had no scholarship system," that is, no system that would have granted social mobility to Gray's villagers.[14]

Some readers find this claim too reductive, but Empson is right in an important way. On reflection, one can hardly imagine a poet of Gray's genius motivated to compose the *Elegy* simply to utter ungrounded maxims such as "The paths of glory lead but to the grave." A careful reading of the poem for more than its "quotations" finds such truths rooted in class tensions and societal observation. The speaker reminds not the "poor" but "the great" – the members of England's power structure – that death levels all. The rural laborers contrast favorably with the elite, marked by "Ambition," "Grandeur," the "boast of heraldry," "pomp of power," and a readiness to "mock" the poor in "disdainful" condescension (29–33).

When Gray's speaker reminds himself that the obscurity of the hamlet's "rude forefathers" limited their potential "crimes" as well as potential virtues, we might expect a more or less equal estimate of both the good and bad deeds of those belonging to "this neglected spot." But if we look at the whole picture of the larger society that Gray paints by negation, we find the villagers escaping many more vices than virtues. One quatrain (61–4) describes their missed opportunities for honorable greatness, while virtually all the rest of the poem's middle section (29–76) critiques the larger world. In addition to being home to Ambition and Grandeur, the *un*-neglected nation fosters the "Proud," "Flattery," "slaughter," merciless warfare, bad conscience, "Luxury," intemperate frivolity – contrasting with the "sober" villagers – and, most famously, the "madding crowd's ignoble strife" (67–74). That phrase is so famous that one may overlook its strong animus against a society of the powerful, a society not only scornful of the illiterate poor but also potentially fatal to a young poet "to fortune and to fame unknown" (118).

Crabbe's *The Village* focuses more intently on its rural setting than does Gray's *Elegy*, but it, too, depicts both the countryside and the country. The relation between the two, however, is not the same as in Gray's poem and not always consistent. Most of Crabbe's debunking of pastoral fictions – "I paint the Cot, / As Truth will paint it, and as Bards will not" (I.53–4) – stresses that country life is as bad as city life and in many ways worse: crime, duplicity, and violence are as common in the village as in the metropolis, but the labor is harder and the conditions harsher. One primary relation between city and village life seems to be cross-contamination. Whatever might once have been the virtues of the "simple life that Nature yields," in the grim Suffolk coastal environs of the late eighteenth century, "Rapine and Wrong and Fear usurp'd her place" (I.110–1). While the villagers lack the sophistication of their metropolitan counterparts, "Yet here Disguise, the city's vice, is seen, / And Slander steals along and taints the Green" (II.39–40). Crabbe goes on to literalize the idea of infection, now transmitted from lord to laborer. In these lines the "clown" is a farm worker, and Cynthia is another name for Artemis or Diana, whose attendant nymphs symbolize virginity:

> Nor are the nymphs that breathe the rural air
> So fair as Cynthia's, nor so chaste as fair:
> These to the town afford each fresher face,
> And the Clown's trull receives the Lord's embrace;

From whom, should chance again convey her down,
The Peer's disease in turn attacks the Clown.

(II.49–54)

Crabbe does not paint his villagers as idealized victims, but in the second half of Book I especially he describes the situation of the elderly poor with real pathos. As the focus narrows from the group to the dying pauper who stands for the group, we see a frail man disdained by his physician ("Who first insults the victim whom he kills"), neglected by his "busy priest" on his deathbed, and finally buried without a funeral because he died on a weekday when the clergyman prefers the "weightier care" of hunting or cards (I.283–317). Crabbe ends this book of *The Village* beautifully by widening the picture to include an uneasy crowd, mainly children, waiting at the graveside and eventually filing away "distressed, / To think a poor man's bones should lie unblessed" (I.345–6). Here the poor epitomize the village and stand in direct contrast to its wealthier and more powerful residents, who, through class, property, or professional education, embody the power of the society. The poor also contrast with the "you" and "ye" invoked at several points in the poem. These pronouns refer generally to wealthy London readers, comfortable enough to imagine they envy the good health the laboring poor must enjoy due to hard work and hearty fare – "such / As you who praise would never deign to touch" (I.171–2). Crabbe's speaker, like Gray's and Goldsmith's, seems to be *from* the city but not entirely *of* it, dwelling in the village but not really of it, either. From this uneasy vantage point, he can envision social realities invisible to both the unlettered rural poor and the complacent metropolitans.

Cowper develops this complex perspective more fully than any other late eighteenth-century poet in *The Task*, and it would be natural to turn now to that work. In order to explore the connection between Cowper's roles as nature poet and social poet, however, I will consider *The Task* throughout the next chapter, partly under the rubric of what would now be called "social ecology." But first, I will conclude this chapter with a few thoughts on the eighteenth-century poet as prophet of modern society through the imagining of its absence.

Social redemption and negative sociology (Pope, Thomson, Thomas Warton, Macpherson, Chatterton)

An unlikely array of very different eighteenth-century poems cast poetry as the agent of social redemption. Pope's *Essay on Man*, Thomson's *Castle of Indolence*,

James Macpherson's Ossianic poetry (largely fabricated in the early 1760s from supposed tales of the third century) and Thomas Chatterton's "Rowley" poems (alleged fifteenth-century works wholly invented in the late 1760s) all reflect the period's readiness to use poetry as a way of thinking about society.

The third epistle of Pope's *Essay*, "Of the State of Man with respect to Society," constructs a theoretical history to manifest the true nature of human society and the modern individual's proper relation to it. In order to posit innate benevolence – because of which society began from "social love" – and still acknowledge evil in human history, Pope constructs a secularized Fall. His fall is not originary, not a Miltonic before-the-beginning of history but rather an interruption of history. Pope starts his narrative of society in a golden age of harmonious patriarchy and religious simplicity, which then declines into monarchy – soon absolute – and superstition-fueled religious tyranny. This long era of false consciousness is brought to an end by great leaders and poets:

> Twas then, the studious head, or gen'rous mind,
> Follow'r of God, or friend of human-kind,
> Poet or Patriot, rose, but to restore
> The Faith and Moral *Nature* gave before;
> Re-lum'd her ancient light, not kindled new;
> If not God's image, yet his shadow drew ...

> (III.283–8)

The crucial verbs are "*restore*" and "*relumed*." The poet helps redeem society from a corrupted state and bring back the best of its primitive simplicity.

This high claim for poetry's role in societal education and progress is symbolized by Pope himself in James Thomson's *Castle of Indolence* (1748), published four years after Pope's death and a few months before Thomson's own. The poem's two Spenserian cantos tell the story of a group enchanted by Indolence in a setting somewhere between Spenser's late sixteenth-century Bower of Bliss (*Faerie Queen*, II.xii) and Tennyson's early nineteenth-century *Palace of Art*. The castle soon turns into a jail. Its prisoners are freed in the second canto by the arrival of the Knight of Arts and Industry – and the poet accompanying him. Thomson placing himself among the indolent – as a bard "more fat than bard beseems" – and identifying the liberating poet – a "little Druid wight" – with Pope typify the poem's gentle humor and generosity, humanizing the gospel of progress that had remained a frozen abstraction in the long monologue *Liberty*.[15] Although the knight Sir Industry could easily free the prisoners by force, the role of liberator goes instead to the poet. He rouses the slaves of Indolence with a speech of some sixteen stanzas, exhorting them to perform the work of the modern world by following Industry:

"Some he will lead to courts, and some to camps;
To senates some, and public sage debates,
Where, by the solemn gleam of midnight-lamps,
The world is pois'd, and manag'd mighty states;
To high discovery some, that new-creates
The face of earth; some to the thriving mart;
Some to the rural reign, and softer fates;
To the sweet muses some, who raise the heart:
All glory shall be yours, all nature, and all art!"

(II, stanza 60)

This message exhibits several interesting tensions, as its energetic modernism pulls against the nostalgic quaintness evoked by Spenserian imitation (an association we saw in Chapter 5) and the genuine appeal of languorous aesthetic reverie in its first canto. Increasingly during the eighteenth century many writers suspect that modernization might steadily enervate poetry, as refinement and luxury replace primitive energy.[16] Thomson seems determined to see poetry as the harbinger of progress, much as the Pope-figure within his poem persuades the prisoners that they can free themselves through a poetry of resolution: "Speak the commanding word—*I will!*—and it is done" (II, stanza 62).

Like Thomson, Thomas Warton endorses modern industry with some visible strain in his *Ode Written at Vale-Abbey in Cheshire* (1777). After dwelling on the beauties of the Gothic ruins and the charms of monastic culture for all but two of the first twenty quatrains, Warton shakes himself into the present. He voices an obligatory rejection of "Superstition" (unreformed Roman Catholicism) and embraces the "freed Religion" that emerged under Henry VIII. He uneasily ignores the historical fact that the English Reformation dissolved the monasteries, including the thirteenth-century abbey that has inspired this poem. It is from the thirteenth century that Warton's own age can be seen as one of "Severer Reason," "Science," "new civilities," and an enlightened "social plan."[17]

Retreating to the past through form or subject matter, then, might seem a way of simply avoiding modern society, but it can afford an indirect means of social analysis, what we might call a "negative sociology." Invoking or creating a world distinctly *not* mid-eighteenth-century England becomes a way of highlighting features *of* mid-eighteenth-century England. Thus James Macpherson in the prefatory "Dissertation" to the poem *Temora*, one of the poems supposedly composed by the third-century bard Ossian, emphasizes the otherness of a world "so contrary to the present advanced state of society." Much of the astonishing popularity of the Ossian poems stems from their allowing Macpherson's readers to have it both ways, persuaded they were experiencing something "primitive" and yet infused with the delicate sensibility usually associated with modernity. Macpherson appeals to "three stages in human society" as an explanation. The first (to which Ossian belonged) is familial, "formed on nature" and thus the "most disinterested and noble." Barbarism, not the first but the second stage, occurs when property is established and maintained by war. The third stage is one of laws and orderly government, a stage more refined and, paradoxically, more sympathetic with primitive society: "Men, in the last, have leisure to cultivate the mind, and to restore it, with reflection, to a primaeval dignity of sentiment."[18]

Both Macpherson and the brilliantly inventive Chatterton, who died at seventeen, imagined distant pasts as salutary alternatives to the present, but they were not simply primitivists. Although motivated first by hopes of fame and gain, both seem to have seen – and their readers to have felt – their "ancient" poetry as contributing something new, oppositional, and necessary for literary progress. Chatterton writes (as the supposed editor rather than author) of the *Bristowe Tragedie or the Dethe of Syr Charles Bawdin* that its simple verses describing a rooster crowing the dawn "are far more elegant and poetical than all the Parade of Aurora's whipping away the Night, unbarring the Gates of the East &c &c."[19] Macpherson announced that Ossian and his contemporaries "give us the genuine language of the heart," a claim Hugh Blair would amplify in his "Critical Dissertation on the poems of Ossian": "His poetry, perhaps more than that of any other writer, deserves to be stiled, *The Poetry of the Heart*."[20]

The pseudo-bardic "measured prose" of Macpherson and the pseudo-medieval poetry of Chatterton will never again seem genuine as they did to readers in the late eighteenth and early nineteenth centuries. Still, readers of today better appreciate their internal contradictions by seeing them as attempts to put modern society in perspective, to comment on one's culture by imagining its absence. In the same essay in which he speaks of "society" as a force ("A City Night-Piece," quoted at the beginning of this chapter) Goldsmith also imagines his society's passing: "There may come a time when this temporary solitude may be made continual, and the city itself, like its inhabitants, fade away, and leave a desart in its room" (Goldsmith, I.431). If such critiques of the "advanced state of society" nearly always reveal ambivalence – there usually being *some* advances few would surrender – that does not render their negative sociology insignificant or merely nostalgic. Such poetry expresses the same progressive hope that a representative young man of letters would voice in 1778, hoping "that the time may not be distant, when the qualities of the heart shall be cultivated with the same general ardour as the powers of the understanding," an era ushered in by a literature that would (re)discover the unity "of sound learning and unsophisticated virtue."[21] Sophistication would not acquire positive connotations until well into the nineteenth century. Johnson's definitions of all forms of "sophisticate" involve adulteration or corruption of what had been genuine or pure, essentially the second definition given in the *Oxford English Dictionary*: "Altered from, deprived of, primitive simplicity or naturalness." One could look back in time to escape sophistication, or to the rural world, as Wordsworth would theorize two decades later, in seeking a place where "our elementary feelings co-exist in a state of greater simplicity, and, consequently, may be more accurately contemplated, and more forcibly communicated."[22] Wordsworth's goal differs significantly from those of Macpherson and Chatterton, but they share the paradoxical project of studying to be simple, of writing new kinds of poetry in search of the primitive.

Chapter 12

Ecological prospects and natural knowledge

"Was it for this?"   199
Nature's people, including humans   201
The ecology of eighteenth-century nature poetry   203
"Physicotheology" and nature poetry   206
The Task and social ecology   210
"Ecographic" poetry?   214

The error of finding the literary origins of modern ecological consciousness in Romanticism dies hard. This chapter explores how we can find a literary precedent for our contemporary ecological perspective by looking harder at eighteenth-century poetry. If an ecological orientation questions anthropocentrism (seeing the world as revolving around humans) and the tendency to regard the natural world as merely the setting for human actions, it arguably shares more with James Thomson, Alexander Pope, and William Cowper (and others) than with Wordsworth, Keats, and Shelley. This fact is usually overlooked because it does not fit the conventionally symbolic opposition of an artificial and mechanical Enlightenment to a natural and organic Romanticism. Thus prominent Romanticist and ecocritic Jonathan Bate credits "Romanticism and its afterlife" with overcoming the eighteenth century's "objectification of the spirit" and undertaking the "imaginative reunification of mind and nature."[1]

But the idea that poetry might reunite mind and nature surfaced more than a century earlier. Milton wrote in *Of Education* (1644) that the purpose of education, in which poetry features prominently, is to "repair the ruin of our first parents," and John Dennis picked up this Edenic vision in 1701 in *The Advancement and Reformation of Modern Poetry*:

> Poetry seems to be a noble Attempt of Nature, by which it endeavours to exalt itself to its happy primitive State; and he who is entertained with an acomplish'd Poem, is, for a Time, at least, restored to Paradise. That happy Man converses boldly with Immortal Beings. Transported, he beholds the Gods ascending and descending, and every Passion, in its Turn, is charm'd, while his Reason is supremely satisfied. Perpetual

Harmony attends his Ear, his Eye perpetual Pleasure. Ten thousand different Objects he surveys, and the most dreadful please him. Tygers and Lions he beholds, like the first Man, with Joy …[2]

Not all nature poetry of the eighteenth century idealizes its subject in quite the way Dennis envisioned, but repeatedly it does seek restorative connection, celebrating what Pope would call the "amazing whole" of the natural world (*Essay on Man*, I.248).

"Was it for this?"

We may gain a fresh perspective on eighteenth-century nature poetry by moving backward from a famous passage in Book I of *The Prelude* that Wordsworth originally composed as the opening of the "Two-Part Prelude" of 1799:

> Was it for this
> That one, the fairest of all rivers, loved
> To blend his murmurs with my nurse's song,
> And, from his alder shades and rocky falls,
> And from his fords and shallows, sent a voice
> That flowed along my dreams?

Revealing differences appear between *The Prelude*'s stance toward nature and that of James Thomson's *Seasons* seven decades earlier when we juxtapose this passage to one superficially like it from *Autumn*:

> … was it then for this ye roam'd the spring,
> Intent from flower to flower? for this ye toil'd
> Ceaseless the burning summer-heats away?
> For this in *Autumn* search'd the blooming waste,
> Nor lost one sunny gleam?[3]

Wordsworth's "Was it for this …?" refers to the poet's own development and current impasse. The lines poignantly intensify Wordsworth's criticism of his own indecision and failure to write the poetry he should, while "Unprofitably travelling toward the grave, / Like a false steward who hath much received / And renders nothing back" (I.267–9). And soon the poet decides that the unprofitable "this" must be made to add up to something more: "For this, didst thou, / O Derwent! … / Where I was looking on, a babe in arms, / Make ceaseless music that composed my thoughts / To more than infant softness …" (274–8). The eventual resolution of this book of *The Prelude* can be seen as the conversion of "this" from a failure to write poetry to the fact of *this* poem that *this* poet is writing. What had been a rueful rhetorical question now takes a real answer: yes, the natural surroundings conspired to produce the poet who now speaks.

Thomson's "was it then for this ...?" differs both in motivation and in destination. His "this" refers not to his poem or to himself but to a biotic community, a colony of bees wantonly destroyed by humans, who plundered rather than harvested the beehive for its honey:

> Ah, see where, robb'd and murder'd, in that pit
> Lies the still heaving hive! at evening snatch'd,
> Beneath the cloud of guilt-concealing night,
> And fix'd o'er sulphur ...

Attempting to represent the act from the bees' vantage, Thomson imagines violence against nature occurring as

> The happy people, in their waxen cells,
> Sat tending public cares, and planning schemes
> Of temperance, for Winter poor; rejoiced
> To mark, full flowing round, their copious stores.
> When humans suffocate the hive with smoke,
>   the tender race,
> By thousands, tumble from their honey'd domes,
> Convolved, and agonizing in the dust.

(1170–3, 1175–81)

Because it participates in a long history of describing bees in humanized, social terms (Mandeville's *Fable of the Bees* derives from Virgil's *Georgics* and other sources), Thomson's use of the word "people" seems apt. Yet we might be surprised to find Thomson's heavily anthropo*morphic* description less anthropo*centric* than Wordsworth's apostrophe. We have learned to suspect versions of the "pathetic fallacy," but metaphorically attributing human qualities to other species does not necessarily cast those creatures as subservient to human desires. In fact, doing so may lead humans to regard other animals – other "people" – as more equivalent. (Environmental philosopher David Abram argues for thinking of language as "a means of attunement" not only "between persons, but also between ourselves and the animate landscape.")[4] It would be a mistake to assume that Thomson's "people" is merely a fanciful, sentimental, or genteel substitution for a more prosaic word. His description of the bees is "environmentally oriented" in at least two senses defined by Lawrence Buell in *The Environmental Imagination*: the "human interest is not understood to be the only legitimate interest" and "human accountability to the environment is part of the text's ethical orientation."[5] In this light, the endings of these two passages become especially significant. This portion of *The Prelude* ends with the poet asserting that the river gave him a promise of "calm" in later years "amid the fretful dwellings of mankind." The passage from *The Seasons*, on the other hand, ends by lamenting human abuses of the non-human environment:

> O Man! tyrannic lord! how long, how long
> Shall prostrate Nature groan beneath your rage,
> Awaiting renovation?
>
> (1187–9)

Nature's people, including humans

The preceding comparison need not elevate Thomson over Wordsworth. The nineteenth and twentieth centuries have deemed Wordsworth the greater poet, and that estimate shows no sign of changing in the twenty-first. But we may now be in a position to regard Thomson's project and that of other eighteenth-century nature poets more sympathetically. Juxtaposing Thomson and Wordsworth helps clarify what "nature poetry" can mean and how we may understand the relationship of characteristic eighteenth-century ways of portraying nature to Romantic modes. From the perspective of ecological criticism, it no longer makes sense to dismiss the poetry of Thomson and his contemporaries as "descriptive" rather than "personal."

Let us now return to the word "people," which looms so large in eighteenth-century poetic diction. The word in fact belongs to a network of terms identified by John Arthos that includes "Band, Breed, Brood, Choir, Citizen, Crew, Flock, Fry, Herd, Host, Inhabitant, Kind, Legion, Nation, Race, Seed, Shoal, Squadron, Train, Tribe, Troop."[6] These words denote biological categories; but "feathered kind," "scaly breed," and so on, are not only scientific but also social groupings: they emphasize the communal existence of insects or flocks of birds or schools of fish. Just how figurative or realistic some of these usages are is hard to know. Sometimes they tend toward mock-heroic: Christopher Smart's turkey hen as "feather'd matron," for example ("On the Omniscience of the Supreme Being," line 68). But often they are more precise than periphrastic, that is, they carefully situate something rather than talk around it. Thus, Thomson's description of poultry as "household feathery people" is no mere euphemism; it highlights a group of shared characteristics, including domestication. It partitions reality differently than, say, the category of "chickens," which would be both less precise and more restrictive. "Chickens" would not construct the same niche, and, since to name something is to suggest what is *not* named, "chickens" – unlike "household feathery people" – would not imply the larger, unmentioned, but fully relevant category of *non*-household feathery people.

But the eighteenth-century tendency to use "people" to refer both to animals and humans dies out by the early nineteenth century. When Wordsworth writes at the start of his career in *Descriptive Sketches* (1793) that "soon a peopled region on the sight / Opens—a little world of calm delight," he means that he sees cottages. His usage seems a long way from Pope's vivid close-up of insect life sixty years earlier:

> Far as Creation's ample range extends,
> The scale of sensual, mental pow'rs ascends:
> Mark how it mounts, to man's imperial race
> From the green myriads in the peopled grass!
>
> (*An Essay on Man*, I.199–202)

Pope's usage is not idiosyncratic in the eighteenth century. These lines may have been influenced by a passage in the first edition of Thomson's *Summer* a few years earlier (1727), in which insects become visible in the sunlight: "by myriads … / Swarming, they … / People the blaze" (244–9).[7] The general idea of plenitude is common property and often expressed in the same vocabulary: even when such fullness is too small for human sight, the poet is certain that "unseen people" fill the air and water (*Summer*, 311).

Do these "people" – myriad, scaly, feathery, finny, household people – have more in common with humans in the eighteenth century for sharing a name? Quite possibly. Let us think for a moment more about "peopled" and the current use of the related word "populated." An area proposed for oil drilling might be said by advocates to be *unpopulated*. If opponents reply that, yes, it is populated, by caribou or sea turtles, their language will seem somewhat unconventional, perhaps a bit polemically poetic; while it is theoretically possible to use *populated* in both senses today, the human sense is our default meaning. That is not the case with *peopled* in the eighteenth century, where the word softens the boundary between human and animal. John Hughes sees a "peopled prospect" (an inhabited landscape) because "Sheep grace the Hills, and Herds or Swains the Fields." Similarly, Dryden describes plains as still "unpeopled" because neither sheep *nor* shepherds have returned to them. For the young Scottish poet Thomas Blacklock in 1746, the "peopled earth" is where one sees an all-inclusive divine "energy prevail / Through Being's ever-rising scale, / From nothing ev'n to God …"[8] The peopled nature poetry of the eighteenth-century offers us a powerful reorientation.

The ecology of eighteenth-century nature poetry

What "*Romantic* ecology" often seems to mean is not so much nature poetry as poetry about the nature of the poet. If we want to grasp origins of "environmental imagination" or even "deep ecology" in earlier poetry, we may put aside Wordsworth for a while and pick up Thomson and Cowper and Pope. *An Essay on Man* recovers its early resonance when read in the context of ecological thought. Pope would not seriously disagree with the founding principles of the "Deep Ecology Platform" formulated by Norwegian philosopher Arne Naess and the American ecologist William Sessions in 1984, namely, that the "flourishing of human and non-human life on Earth has intrinsic value" and the "value of non-human life forms is independent of the usefulness these may have for narrow human purposes."[9] In Pope's world only the absurdly proud man could believe that everything was created for him, murmuring to himself,

> "For me, the mine a thousand treasures brings;
> For me, health gushes from a thousand springs;
> Seas roll to waft me, suns to light me rise;
> My footstool earth, my canopy the skies."

> (I.137–40)

With an ecological orientation in mind we can also turn with fresh eyes to the closing book of William Cowper's *The Task* (1785). There, Cowper celebrates what would now be called "biophilia," defined by biologist E. O. Wilson as a natural affinity among humans for living things.[10] Cowper regards such an affinity as a moral norm:

> The heart is hard in nature, and unfit
> For human fellowship, as being void
> Of sympathy, and therefore dead alike
> To love and friendship both, that is not pleased
> With sight of animals enjoying life,
> Nor feels their happiness augment his own.[11]

Like virtually all of his contemporaries Cowper accepts the pronouncement in Genesis that man shall have dominion over the animals; but he anticipates some current theologians in seeking to define dominion as stewardship, and he echoes less-cited verses from Exodus, Job, Deuteronomy, and Numbers that imply strict limits on anthropocentrism.[12] A few hundred lines later in *The Task*, Cowper sums up human obligations to the animal creation, a part of the environment, incidentally, that appears rather rarely in Romantic poetry, birds excepted. What we would call ecology Cowper calls the "oeconomy of nature's realm" (VI.579). In the following lines the word "convenience" has more moral weight than our "ease," meaning ethical fitness, suitability, propriety:

> The sum is this: if man's convenience, health,
> Or safety interfere, his rights and claims
> Are paramount, and must extinguish theirs.
> *Else they are all*—the meanest things that are,
> As free to live and to enjoy that life,
> As God was free to form them at the first,
> Who in his sovereign wisdom made them all.

(VI.581–7)

The italics are mine, but the emphasis is surely Cowper's. I will return to *The Task* later in this chapter.

The responsibility to care for the natural world – today's "stewardship" – surfaces in eighteenth-century poetry in a word we may easily misinterpret, "imperial." We encountered it above in Pope's lines on the "peopled grass," in which sensory and mental capacities rise from the insects up to "man's imperial race." While the phrase assumes an earthly hierarchy with humans at the top, its usual contexts consistently imply responsibility rather than arbitrary power. Again and again in the period the concept opposed to "imperial" man is "tyrannic" man, as in Thomson's lines on the ravaged beehive ("O Man! tyrannic lord!"). In Pope's *Windsor-Forest* the "tyrant" Normans exploited the forest environment so selfishly that they "dispeopled Air and Floods," quickly becoming "lonely Lords of empty Wilds and Woods" (47–52). In Mary Leapor's "Man the Monarch" the animals' "Tyrant, Man," fancies himself entitled to "despotic sway" over his "mute Brethren" who justly punish his hubris by shunning or threatening him. In Thomson's *Autumn* (1730) the "steady tyrant Man" is steady only in his "thoughtless insolence of power" and love of hunting. "Inflamed, beyond the most infuriate wrath" of beasts, such a man kills animals for "sport alone" (390–4). For William Somerville in *Field-Sports* (1742), "Tyrant Man" is a "Free-booter" – that is, a pirate – who "Destroys at will / The whole Creation, Man and Beasts."[13] In contrast, characterizing the human species as "imperial" in eighteenth-century writing underscores participation and responsibility rather than exceptionalism. In the later eighteenth century, moralist Abraham Tucker expressed in emphatic form a view most poets would have agreed with, that as we become properly "lords and not tyrants" of our environment we will understand that we are not the "sole care of heaven." We can then learn to "exercise government by employing our superior skill and power for the benefit of the governed."[14] That humans are not heaven's sole care underlies Pope's insistence in *An Essay on Man* on an "equal" God, a Creator

> Who sees with equal eye, as God of all,
> A hero perish, or a sparrow fall,
> Atoms or systems into ruin hurl'd,
> And now a bubble burst, and now a world.
>
> (I.87–90)

Perhaps none of Pope's readers could really envision what he asked them to, a scene where atoms and solar systems, bubbles and planets, are equivalent; but that challenge is the point. The passage enacts an imaginative experience of anthropocentrism's limits, an experience that occurs as outlook and insight merge.

Eighteenth-century nature poetry is "ecological" not only in its interest in the finely linked "chain of being" but in its unique comfort with science. If the "new philosophy" called "all in doubt" for Donne in the early seventeenth century, it seems to have inspired faith – religious and poetic – in the eighteenth. In his *Essay on the Application of Natural History to Poetry* (1777), John Aikin (brother of the poet Anna Laetitia Barbauld) could urge poets to energize their art by turning to current botany and zoology. But the easy commerce between poetry and science would grow strained by the century's end. In the 1802 Preface to *Lyrical Ballads*, Wordsworth would eschew the conventional opposition of poetry to prose for a "contradistinction between … Poetry and Matter of Fact, or Science." And Keats, in a well-known passage from *Lamia* (1820), would blame the "cold Philosophy" of science for spoiling nature's poetic "charms":

> There was an awful [awe-inspiring] rainbow once in heaven:
> We know her woof, her texture; she is given
> In the dull catalogue of common things.
> Philosophy will clip an Angel's wings,
> Conquer all mysteries by rule and line,
> Empty the haunted air, and gnomed mine—
> Unweave a rainbow …
>
> (II.231–7)

James Thomson and Mark Akenside, like most eighteenth-century poets, saw the role of science in nature poetry quite differently. Both felt that scientific knowledge could increase rather than dissipate aesthetic appreciation. The person who understands the optics of "mighty" Newton, writes Thomson, sees the rainbow's "prism" with "Philosophic Eye" (vision informed by science). In

The Pleasures of Imagination (1744), Akenside links scientific knowledge and pleasure even more closely:

> Nor ever yet
> The melting rainbow's vernal-tinctur'd hues
> To me have shone so pleasing, as when first
> The hand of science pointed out the path
> In which the sun-beams gleaming from the west
> Fall on the watry cloud ...[15]

William Blake's conviction that he must reject Newton (along with Bacon and Locke) in order "To cast aside from Poetry all that is not Inspiration" may have been extreme, but it signals the distance between science and poetry that would persist through the nineteenth century and much of the twentieth.[16]

"Physicotheology" and nature poetry

The noun "physicotheology" came into English in 1713, thanks to William Derham, the man who literally wrote the book. Derham's subtitle for *Physicotheology* – "*a Demonstration of the Being and Attributes of God, from His Works of Creation*" – effectively explains the word's meaning. Derham did not, of course, invent the idea that the more thoroughly we study the book of Nature the closer we come to its Author. He was influenced by John Ray's *The Wisdom of God Manifested in the Works of the Creation* (1691) and a broader current of "natural theology" that strengthened from the mid-seventeenth century. In fact, the adjectival form of the word had already been introduced in 1652 by Walter Charleton, in *The Darkness of Atheism, Dispelled by the Light of Nature: A Physico-theologicall Treatise*, and used by the scientist and Christian apologist Robert Boyle in the 1670s and 1680s. Much, perhaps most, eighteenth-century nature poetry rests at least implicitly on physicotheology. The most ambitious successful nature poem of the era, Thomson's *Seasons*, makes explicit its foundation in natural theology. *A Hymn on the Seasons*, the postscript to Thomson's work, designates the changing seasons themselves "the varied God," to whom, Thomson says, the "rolling year" is "full of thee."

But we do not need to rely on the postscript to discern Thomson's physicotheological commitment. Within the body of the poem each of the four seasons contributes to a massive if unsystematic "argument from design," attempting to prove God's existence from the text of Creation. Thomson repeatedly celebrates nature as itself the celebration of the "Almighty Father," the "eternal cause, support, and end of all" (*Summer* 186–91). In the sun's warm brilliance

God "shines out"; in the "latest glooms" of "Dread Winter" the thoughtful observer will see divine "Power" and "Wisdom—oft arraigned" (*Summer*, 96; *Winter*, 1024, 1051–2). But Thomson does not glimpse infinitude only in the inorganic forces that preoccupy some later poets of the sublime. He writes with particular force about the organic world of nature-in-process. Some of the most ardent parts of *The Seasons* address the sexual energy manifest in the spring mating of animals, including some whose copulation one assumes Thomson imagined rather than observed. Thus, jungle beasts "growl their horrid loves" and whales "flounce and tumble in unwieldy joy" (*Spring*, 824–30). All this instinctual sexuality may amuse or fascinate us, but ultimately for Thomson it reflects divinity. The mating of birds provides more evidence still of providential immanence:

> What is this *mighty Breath*, ye Curious, say,
> That, in a powerful Language, felt not heard,
> Instructs the Fowls of Heaven, and thro' their Breast
> These Arts of Love diffuses? What, but GOD?
> Inspiring GOD! who, boundless Spirit all,
> And unremitting Energy, pervades,
> Adjusts, sustains, and agitates the whole.
>
> (*Spring*, 849–55)

Thomson typifies an interesting tension in the period's nature poetry between system and sensuous detail, one that requires the reader to shift from large-scale comprehension to close-up partiality and back again. In this next passage, Thomson ranges from grand scheme to particulars of glance and palate:

> I solitary court
> Th' inspiring Breeze: and meditate the Book
> Of Nature, ever open; aiming thence,
> Warm from the Heart, to learn the moral Song.
> And, as I steal along the sunny Wall,
> Where Autumn basks, with Fruit empurpled deep,
> My pleasing Theme continual prompts my Thought:
> Presents the downy peach; the shining Plumb,
> With a fine blueish Mist of Animals
> Clouded; the ruddy Nectarine; and dark,
> Beneath his ample Leaf, the luscious Fig.
>
> (*Autumn*, 669–79)

The "animals" on the surface of the plum, too tiny to see except as collectively causing a mist, were supposed by some late seventeenth-century scientists to cause a sensation of sharpness because they "bite you by the tongue."[17]

This nearly microscopic focus proceeds from a more abstract desire to attain "the moral song"; the "theme" of the project more than the logic of the walk "presents" peach, plum, nectarine, and fig.

The interdependence of concept and percept in nature poetry does not render the sensuous image unimportant. With Thomson's abundant fruit let us juxtapose Christopher Smart's lines from *A Song to David* (1762):

> Now labour his reward receives,
> For ADORATION counts his sheaves
> To peace, her bounteous prince;
> The nectarine his strong tint imbibes,
> And apples of ten thousand tribes,
> And quick peculiar quince.

> (349–54)

The various fruits all exist as part a world that both manifests and praises the Creator. As pieces of the ADORATION that the creation pays to God they are conceived of as generic and collective; but in Smart's poetic perception each is bursting with individual life: "quick" and keenly "peculiar."

Smart's *Song to David*, not primarily a physicotheological poem, draws its theology more from scripture than from nature. But much of Smart's poetry relies heavily on natural observation, including his early prize-winning, formative poems on the "Perfections or Attributes" of God. (The annual Seatonian Prize for such poems was established at Cambridge in 1750, and by 1756 Smart had won it four times.) Smart finds those divine perfections and attributes, as had Thomson, in the creation. *On the Omniscience of the Supreme Being* (1752) resembles *Spring* (and *An Essay on Man*, III.83–98) in its celebration of animal instincts, which, in their certainty, reflect God's knowledge and show the imperfection of man's. Smart sees humanity as fallen, of course, but nature's charms do much to compensate for mortal limitations:

> tho' no more
> Is Paradise our home, but o'er the portal
> Hangs in terrific pomp the burning blade;
> Still with ten thousand beauties blooms the Earth
> With pleasures populous, and with riches crown'd.
> Still is there scope for wonder and for love
> Ev'n to their last exertion – show'rs of blessings …[18]

The possibility that aesthetic responsiveness to nature should have a redemptive function runs through several of Smart's poems of the next decade as well. In *The Sweets of Evening* (1764) the "softer scenes of nature" lead to a religious moment of self-transcendence,

>   when thoughts themselves sublime,
> And with superior natures chime
>   In fancy's highest sphere.[19]

Earlier in the century, in *A Nocturnal Reverie* (1713), Anne Finch had identified the perfect composure of a quiet natural scene with spiritual epiphany. I
discussed this poem briefly in Chapter 2 for its opening syntactic tour de force.
As the poem progresses, the scene is not seen but heard and smelled, as the
experience unfolds in darkness:

> When a sedate Content the Spirit feels,
> And no fierce Light disturbs, whilst it reveals;
> But silent Musings urge the Mind to seek
> Something, too high for Syllables to speak;
> Till the free Soul to a compos'dness charm'd,
> Finding the Elements of Rage disarm'd,
> O'er all below a solemn Quiet grown,
> Joys in th' inferiour World, and thinks it like her Own …

> (39–46)

Many eighteenth-century poems of course eschew nature's softer moments, when
soul and scene are so much in harmony that speech is inadequate, favoring instead
the strife and "sublime" violence that threaten to overwhelm the spectator.

Thomson's *Seasons* had its beginning as a short version of *Winter* (1726) with
a heavy emphasis on a life-threatening snow storm. Finch herself wrote one of
the period's most ambitious poems by a woman, *Upon the Hurricane*, a Pindaric ode about the great storm of 1703, in which the wind's destructive force
bespeaks God's presence unmistakably if mysteriously. These and poems like
Ambrose Phillips's popular *A Winter-Piece* (1709) emphasize nature's "wild disorder," focusing more conspicuously on force than design. But they still tend to
share the natural theologian's premise that the text of creation reveals its Creator. Understanding the pervasiveness of this premise in eighteenth-century
poetry helps prepare us for some of the ways in which poets are likely to avoid
the very element we have gotten used to looking for in later "nature" poetry –
namely, autobiography – in favor of a relatively impersonal perspective.

The tendency to exclude or minimize dramas of the self in favor of presentation of the natural environment often seems unpoetic to readers schooled on
Wordsworth rather than on Thomson or Cowper. It reflects the physicotheological poet's commitment to reveal the author of Creation over the author of the
poem. I suggested earlier that this emphasis might harmonize more closely with
some recent developments in Christian theology than with the dominant nine-
teenth- and twentieth-century theologies of redemption. One major proponent

of what is now loosely called "ecotheology" calls it a study that "understands its context to be the well-being of the planet" and takes as its subject the "entire cosmos with all its creatures, human and otherwise."[20] While ecotheology is not simply eighteenth-century physicotheology revived – Darwin irrevocably complicated the assumptions of harmonious design that reassured physicotheologians – for our purposes a general analogy is relevant. Ecotheology comprises a variety of approaches that tend (as, broadly speaking, had physicotheology) to focus more on the Creation than on individual salvation, or, in James Gustafson's phrase, to adopt a "theocentric perspective."[21] Pope's equivalent of this orientation is to focus on the "*general good*" (his italics). The phrase is abstract, but in the most ecological passage of *An Essay on Man* Pope stages a prospect from which readers can "see" the abstraction as a physical system:

> Look round our world: behold the chain of love
> Combining all below, and all above.
> See, plastic Nature working to this end,
> The single atoms each to other tend,
> Attract, attracted to, the next in place,
> Form'd and impell'd, its neighbour to embrace.
> See matter next, with various life endu'd,
> Press to one centre still, the *general good.*
> See dying vegetables life sustain,
> See life dissolving vegetate again.
> All forms that perish other forms supply,
> By turns they catch the vital breath, and die;
> Like bubbles on the sea of matter born,
> They rise, they break, and to that sea return.
> Nothing is foreign …

                                                                    (III.7–21)

"*Homo sum, humani nil a me alienum puto,*" runs the best-known line by Terence, the Roman playwright (*The Self-Tormenter*, 163 BCE): I am human, I consider nothing human foreign to me. Pope's statement expands this traditional humanist ideal to the non-human world as well, taking into account all of creation, animals and plants, worlds peopled and unpeopled. Pope's deeply ecological vision is one where, with or without our special interests, nature is whole: *nothing is foreign*.

The Task and social ecology

Although it bears many possible applications, the phrase "social ecology" here refers to an orientation that sees ecological problems as parts of broader social and political problems, particularly unequal and exploitative relations. Murray Bookchin, one of its more prolific proponents, connects social ecology with the advocacy of communalism and "anarchistic" decentralization, that is, with a radical revision of capitalism and breaking up large cities and power structures into smaller, more sustainable units.[22] The more general premise of social ecology is that overcoming environmental damage done by humans will require eliminating the damage humans do to each other. (Ecofeminism, which connects unjust male domination of women with unjust male domination of the environment, might arguably be considered a particular form of social ecology.)

As we have seen, Pope's *Essay on Man* tends to make the societal and ecological connection through a narrative "fall" in which human despotism and animal butchery occur in the same stage of society. But it is Cowper who ponders the connection between interpersonal and interspecies relations at such length and in such depth that it becomes the unifying subject of his major work. *The Task* is so firmly associated with the celebration of rural retirement that we can easily forget how much of it is about modern England and particularly London. This focus is so persistent that in some respects Cowper's poem anticipates the "condition of England" novels of the next century.

Cowper's constitutional biophilia, touched on above, operates as an important moral index in his poem: as we have seen, anyone "not pleased / With sight of animals enjoying life" is "unfit / For human fellowship" (VI.321–4). But Cowper departs from natural theology by reversing the assumption that the love of nature leads to love of God. For Cowper, divine grace first liberates believers from the "slavish state of man by nature" and *then* grants a proper "relish of the works of God" ("Argument" for Book V). Biophilia is "Nature's dictate" (I.413), and the person lacking it is unredeemed, "self-imprison'd," and still in the thrall of unnatural, urban values. The poem's most famous line, "God made the country, and man made the town" (I.749), is less a rationale for natural description than for the study of what man *has* made, especially the "gain-devoted cities," and of what humans *should* be making. Cowper abhors large cities, but he is no primitivist. Not surprisingly, this most civilized of poems sees the "mild / And genial soil of cultivated life" as essential to the growth of virtue: the norm seems to be village life (I.678–82).

Cowper emphasizes the distance between his rusticated life and London life throughout *The Task*. Nearly every sustained celebration of rural beauty or simplicity marks a contrast with urban decadence or insensibility. Book III ends with Cowper's long "apostrophe to the metropolis" ("Argument"), the city whose pseudo-charms "unpeople all our counties"; the gullible and corruptible make their way to town, and "London ingulfs them all" (III.816, 831). London is not the only source of corruption for Cowper. Book II launches a sustained critique of "Profusion," a consumerist vice encouraged by miseducation at the universities, and Book IV explores the corrupting influence of widespread military training. The common thread is what Cowper calls "bodies corporate" ("Argument" to Book IV), by which he seems to mean aggregates of greed and power that supplant fully human communities. Society humanizes

> But man associated and leagued with man
> By regal warrant, or self-joined by bond
> For interest-sake, or swarming into clans
> Beneath one head for purposes of war

becomes capable of great evil, just as burghers "once combined" turn into a "loathsome body" or merchants once "incorporated" grow less humane. Such corporations

> disclaiming all regard
> For mercy and the common rights of man,
> Build factories with blood, conducting trade
> At the sword's point, and dying the white robe
> Of innocent commercial justice red.

> (IV.660–83)

Individual merchants in Cowper's view would never become slave masters, but corporations naturally do so. The connections between human and environmental exploitation develop more theoretically in the fifth and sixth books.

Although Cowper is usually thought of as politically conservative, fearful of disorder and quick to urge loyalty and patience, much of Book V stresses the evils of monarchy and the king's obligation to observe strict constitutional limits to deserve his subjects' loyalty. The general idea of constitutional restraints on the king was commonplace, especially from 1688 onward, but Cowper's stance was emphatic enough to gain the surprised admiration of bluestocking and poet Anna Seward. In her copy of *The Task* she marked the long passage (V.293–343) which concludes that the king "is ours, / To administer, to guard, to adorn the state, / But not to warp or change it," and wrote in the margins: "I wonder after the publication of these two pages that Cowper has escaped the title of Democrat lavished upon numbers who have never avowed principles so unequivocally democratic."[23] The title might not have wholly pleased Cowper, but the latter books of the poem mount a spirited defense of liberty and rights – human and animal. The poet's lament "That man should thus encroach on fellow man" (V.435) grows in the last book to a longer condemnation of unnecessary encroachments on the lives and liberties of non-human creatures.

In the "Argument" to Book V, Cowper thus refers to this part of the poem: "Of cruelty to Animals. That it is a great crime proved from Scripture." Cowper had trained as a lawyer, and he insists legalistically that his readers study the Bible carefully before taking for granted a blanket right to use animals for human purposes:

> The charter was conferr'd by which we hold
> The flesh of animals in fee, and claim
> O'er all we feed on, power of life and death.
> But read the instrument, and mark it well.
> Th' oppression of a tyrannous controul
> Can find no warrant there.

(VI.451–6)

The connection between the constitutional politics of Book V and the celebration of animal creation in Book VI lies in Cowper's contractual view of the Bible. The Christian's obligation is to "read the instrument, and mark it well" in order to rise above an ethics of encroachment.

One of *The Task*'s most poignant moments occurs in the course of "The Winter Evening" (Book IV) when the warm and comfortable poet contemplates the situation of those less "distinguished" (IV.388) by divine mercy or human benevolence. He first imagines a hearty wagoner braving the snow to complete his work, and then a poor family shivering in their bare cottage, husband and wife at a distance from the meager brushwood fire so that the children may crowd by the hearth. As the poet details the struggles of their day it becomes clear that the scene is not imagined but remembered:

> The taper soon extinguished, which I saw
> Dangled along at the cold fingers' end
> Just when the day declined, and the brown loaf
> Lodged on the shelf half-eaten without sauce
> Of sav'ry cheese, or butter costlier still …

(IV.391–5)

Most penetrating is the realization that the many frugal measures of their "ingenious parsimony" can not suffice: "With all this thrift they thrive not" (399–400).

The bleak wit of this summary intensifies when we recall that "thrift" meant prospering before it meant doing with less.[24] One might conclude that Cowper devotes so much of the last book of the poem to cruelty to animals because the problems of exploited people seem so intractable. But from another perspective *The Task* is a poem about thrift, capaciously conceived. Whatever the limits of Cowper's political analysis, *The Task*'s imaginative vision may strike us freshly as one in which humans and animals can flourish only together.

"Ecographic" poetry?

The point of looking at eighteenth-century poetry with ecological concerns in mind should not be to trick up old poems in new dress. Putting the prefix "eco" on something does not render it ecological in any meaningful sense. Readers have long recognized that the eighteenth century produced a great deal of topographical or locodescriptive poems. To begin calling these instead "ecographical" or "ecodescriptive" poems adds little to our reading and may in most cases be simply inaccurate. It is clearly not true that every descriptive nature poem of the eighteenth century raises questions of ecological relatedness or of the responsibilities of stewardship. What I have tried to call attention to in this chapter is the fact that many notable eighteenth-century poems do entertain such questions and that we may overlook their significance either because of the conventional assumption that "green" thinking began with the Romantics, or because we may miss the resonance of certain words and categories, or in some cases simply because relevant poems have been too little studied.

If we approach eighteenth-century nature poems looking for certain markers of "ecological correctness" we will be disappointed. Pope welcomes the building of canals, the improvement of roads, and the draining of swamps (wetlands, now) in the concluding lines of the *Epistle to Burlington*, and so does virtually every other poet I know of who addresses such topics in an era in which communications were poor and underpopulation could often seem more of a threat than overpopulation.[25] Nor will we find untouched wilderness celebrated until well into the nineteenth century, and then it is likelier to be a sublime spectacle (with the adjective "sublime" replacing "horrid") than something worthy of study. Even in America, Thoreau took a minority position in the essay "Walking" (1862), when he proclaimed that "in Wildness is the preservation of the world." In England through most of the eighteenth century, as in most pre- or early industrial societies, wilderness is more often associated with death or damnation than with salvation.

But these differences should not blind us to meaningful connections. One of the most helpful assessments of Pope as an ecological poet has come not from an eighteenth-century specialist but from a fellow poet. The contemporary American poet and environmental thinker Wendell Berry has written tellingly of Pope's poetry, especially *An Essay on Man* and the *Epistle to Burlington*, in the long essay "Poetry and Place" (1983). The section on Pope begins, "Few poets that I know have been so explicitly appreciative of the human kinship with the natural world as Alexander Pope, and few have been so carefully attentive to the spiritual, moral, and practical implications of that kinship."[26] Berry's essay, which ranges from the Renaissance to the mid-twentieth century, avoids the mistake of assuming that eighteenth century perspectives on nature must be remote from ours. More broadly, one of Berry's later poems, *In a Hotel Parking Lot, Thinking of Dr. Williams*, bears on the challenge of not distancing ourselves irresponsibly from the works we study, whatever their subjects:

> To remember,
> to hear and remember, is to stop
> and walk on again
>
> to a livelier, surer measure.
> It is dangerous
> to remember the past only
>
> for its own sake, dangerous
> to deliver a message
> that you did not get.[27]

We should not, of course, set out to remake the poetry of past in the image of our own time. But when its connections with our moment are genuine, to ignore them is to reduce the vital transmission of literary experience to antiquarian repetition, a dangerous devaluation.

A concluding note: then and now

A hazard of literary scholarship to which eighteenth-century specialists may be especially liable is a tendency toward selective identifications with some of the authors we study, identifications that are selective in two senses. One imagines a special kinship with only some authors – Swift, say, rather than Johnson, or vice versa – and with only some features of those authors. So, I align myself with Swift's views on imperialism but not on the deference due to a national church. When I think, "If Swift were alive today he would satirize ——,"the blank fills in with the current object of my own indignation. This ethical idealization has a formal equivalent, usually a kind of aesthetic nostalgia: "If Pope were alive today, he'd be writing real poetry, not the kind of obscure mush published by ——." Here one may fill in the name of a least favorite contemporary magazine or poet, while imagining Pope (or Johnson, or Cowper) valiantly holding up formalist standards against an amorphous twenty-first century. Arguably, however, if Pope were alive today "he" would be writing free verse.

This view may be wrong, as well as ill-advised. As George Eliot remarks in *Middlemarch*, "Among all forms of mistake, prophecy is the most gratuitous" (chapter 10, opening). But it seems a more convincing image than one of Pope clinging to the heroic couplet three centuries after he began refining it. Of course, this whole mode of supposition begins quickly to unravel, there being no "Pope" abstracted from the historical particularity that produced him. But just before we abandon it entirely, we might recall that Pope was always an experimental modernist. Whatever his reverence for the Ancients, he believed that the poetry of his day could and should progress, and he never tried to revive an antiquated style. Edward Young wrote in 1759 that the way to imitate Homer is not to imitate Homer (a view Johnson considered uncontroversial), and the same might be said of imitating Pope or of imagining eighteenth-century poetry more broadly.[1]

The significant continuities, then, between the period's poetry and that of our own are to be found in energy, flexibility, capaciousness, and, often, in a readiness to create a poetry that shares some of the values generally associated with prose, such as lucidity, accessibility, and colloquial familiarity. We may be in a better position now than even a few decades ago to appreciate the vocal and visionary range of eighteenth-century poetry. Postmodern poets have been open to conversational poems, epistolary poems, even poetic "essays" and "georgics of the mind," in the phrase Francis Bacon used for works meant to improve thinking in ways that could affect conduct.[2] A few late twentieth-century American examples that come to mind are A. R. Ammons's *Essay on Poetics* (1970) and *Sphere: The Form of a Motion* (1974), Robert Pinsky's *Essay on Psychiatrists* (1975), and Charles Bernstein's *Artifice of Absorption* (1987) – all poems that mix metapoetic self-consciousness and leisurely conversation.[3]

Shortly before World War II erupted, the philosopher R. G. Collingwood argued against what he saw as a prevailing "individualistic theory of art" and for a poetry instead that would be public and accessible. Collingwood's poet would become the "spokesman of his community," uttering collective "secrets" rather than his own. This role is crucial because "no community altogether knows its own heart." Collingwood's call is in some respects "neoclassical," casting the poet in a social and didactic role; but it is also romantic in its vatic urgency. The poet must reveal the community's heart to itself to avert catastrophe:

> by failing in this knowledge a community deceives itself on the one subject concerning which ignorance means death. For the evils which come from that ignorance the poet as prophet suggests no remedy, because he has already given one. The remedy is the poem itself. Art is the community's medicine for the worst disease of mind, the corruption of consciousness.[4]

The terms are as Coleridgean as Popean. In *Biographia Literaria* (1817) Coleridge had said that good poetry "is at all times the proper food of the understanding; but in an age of corrupt eloquence it is both food and antidote" (chapter 22). One imagines the need for an antidote to "corrupt eloquence" being felt especially keenly in 1938 when Collingwood is writing. But in fact the corruptions of consciousness and eloquence are perennial, as is the hope that poetry might be a counter-voice, an uncorrupted and thus curative eloquence. In this spirit, Pope had opposed the alienated poetic voice of *The Dunciad* against the popular voices of the dunces.

One can think of the corruption of consciousness that Pope, Coleridge, and Collingwood want poetry to counter as primarily political in origin. Thus, Allen Ginsberg writes, in *Wichita Vortex Sutra* (1966), "almost all our language has been taxed by war."[5] Ginsberg's dark play on "taxed," on the costs of both funding and rationalizing violence, diagnoses our predicament politically and hints at the bare possibility of a language less strained and compromised by official formulas. An alternative or complement to this political diagnosis is to think of corrupt consciousness as the result of internalized popular culture. English poet and theorist Denise Riley argues that while we might like to imagine our "inner speech" as pure because private, even the language in our heads is

> thickened with reiterated quotation, choked with the rubble of the over-heard, the strenuously sifted and hoarded, the periodically dusted down then crammed with slogans and jingles, with mutterings of remembered accusations, irrepressible puns, insistent spirits of ancient exchanges, monotonous citation, the embarrassing detritus of advertising, archaic injunctions from hymns, and the pastel snatches of old song lyrics.[6]

Whether our cluttered compulsions and duncical distractions result from specifically political or broadly cultural discourses, the voices of poetry, listened to carefully, can yield small but real alternatives to them. The poems published between 1700 and 1785 offer many kinds of voices and visions, and we could well use the whole range. Because of their distance and difference, we can find in our imaginative production of eighteenth-century poems something restorative and clarifying, something that, in Pope's phrase and at our best, "gives us back the image of our mind."

Notes

Introduction

1 Sylvia Plath, *The Bell Jar* [1971] (New York: Harper Collins, 1996), p. 139.

2 A. R. Ammons, *Sphere: The Form of a Motion* (New York: W. W. Norton, 1974), p. 29 (section 41).

3 The remark is usually attributed to Mark Twain, but Twain attributes it to Edgar Wilson ("Bill") Nye; Twain, *Autobiography*, 2 vols., ed. Albert Bigelow Paine (New York: Harper Brothers Publishers, 1924), I, 338.

4 Wallace Stevens, "The Noble Reader and the Sound of Words," *The Collected Poetry and Prose*, ed. Frank Kermode and Joan Richardson (New York: Library of America, 1997), p. 663.

5 Allen Grossman, *True-Love: Essays on Poetry and Valuing* (University of Chicago Press, 2009), p. 159.

6 Important studies of women poets include Paula Backscheider, *Eighteenth-Century Women Poets and Their Poetry* (Baltimore: Johns Hopkins University Press, 2005); Moira Ferguson, *Eighteenth-Century Women Poets: Nation, Class, and Gender* (Albany: State University Press of New York, 1995); Carole Barash, *English Women's Poetry, 1649–1714: Politics, Community, and Linguistic Authority* (Oxford: Clarendon Press, 1996), and (treating men and women poets comparatively) Jennifer Keith, *Poetry and the Feminine from Behn to Cowper* (Newark: University of Delaware Press, 2005). See the Further Readings for the recent anthology of women poets edited by Paula R. Backscheider and Catherine Ingrassia.

1 Voice in eighteenth-century poetry

1 *Jubilate Agno* (B 239), quoted from Karina Williamson and Marcus Walsh, eds., *Christopher Smart: Selected Poems* (London: Penguin Books, 1990), p. 77.

2 The various editions of the Preface, including its Appendix on "poetic diction," are available in R. L. Brett and A. R. Jones, eds., *Lyrical Ballads* (London: Methuen, 1963, rev. 1965); see pp. 252–3 for the discussion of Gray's sonnet.

3 John Stuart Mill, "Thoughts on Poetry and Its Varieties" [1833], in *The Collected Works of John Stuart Mill*, 8 vols. (Indianapolis: Liberty Fund, 2006), I, 348.

4 Henry Home, Lord Kames, in his *Elements of Criticism*, 3 vols. (Edinburgh, 1762), remarked that "there is, in every line, one accent that makes a greater figure than the rest," stipulating that it occurs, or should occur, just before the "capital pause," that is, the main caesura (II, 417). Fortunately, eighteenth-century practice varies more than this. In my reading the "strongstress" is often determined more by sense than by position.

5 The Chadwyck-Healey electronic database *English Poetry*, which contains texts of approximately 165,000 poems from 600 to 1900, is searchable by literary period, and, among other variables, rhymed or unrhymed poetry. The latter are perhaps undercounted, however, because miscoded; for example, unrhymed odes by William Collins and Anna Laetitia Barbauld are classified as rhymed, perhaps because of their titles.

6 Adam Smith, *Theory of Moral Sentiments*, ed. D. D. Raphael and A. L. Macfie (Oxford: Clarendon Press, 1976; rpt. Indianapolis: Liberty Classics, 1982), p. 198.

2   The heroic couplet continuum

1 *A Tuft of Flowers* from Robert Frost, *A Boy's Will* (New York: Henry Holt and Company, 1915), p. 47; *My Last Duchess*, lines 5–12, from Donald Smalley, ed., *Poems of Robert Browning* (Boston: Houghton Mifflin Company, 1956), pp. 49–50; *The Wife of Bath's Prologue*, lines 195–200, Larry Benson *et al.*, eds., *The Riverside Chaucer*, 3rd edn. (Boston: Houghton Mifflin Company, 1987), p. 107.

2 Dryden, *Mac Flecknoe*, lines 1–6, in H. T. Swedenberg, Jr. and Vinton A. Dearing, eds., *The Works of John Dryden: Poems 1681–1684* (Berkeley and Los Angeles: University of California Press, 1971), p. 54; Pope, *An Essay on Man*, II.1–8, in *The Works of Alexander Pope, Esq; Vol. II. Containing his Epistles and Satires* (1735), p. 20; Johnson, *The Vanity of Human Wishes* [lines 73–8] (1749), pp. 8–9.

3 Dryden, Dedication to Roger, Earl of Orrery, prefaced to *The Rival Ladies*, in George Watson, ed., *Of Dramatic Poesy and Other Critical Essays*, 2 vols. (London: J. M. Dent and Sons, 1962), I, 7; Pope, *The First Epistle of the Second Book of Horace Imitated* (1737), p. 16 [lines 267–9]. Richard Bradford's survey, *A Linguistic History of English Poetry* (London and New York: Routledge, 1993), is valuable throughout for its analysis of historical changes in what he terms the "double pattern" of poetic lines and sentence syntax; for his observations on the Restoration and eighteenth-century heroic couplet see pp. 66–76.

4 Pope, *An Essay on Criticism*, lines 362–3; the poem first appeared in 1711, but Pope added this couplet when the *Essay* was republished in *The Works of Mr. Alexander Pope* in 1717, quoted here.

5 Daniel Hallows, *Poems on the Principal Festivals and Fasts of the Church of England. I. On the Annunciation of the Blessed Virgin Mary*, 1733, p. 19.

6 Quotations from Donne and Pope's modernization of Donne are from *The Works of Alexander Pope, Esq; vol. II. Containing his Epistles and Satires* (1735), in which Pope printed Donne's text on the verso and his on the recto.

7 For an excellent brief overview of period readership see Barbara M. Benedict, "Publishing and Reading Poetry," in John Sitter, ed., *The Cambridge Companion to Eighteenth-Century Poetry* (Cambridge University Press, 2000), pp. 63–82.

8 Parnell's modernization of Donne's third satire first appeared, attributed to Parnell and accompanied by Donne's poem, in *The Works of Alexander Pope, Esq; Vol. II. Part II.* (1738), pp. 138–49.

9 Pope's translation of the *Iliad* appeared in six volumes from 1715 to 1720. The third volume, containing Sarpedon's speech (Book XII, lines 371–96), appeared in 1717, the year in which Pope added Clarissa's speech to *The Rape of the Lock.*

10 *Retirement*, lines 381–4, in *Poems by William Cowper, of the Inner Temple, Esq.* (1782), p. 277.

11 Hayden Carruth, "The Question of Poetic Form," in Donald Hall, ed., *Claims for Poetry* (Ann Arbor: University of Michigan Press, 1982), pp. 50–61; the quotation is from p. 59.

12 *Biographia Literaria*, chapter 1; see H. J. Jackson, ed., *Samuel Taylor Coleridge: The Oxford Authors* (Oxford University Press, 1986), p. 165.

13 Anne Finch, *A Nocturnal* Reverie, lines 1–16, in her *Miscellany Poems* (1713), p. 291.

14 Mary Leapor's poetry was collected in two volumes (published shortly after her death in 1746, while in her early twenties), *Poems upon Several Occasions* (1748, 1751). This quotation of lines 1–23 of *Man the Monarch* is from the latter volume, pp. 7–8. Poems from both are available in the excellent modern edition by Richard Greene and Anne Messenger, eds., *The Works of Mary Leapor* (Oxford University Press, 2003).

3 Vocal engagement: reading Pope's *An Essay on Criticism*

1 Thomas Berger, *Little Big Man* (New York: Fawcett, 1963), p. 133. Jack Crabb is recalling *An Essay on Man*, but one suspects the teenage boy would not have responded much differently to *An Essay on Criticism*.

2 Lines 574–5. Pope, *An Essay on Criticism* (1711), p. 3 [lines 1–6]. Quotations are from this edition except where noted.

3 Terry Eagleton, *How to Read a Poem* (Oxford: Blackwell, 2007), p. 89.

4 In his classic discussion of Pope's *Epistle to Dr. Arbuthnot*, "The Muse of Satire," *Yale Review* 41 (1951), 80–92, Maynard Mack distinguishes three voices in that poem: 1) the *vir bonus* or Stoic "plain good man," 2) the *naif* or *ingénu* who is so innocent in the ways of the world that he spontaneously tells the truth, and 3) the "public defender" or "satirist as hero" who cannot rest while corruption threatens the country. The two poems are very different, but perhaps one can see the early manifestation of the voice Mack calls the public defender in the figure I call the "Poet" in *An Essay on Criticism*, who regards bad criticism as a public danger.

5 The Bodleian Library manuscript of *An Essay on Criticism* in Pope's hand is available in facsimile and with extensive commentary in Robert M. Schmitz, *Pope's Essay on Criticism, 1709* (St. Louis: Washington University Press, 1962).

6 Pope added a table of contents to the *Essay* many years later. I quote his summary from *The Works of Alexander Pope, Esq; Vol. I. With Explanatory Notes and Additions Never before Printed* (1736), p. 103.

7 David B. Morris is particularly helpful on this point: "Pope and the Arts of Pleasure," in G. S. Rousseau and Pat Rogers, eds., *The Enduring Legacy: Alexander Pope Tercentenary Essays* (Cambridge University Press, 1988), pp. 95–117. I am indebted also to Morris's reading of *An Essay on Criticism* in his *Alexander Pope: The Genius of Sense* (Cambridge, MA: Harvard University Press, 1984), pp. 47–74.

8 Johnson, *Life of Cowley*, paragraph 54; Roger Lonsdale, ed., *The Lives of the Poets*, 4 vols. (Oxford: Clarendon Press, 2006), vol. I, p. 200.

9 Keats, 27 February 1818 to John Taylor, in Robert Gittings, ed., *John Keats: Selected Letters* (Oxford University Press, 2002), p. 66; Ralph Waldo Emerson, "Self-Reliance" (1841), opening paragraph.

4   Talking in tetrameter

1 See E. San Juan, Jr., "The Anti-Poetry of Jonathan Swift," *Philological Quarterly* 44 (1965), 387–96, and the interesting discussion of Swift's "Presentation of Self in Doggerel Rhyme" in Robert C. Elliott's *The Literary Persona* (University of Chicago Press, 1982), pp. 144–64.

2 The quotations from *Strephon and Chloe* [lines 25–6], *Phyllis, or The Progress of Love* [lines 67–72], and from all other poems except the posthumously published *Satirical Elegy*, are from *The Works of J. S., D.D, D. S.P.D*, 4 vols. (Dublin: Printed by and for George Faulkner, 1735), vol. II.

3 Finch, *Sir Plausible*, in Barbara McGovern and Charles H. Hinnant, eds., *The Anne Finch Wellesley Manuscript Poems* (Athens, GA: University of Georgia Press, 1996), p. 53.

4 Canto I, lines 499–508, quoted from John Wilders, ed., *Hudibras* (Oxford: Clarendon Press, 1967), p. 16.

5 Letter to Charles Wogan, July or August 1732, in David Wooley, ed., *The Correspondence of Jonathan Swift, D. D.*, 4 vols. (Frankfurt am Main: Peter Lang, 1999–2007), III, 515; *Verses on the Death of Dr. Swift*, lines 49–50.

6 *Alma* first appears in Prior's *Poems on Several Occasions* (1718), pp. 319–81, without line numbers. I include here the line numbers from the definitive scholarly edition: H. Bunker Wright and Monroe K. Spears, eds., *The Literary Works of Matthew Prior*, 2 vols. (Oxford: Clarendon Press, 1971).

7 W. H. Auden, *Lectures on Shakespeare*, reconstructed and edited by Arthur Kirsch (Princeton University Press, 2000), p. 24.

8 Elizabeth Tollet, *Poems on Several Occasions* (1724), p. 23.

9   Mary Alcock, *Poems* (1799), pp. 89–90.

10 *A Ramble in St. James's Park*, lines 57–62, in Keith Walker and Nicholas Fisher, eds., *John Wilmot, Earl of Rochester: The Poems and Lucina's Rape* (Malden, MA: Wiley-Blackwell, 2010), p. 83.

11 See Doody's "Women Poets of the Eighteenth Century," in Vivien Jones, ed., *Women and Literature in Britain, 1700–1800* (Cambridge University Press, 2000), pp. 217–37.

12 See, e.g., Derek Attridge, *Poetic Rhythm: An Introduction* (Cambridge University Press, 1995), pp. 153–61.

13 Mary Barber, *Poems on Several Occasions* (1734), p. 72 [lines 15–22].

14 Mary Leapor, *Poems upon Several Occasions* (1748), p. 102 [lines 28–33].

15 Leapor, *Poems upon Several Occasions* (1751), pp. 68–9 [lines 7–18].

16 *Epistle* I.vii, 1–4, *The Works of Alexander Pope, Esq.*, 2 vols. (1738), II, 72.

17 This poem was first published in 1765; I quote it from *The Works of Dr. Jonathan Swift, Dean of St. Patrick's, Dublin. Collected and revised by Deane Swift*, 8 vols. (1765), VIII, 168 [lines 11–18].

18 Mary Chudleigh, *Essays upon Several Subjects in Prose and Verse* (1710), p. 236; the essay and poem are both included in the excellent modern edition, *The Poems and Prose of Mary, Lady Chudleigh*, ed. Margaret J. M. Ezell (Oxford University Press, 1993), as is Chudleigh's ambitious ode *Solitude*.

19 *Poems on Several Occasions. Written by Dr. Thomas Parnell, Late Arch-Deacon of Clogher: and Published by Mr. Pope* (1722), p. 152.

20 *The Bird*, lines 1–4, in Myra Reynolds, ed., *The Poems of Anne Finch, Countess of Winchilsea* (University of Chicago Press, 1903), p. 266; *The Tree*, lines 1–4, 15–20, in Finch, *Miscellany Poems* (1713), pp. 289–90.

21 B. H. Fairchild, Jr., "Melos and Meaning in Blake's Lyric Art," *Blake Studies* 7.2 (1975), 125–41.

22 *A Hymn to Contentment* (entitled *Hymn on Contentment* when it appeared in a collection in 1714) is included by Pope in his 1722 edition of Parnell's *Poems*, followed here; but much of his poetry, especially his religious poetry, was not published until 1758 and some only recently in the indispensable *Collected Poems of Thomas Parnell*, ed. Claude Rawson and F. P. Lock (Newark: University of Delaware Press, 1989).

23 The ode version first appeared in Richard Savage, ed., *Miscellaneous Poems and Translations. By Several Hands* (1726), pp. 60–6, the couplet version the same year in D[avid] Lewis, ed., *Miscellaneous Poems, by Several Hands*, pp. 223–31.

24 *The Works of Dr. Jonathan Swift, Dean of St. Patrick's, Dublin. Collected and Revised by Deane Swift*, 3 vols. (1765), III, 184–5.

25 Nicholas Amhurst, *The British General; A Poem, Sacred to the Memory of His Grace John, Duke of Marlborough* (1722).

26 Lines 198–205. I follow the text of vol. II of Swift's 1735 *Works* (see note 2 above); the reader new to Swift's poem will be well guided by Pat Rogers's beautifully annotated modern-spelling edition, *Jonathan Swift: The Complete Poems* (London: Penguin Books, 1983), from which line numbers are supplied.

5 Blank verse and stanzaic poetry

1 Joseph Spence, *Observations, Anecdotes, and Characters of Books and Men*, 2 vols., ed. James M. Osborn (Oxford: Clarendon Press, 1966), I, 173.

2 Unless otherwise noted, quotations from Young are from Stephen Cornford, ed., *Night Thoughts* (Cambridge University Press, 1989).

3 Life of Young, in *The Lives of the Most Eminent Poets*, 4 vols., ed. Roger Lonsdale (Oxford: Clarendon Press, 2006), IV, 164; Eliot's "Worldliness and Other-Worldliness: The Poet Young" is most easily consulted online through Project Gutenberg in *The Essays of George Eliot*.

4 Philips, *The Splendid Shilling. An Imitation of Milton. Now First Correctly Publish'd* (1705), p. 3 [lines 35–40].

5 Smart, *The Hop-Garden*, line 7, in *Poems on Several Occasions* (1752), p. 103.

6 Watts's *Horae Lyricae* was first published in 1706; the statement is from his Preface to the revised edition of 1709, p. cv, quoted in Dustin Griffin's excellent study of Milton's influence, *Regaining Paradise: Milton and the Eighteenth Century* (Cambridge University Press, 1986), p. 98.

7 *Autumn*, 910–15, 919–22. Unless otherwise noted, quotations are from James Thomson, *The Seasons*, ed. James Sambrook (Oxford: Clarendon Press, 1981).

8 Johnson, *Prologue Spoken by Mr. Garrick* [line 32], in *Prologue and Epilogue Spoken by Mr. Garrick, At the Opening of Drury-Lane Theatre in 1747* (1747), p. 3.

9 Anna Laetitia Barbauld, *Poems* (1773), pp. 132–3 [lines 18–28].

10 Edward Young, *The Consolation. Containing, among other things, I. A Moral Survey of the Nocturnal Heavens. II. A Night-Address to the Deity …* (1745), p. 39 [Night IX, lines 744–53 in later editions].

11 William Cowper, *The Task, A Poem, In Six Books* (1785), pp. 151–2 [IV.284–95]. All quotations are from this first edition, with line numbers supplied from the definitive scholarly edition, John D. Baird and Charles Ryskamp, eds., *The Poems of William Cowper*, 3 vols. (Oxford: Clarendon Press, 1980–95).

12 Coleridge, *Fears in Solitude, Written in 1798, during the Alarm of an Invasion. To which are added, France, an Ode; and Frost at Midnight* (1798), p. 20. Coleridge revised the passage substantially in 1817 and 1834.

13 Edward Young, *Conjectures on Original Composition* (1759), p. 60.

14 Goldsmith's introductory note to Gray's *Elegy* in his anthology, *The Beauties of English Poesy*, 2 vols. (London, 1767), I, 53.

15 Quoted from the second edition of *Miscellanies in prose and verse. In two volumes. By Jonathan Swift, D. D. and Alexander Pope* (1728), p. 45 [lines 10–18].

16 Shenstone, *The School-Mistress. A Poem. In Imitation of Spencer's Stile* (1742), n.p., stanza xvii.

17 Beattie, *The Minstrell; or, The Progress of Genius. A Poem. Book the First* (1771), p. 31 [lines 518–19].

18 I quote from the second edition of *A Song to David*, printed following the main text of *A Translation of the Psalms of David, Attempted in the Spirit of Christianity, and Adapted to the Divine Service* (1765), p. 191 [stanza 51].

19 *Poems, And a Tragedy. By William Julius Mickle* (1794), p. 122.
20 Isaac Watts, *Few Happy Matches*, lines 31–6, in *Horae Lyricae* (1709), p. 226.
21 Gray, *Designs by Mr. R. Bentley for Six Poems by Mr. T. Gray* (1753), pp. 6–7 [lines 31–6].

6 Satiric poetry

1 Edward W. Rosenheim, Jr., *Swift and the Satirist's Art* (Chicago and London: University of Chicago Press, 1963), pp. 1–34; he defines satire on p. 31.
2 Quintilian, *Institutes* 10.1.93. In the phrase of one eighteenth-century translator, "The Province Satyr is wholly ours"; William Guthrie, *M. Fabius Quinctilianus his Institutes of Eloquence*, 2 vols. (1756), II, 354.
3 John Dryden, *Of Dramatic Poesy and Other Critical Essays*, ed. George Watson, 2 vols. (London: J. M. Dent and Sons, 1962), II, 130.
4 Unfortunately, there is no modern edition of Young's satires. The 1752 edition of *Love of Fame* is currently available online through Google Books.
5 Brief sketches of type characters, such as the miser, the braggart, and so on, go back at least to Theophrastus (*c.* 372–287 BCE). In the same year that Young began publishing his satires, Henry Gally's translation of the Greek philosopher, naturalist, and caricaturist appeared under the title *Theophrastus, Moral Characters, with notes and a critical essay on Characteristic Writings*.
6 Mary Leapor, *Poems upon Several Occasions* (1751), p. 46.
7 Thomas Creech, *The Odes, Satyrs, and Epistles of Horace Done into English* (1684), p. 420.
8 Dryden's Preface to *Epistles of Ovid, Translated by Several Hands* (1680); see George Watson, ed., *Of Dramatic Poesy and Other Critical Essays*, 2 vols. (London: Dent, 1962), I, 268.
9 The full title of the first edition (followed here) emphasizes the poem's local immediacy: *The First Satire of the Second Book of Horace, Imitated in a Dialogue between Alexander Pope, of Twickenham, in Com. Midd. Esq; on the One Part, and his Learned Council on the Other* (1733).
10 Samuel Johnson, *Lives of the Poets*, 4 vols., ed. Roger Lonsdale (Oxford University Press, 2006), IV, 55: "When he wanted to sleep he *nodded in company*; and once slumbered at his own table while the Prince of Wales was talking of poetry."
11 *Verses on the Death of Dr. Swift*, lines 7–10; for this poem I follow the text as established by Harold Williams, ed., *The Poems of Jonathan Swift*, 3 vols. (Oxford: Clarendon Press, 1937, rev. edn., 1958), II, 553–72.
12 Pope to Swift, 15 October 1725, *Correspondence of Alexander Pope*, ed. George Sherburn, 5 vols. (Oxford: Clarendon Press, 1956), II, 333; Swift to Pope, 26 November 1725, *The Correspondence of Jonathan Swift, D. D.*, 4 vols., ed. David Woolley (Frankfurt am Main: Peter Lang, 1999–2007), II, 623.

13 Maxims # 2 and 19 in *Moral Reflections and Maxims, Written by the late Duke de la Rochefoucauld* (1706).
14 Or 182 lines in the modern text edited by Pat Rogers, *Jonathan Swift: The Complete Poems* (London: Penguin Books, 1983), pp. 485–98, who inserts four lines from manuscript sources following line 301.
15 See Irwin Ehrenpreis, *Swift: The Man, His Works, and the Age*, 3 vols. (Cambridge, MA: Harvard University Press, 1962–83), III, 877–8.
16 Fish, "Short People Got No Reason to Live: Reading Irony," *Daedelus* 112, 1 (Winter, 1983), 175–91, referring to Barry Slepian, "The Ironic Intention of Swift's Verses on his own Death," *Review of English Studies* 14 (1963), 249–56.
17 See Chapter 3, endnote 4.
18 *Epistle to Dr. Arbuthnot*, lines 323, 325. Dated 1734, the poem first appeared in January 1735, without some lines that Pope included the next year. I quote from the first complete edition, in *The Works of Alexander Pope, Esq; Vol. II. Containing his Epistles and Satires* (1736), pp. 78–96.
19 In his *Dictionary* of 1755 Samuel Johnson underscores the differentiation: "Proper *satire* is distinguished, by the generality of the reflections, from *lampoon*, which is aimed against a particular person."
20 *London. A Poem. In Imitation of the Third Satire of Juvenal* (1739), p. 18 [lines 248–53].
21 Churchill, *The Apology. Addressed to the Critical Reviewers. By C. Churchill* (1761), pp. 18–19.
22 *Night, an Epistle to Robert Lloyd* (1760), p. 1 [lines 7–10].
23 *Table-Talk*, lines 675–83; *Table-Talk*, *Charity*, and *Hope* all first appeared in *Poems by William Cowper, of the Inner Temple, Esq.* (1782), the text followed here. Quotations from *The Task* here and in later chapters are from *The Task, a Poem, in Six Books. By William Cowper, of the Inner Temple, Esq.* (1785).

7   Pope as metapoet

1 Stein, "Composition as Explanation," in *What Are Masterpieces* (New York: Pitman Publishing Corporation, 1970), pp. 27–8.
2 *The Life of David Hume, Esq. Written by Himself* (Dublin, 1777), p. 4; Hume echoes ironically Pope's "All, all but Truth, drops dead-born from the Press," *One Thousand Seven Hundred and Thirty Eight. Dialogue II* [later renamed *Epilogue to the Satires*] (1738), line 226.
3 W. J. Bate, *The Burden of the Past and the English Poet* (Cambridge, MA: Harvard University Press, 1970), pp. 3–4. Bate does not give a source for the statement but attributes it to Khakheperresenb. The name is also transliterated as Khakheperre-sonb, and the remark may be read in context in Miriam Lichtheim, *Ancient Egyptian Literature: A Book of Readings*, 3 vols. (University of California Press, 1973), I, 146.

4 Dryden's poem *To My Dear Friend Mr. Congreve, on his Comedy Call'd The Double-Dealer* prefaced Congreve's play in the first edition in 1694.

5 *The Pastorals* (first published in 1709), *Windsor-Forest* (1713), *The Temple of Fame* (1715), *Eloisa to Abelard and Verses* [later *Elegy*] *on the Death of an Unfortunate Lady* (both 1717), are all quoted from *The Works of Mr. Alexander Pope* (1717).

6 Closing line of *To Mr. Jervas, with Fresnoy's Art of Painting* and "Preface" (unpaginated, para. 11), both quoted from *Works* (1717).

7 The phrase is the title of Thomas Nagel's *The View from Nowhere* (New York: Oxford University Press, 1986). For more about Pope's choice of perspective in *An Essay on Man* see, pp. 129–31.

8 Joseph Spence, *Observations, Anecdotes, and Characters of Books and Men*, 2 vols., ed. James M. Osborn (Oxford University Press, 1966), I, 45. Samuel Johnson refers to the plausibility of Addison's advice in his "Life of Pope," paragraphs 55–6; see *The Lives of the Poets*, 4 vols., ed. Roger Lonsdale (Oxford University Press, 2006), IV, 10. The major changes appeared in 1714; Clarissa's speech was added to the opening of Canto V in 1717.

9 Especially helpful, for its inclusion of background materials as well as the 1712 text, is Cynthia Wall, ed., *The Rape of the Lock* (Boston and New York: Bedford Books, 1998).

10 Quotations from *The Rape of the Lock* follow the text of *The Works of Mr. Alexander Pope* (1717), which includes the last major change to the poem, the addition of Clarissa's speech in Canto V. Pope made additional minor changes in 1736, none of which are pertinent to this commentary.

11 *Miscellaneous Poems and Translations. By Several Hands* (1712), p. 362.

12 Canto IV, lines 175–6. Curiously, in the 1712 poem these lines were spoken not by Belinda but by Thalestris.

13 J. V. Guerinot, *Pamphlet Attacks on Alexander Pope, 1711–1744: A Descriptive Bibliography* (New York University Press, 1969).

14 The best is A. D. Hope's *The Dunciad Minor* (Melbourne University Press, 1970). See also *A Modern Dunciad* by Richard Nason (New York: The Smith, 1978).

15 *Dunciad Variorum*, III, 75–8. In light of the complicated textual history of *The Dunciad*, I follow the standard modern edition by James Sutherland, which includes both the 1729 and 1743 versions of the poem, vol. V (3rd edn., 1963) of John Butt (gen. ed.), *The Twickenham Edition of the Poems of Alexander Pope* (London: Methuen; New Haven: Yale University Press, 1938–68). For an even more fully annotated edition of the 1743 poem see Valerie Rumbold, ed., *The Dunciad in Four Books* (Harlow: Pearson Education Limited, 1999, rev. edn., 2009).

16 Pope first referred to the *Dunciad* as the "Temple of Infamy" in 1735. I compare the *Dunciad* and the *Temple of Fame* in *The Poetry of Pope's "Dunciad"* (Minneapolis: University of Minnesota Press, 1971), pp. 66–117.

17 Quotations from *An Essay on Man* are from *The Works of Alexander Pope, Esq; Vol. II. Containing his Epistles and Satires*. The remark from "The Design" is on p. 2.

18 Pope put the two lines in quotation marks when the *Epistle to Bathurst* was included in *The Works of Alexander Pope, Esq; Vol. II. Containing his Epistles and Satires* (1735), p. 36. They appeared following line 148 of the second epistle of *An Essay on Man*; Pope removed them from the *Essay* in 1735. The couplet is included in the textual apparatus of the Twickenham Edition of *An Essay on Man*, edited by Maynard Mack: *The Poems of Alexander Pope*, vol. III.i (London and New York, Methuen, 1950), p. 72.

19 Spence, *Observations, Anecdotes, and Characters of Books and Men*, I, 130.

20 "The Author's Apology for Heroic Poetry," in John Dryden, *Of Dramatic Poesy and Other Critical Essays*, ed. George Watson, 2 vols. (London: J. M. Dent and Sons, 1962), I, 200.

21 *An Epistle to the Right Honourable Richard Lord Visct. Cobham* (dated 1733, published 1734), p. 4 [line 61].

8   Metapoetry beyond Pope

1 A complete edition of Finch's work is in progress under the editorship of Jennifer Keith and Claudia Kairoff for Cambridge University Press. The following quotations from *To the Nightingale* and *The Spleen* are from Finch's *Miscellany Poems* (1713).

2 Myra Reynolds, ed., *The Poems of Anne, Countess of Winchilsea* (University of Chicago Press, 1903), p. 15.

3 *An Essay on the Different Stiles of Poetry* (1713), pp. 17 and 24 [lines 237–40, 335–8].

4 *Poems on Several Occasions. Written by Dr. Thomas Parnell, Late Arch-Deacon of Clogher: and Published by Mr. Pope* (1722), pp. 119–22.

5 *Piety: Or, The Vision*, lines 107–10, in Claude Rawson and F. P. Lock, eds., *Collected Poems of Thomas Parnell* (Newark: University of Delaware Press, 1980).

6 *Autumn*, lines 1020–3 in *The Seasons* (1746), p. 167, corresponding to lines 1010–13 in James Sambrook, ed., *The Seasons and Castle of Indolence* (Oxford University Press, 1972).

7 Thomas Warton, *The Pleasures of Melancholy. A Poem* (1747), p. 14 [lines 158–63].

8 Joseph Warton, *The Enthusiast: or, The Lover of Nature. A Poem* (1744), pp. 9, 12, 14 [lines 79, 111, 124].

9 *Ode to Pity* [lines 37–42] in *Odes on Several Descriptive and Allegoric Subjects* (dated 1747, published 1746), p. 4. Other quotations from Collins's odes are from this edition.

10 William Duff, *An Essay on Original Genius; and Its Various Modes of Exertion in Philosophy and the Fine Arts, Particularly in Poetry* (1767), p. 159.

11 The remark occurs in Barbauld's important edition, *The Poetical Works of William Collins* (1797), p. xxiv.

12 Harold Bloom, *The Visionary Company: A Reading of English Romantic Poetry* (Ithaca: Cornell University Press, 1971), pp. 14 and 217, referring to Collins, Smart, Chatterton, Cowper, and "other bards of sensibility."

13 *Odes by Mr. Gray* (1757), p. 7 [*Progress of Poesy*, lines 42–7].

14 *Poems by Mr. Gray* (1768), p. 38.

15 Mark Akenside, *The Pleasures of Imagination. A Poem in Three Books* (1744), p. 19 (Book I, line 277).

16 Karina Williamson and Marcus Walsh, eds., *Christopher Smart: Selected Poems* (London: Penguin Books, 1990), p. 85.

17 *The Task, a Poem, in Six Books. By William Cowper* (1785), p. 269 [VI, 747–50].

18 Kevis Goodman's excellent reading of *The Task* in *Georgic Modernity and British Romanticism: Poetry and the Mediation of History* (Cambridge University Press, 2004), pp. 67–105, emphasizes Cowper's immersion in news accounts during the composition of the poem.

9   Reading visions

1 *Summer*, lines 1435–7. As in Chapter 5, quotations from Thomson's *Seasons* are from James Sambrook, ed., *The Seasons* (Oxford: Clarendon Press, 1981).

2 Quoted by Donald Davie, *Purity of Diction in English Verse* (New York: Schocken Books, 1967; originally published 1952), p. 40, and by Chester Chapin, *Personification in Eighteenth-Century English Poetry* (New York: Columbia University Press, 1955), p. 63. I am indebted greatly to both of these foundational studies in this and the following chapter.

3 *Verses on the Death of Dr. Swift*, lines 35–6; here and elsewhere quotations from this poem are from Harold Williams, ed., *The Poems of Jonathan Swift*, 3 vols. (Oxford: Clarendon Press, 1937, rev. edn., 1958), II, 553–72.

4 Richard Savage, *The Authors of the Town, a Satire* (1725), p. 15.

5 *The Vanity of Human Wishes. The Tenth Satire of Juvenal, Imitated by Samuel Johnson* (1749), p. 19 [lines 237–40].

6 Henry Howard, Earl of Surrey, *Poems*, ed. Emrys Jones (Oxford: Clarendon Press, 1964), p. 2.

7 *Windsor-Forest* (1713), p. 13 [line 291n.].

8 In *Arguments of Augustan Wit* (Cambridge University Press, 1991), pp. 43–54, 180–1, I elaborate this distinction more fully. Thomas Kaminski nicely explicates the "disguised concreteness" of Johnson's writing in "Some Alien Qualities of Samuel Johnson's Art," in Jonathan Clark and Howard Erskine-Hill, eds., *Samuel Johnson in Historical Context* (New York: Palgrave, 2002), 222–38.

10   Personification

1 Wordsworth, Preface to *Lyrical Ballads* (1800); R. L. Brett and A. R. Jones, eds., *Lyrical Ballads* (London: Methuen, 1963, rev. 1965), pp. 250–1.

2 "Personification" in Alex Preminger and T. V. F. Brogan, eds., *The New Princeton Encyclopedia of Poetry and Poetics* (Princeton University Press, 1993), p. 902.

3 Joseph Priestley, *A Course of Lectures on Oratory and Criticism* (1777), pp. 253–4 (Lecture 19); Henry Home, Lord Kames, *Elements of Criticism*, 3 vols. (Edinburgh, 1762), III, 64–72 (ch. 20); the following quotations from Hugh Blair are from *Lectures on Rhetoric and Belles Lettres*, 2 vols. (1783), I, 326–31 (Lecture 16).

4 James Sutherland points out the change in his anthology, *Early Eighteenth Century Poetry* (London: Edward Arnold, 1965), p. 181, speculating that Thomson may have come to regard the original "Unlist'ning" as unclear.

5 Donald Davie, *Purity of Diction in English Verse* [1952] (New York: Schocken Books, 1967), p. 32.

6 James Harris, *Hermes: or, A Philosophical Inquiry concerning Language and Universal Grammar* (1751), pp. 41–51.

7 This cultural association may finally be fading, but it was still prominent enough for Mary Ellmann to include it as one of the major "feminine stereotypes" in her incisive *Thinking About Women* (New York: Harcourt, Brace, and World, 1968), where she connected its construction with the "apathy" popularly attributed to African Americans (p. 81).

8 The two 1743 editions of Robert Blair's *The Grave* and several subsequent editions through 1764 use the feminine pronoun for Death. The phrase "his Fellness" (referring to Death's fearful power) first appears in the Edinburgh edition of 1767 and is adopted in London editions of 1780 and 1791.

9 *Fancy: An Irregular Ode* [lines 63–4], quoted from Chadwyck-Healey English Poetry database, which draws from James Grainger, *Poetical Works*, 2 vols. (1836).

10 For Cowper summer "has her riches" in Book III of *The Task* (1785) [line 427]; William Stevenson refers to Summer as Spring's "elder sister" in *Vertumnus, or The Progress of the Spring* [I.179] in his *Original Poems on Several Subjects*, 2 vols. (1765), I, 13.

11 Thomas Cooke, *The Works of Hesiod Translated from the Greek*, 2 vols. (1728), II, 27; James Beattie, *Original Poems and Translations* (1761), p. 1.

12 Collins's "Lines Addressed to James Harris," lines 21–2; this manuscript poem, which probably dates from 1744, was first printed in J. S. Cunningham, ed., *Drafts and Fragments of Verse* (Oxford: Clarendon Press, 1956), pp. 19–20.

13 James Cawthorn, *Poems* (1771), pp. 188–209. Mary Masters, *Poems* (1733), pp. 8–10.

14 *The Ghost. By C. Churchill. Book III* (1762), p. 95; Brown's poem on satire aspires to "fix her equal Law," *An Essay on Satire, Occasioned by the Death of Mr. Pope. Inscribed to Mr. Warburton* (2nd edn., 1749), p. 8; Cowper, *Table-Talk*, line 728, *Charity*, line 492, in *Poems by William Cowper, of the Inner Temple, Esq.* (1782), pp. 38, 204.

15 For cognitive discussions of prototypes see Eleanor Rosch, "Natural Categories", *Cognitive Psychology* 4 (1973), 328–50, and Rosch and Carolyn B. Mervis, "Family Resemblances: Studies in the Internal Structure of Categories", *Cognitive Psychology* 7 (1975), pp. 573–605.

16 Jerry A. Fodor, *Hume Variations* (Oxford: Clarendon Press, 2003), p. 134.

17 George Lakoff and Mark Turner, *More than Cool Reason: A Field Guide to Poetic Metaphor* (University of Chicago Press, 1989), esp. pp. 72–80. Personification is treated more briefly as a way to "make sense of the phenomena of the world in human terms" in George Lakoff and Mark Johnson, *Metaphors We Live By* (University of Chicago Press, 1980), pp. 33–4.

18 Joseph Butler, *The Analogy of Religion … To which are added Two Brief Dissertations* (1736), p. 311. The quotation is from the second of these dissertations, "Of the Nature of Virtue," paragraph two.

19 Paul M. Churchland, *A Neurocomputational Perspective: The Nature of Mind and the Structure of Science* (Cambridge, MA: MIT Press, 1989), pp. 7–8.

20 R. N. McCauley (2000), "The Naturalness of Religion and the Unnaturalness of Science," in F. Keil and R. Wilson, eds., *Explanation and Cognition* (Cambridge, MA: MIT Press), pp. 61–85; p. 70.

21 Stephen Toulmin, *Cosmopolis: The Hidden Agenda of Modernity* (University of Chicago Press, 1990), p. 112.

22 Adam Smith, *Theory of Moral Sentiments*, ed. D. D. Raphael and A. L. Macfie (Oxford: Clarendon Press, 1976; rpt. Indianapolis, IN: Liberty Classics, 1982), pp. 184–5 (Part 4, ch. 1, para. 10).

23 *Miscellany Poems, on Several Occasions. Written by a Lady* (1713), p. 29. When not otherwise noted, quotations from Finch are from this volume.

24 *Song to David* (1763), quoted from Smart, *A Translation of the Psalms of David, Attempted in the Spirit of Christianity, and Adapted to the Divine Service* (1765), pp. 191–2.

25 Cf. Hugh Blair, *Lectures on Rhetoric and Belles Lettres*, 2 vols. (1783), I, 325 [Lecture 16]: "Indeed, it is very remarkable, that there is a wonderful proneness in human nature to animate all objects. Whether this arises … from a propension to spread a resemblance of ourselves over all other things, or from whatever other cause it arises, so it is, that almost every emotion, which in the least agitates the mind, bestows upon its object a momentary idea of life."

11   Prophecy and prospects of society

1 *Collected Works of Oliver Goldsmith*, 5 vols., ed. Arthur Friedman (Oxford University Press, 1966), I, 432.

2 Cowper, *The Task* (1785) [IV.495–9]; other quotations from the poem are from this edition, with book and line numbers noted parenthetically.

3 Raymond Williams, *Keywords: A Vocabulary of Culture and Society*, revised edition (New York: Oxford University Press, 1985), p. 292; in addition to the entry on "Society," the entries "Culture" and "Determine" are helpful here.

4 Collins, *Odes on Several Descriptive and Allegoric Subjects* (dated 1747, published 1746), p. 41; *The Poems of Mark Akenside, M. D.* (1772), p. 291.

5 In her strong reading of Thomson's use of personification, Heather Keenleyside notes that "Thomson frequently describes human beings as animated from without; see "Personification for the People: On James Thomson's *The Seasons*," *ELH*, 76, 2 (Summer, 2009), 447–72 (p. 457).

6 *The Second Epistle of the Second Book of Horace Imitated* (1737), p. 17 [lines 278–81]. Pope was particularly sensitive to charges that the *Essay on Man* espoused determinism and particularly grateful to Rev. William Warburton's defense of the poem's Christian orthodoxy against the attack of Jean-Pierre de Crousaz. The issues and episode are explained in Maynard Mack's authoritative biography, *Alexander Pope: A Life* (New Haven: Yale University Press, 1985), pp. 736–41.

7 Wordsworth, *Poems in Two Volumes* (1807), I, 18; Elizabeth Tollet, *Poems on Several Occasions* (1755), p. 152.

8 Thomson, *The Prospect: Being the Fifth Part of Liberty* (1736), pp. 4, 35. Glover, *London: Or, The Progress of Commerce* (2nd edn., 1739), p. 2.

9 See Suvir Kaul's excellent *Poems of Nation, Anthems of Empire: English Verse in the Long Eighteenth Century* (Charlottesville: University Press of Virginia, 2000). The quoted phrases are from pp. 1 and 33.

10 See James Sutherland, ed., *The Dunciad*, vol. V (3rd edn., 1963) of John Butt (gen. ed.), *The Twickenham Edition of the Poems of Alexander Pope* (London: Methuen; New Haven: Yale University Press, 1938–68), p. 205.

11 Goldsmith, *The Deserted Village. A Poem* (2nd edn., 1770), p. 22 [lines 398, 403–7].

12 Goldsmith, *The Traveller, or a Prospect of Society. A Poem* (1764), pp. 17–18 [lines. 328–34].

13 Johnson, "Gray," final paragraph, in Roger Lonsdale, ed., *The Lives of the Poets*, 4 vols. (Oxford: Clarendon Press, 2006), IV, 184.

14 William Empson, *Some Versions of Pastoral* (New York: New Directions, 1950), p. 4. For a provocative discussion and extension of Empson's political reading of Gray's *Elegy* see John Guillory, *Cultural Capital: The Problem of Literary Canon Formation* (University of Chicago Press, 1993), pp. 85–124.

15 Joseph Warton takes it as a given that the "little Druid wight" of II, stanza 33, is Pope in his *Essay on the Genius and Writings of Pope* (1782), II, 399–400.

16 See W. J. Bate, *The Burden of the Past and the English Poet* (Cambridge, MA: Harvard University Press, 1970), esp. pp. 46–65.

17 The "ode," in fact modeled closely on Gray's *Elegy*, was first published in Warton's *Poems* of 1777.

18 *Temora, an Ancient Epic Poem, in Eight Books: Together with Several Other Poems, Composed by Ossian, the Son of Fingal. Translated from the Galic Language, by James Macpherson* (1763), pp. xvii and xii.

19 *The Complete Works of Thomas Chatterton*, 2 vols. ed. Donald S. Taylor (Oxford: Clarendon Press, 1971), I, 6.

20 Blair's work is reprinted in *The Poems of Ossian and Related Work*, ed. Howard Gaskill (Edinburgh UP, 1996), pp. 345–99; the quotation is from p. 356.

21 Vicesimus Knox, *Essays, Moral and Literary*, 2 vols. (1778), I, 326.

22 Wordsworth, Preface (of 1800) in R. L. Brett and A. R. Jones, eds., Wordsworth and Coleridge, *Lyrical Ballads* (London: Methuen, 1963), p. 245.

12 Ecological prospects and natural knowledge

1 Jonathan Bate, *Song of the Earth* (London: Picador, 2000), pp. 78, 245, 252. Similar assumptions operate in Karl Kroeber's *Ecological Literary Criticism: Romantic Imagining and the Biology of Mind* (New York: Columbia University Press, 1994) and Bate's earlier *Romantic Ecology: Wordsworth and the Environmental Tradition* (London: Routledge, 1991).

2 E. N. Hooker, ed., *The Critical Works of John Dennis*, 2 vols. (Baltimore: Johns Hopkins University Press, 1939–43), I, 257, 264.

3 The passage from Wordsworth is lines 1–6 of the reconstructed "Two-Part Prelude of 1799," lines 271–6 of book one of the 1805 *Prelude*, and lines 269–74 in the 1850 text; see Jonathan Wordsworth, M. H. Abrams, and Stephen Gill, eds., *The Prelude: 1799, 1805, 1850* (New York: W. W. Norton, 1979). The passage from Thomson appeared as lines 1085–89 in *Autumn. A Poem* (1730), p. 62; they are lines 1182–6 in James Sambrook, ed., *The Seasons* (Oxford: Clarendon Press, 1981).

4 David Abram, *The Spell of the Sensuous: Perception and Language in a More-than-human World* (New York: Pantheon, 1996), p. 263.

5 Lawrence Buell, *The Environmental Imagination: Thoreau, Nature Writing, and the Formation of American Culture* (Cambridge, MA: Harvard University Press, 1995), pp. 7–8.

6 The list comes from the Appendix to John Arthos's monumental study, *The Language of Natural Description in Eighteenth-Century Poetry* (Ann Arbor: University of Michigan Press, 1949).

7 Samuel Boyse would in turn echo Pope closely a few years later, surveying creation "From the unwieldy Whale's enormous Mass, / To the small Insect on the peopled Grass"; *Retirement*, in *Translations and Poems, Written on Several Occasions* (1738), p. 153.

8 John Hughes, *To Mr. Constantine, on his Paintings*, in *Poems on Several occasions. With some Select Essays in Prose*, 2 vols. (1735), I, liv; Dryden, Georgic III, 719–20, in *The Works of Virgil containing his Pastorals, Georgics and Aeneis … Translated into English Verse by Mr. Dryden* (1697), p. 117; Thomas Blacklock, *An Hymn to Benevolence*, in *Poems on Several Occasions* (Glasgow, 1746), pp. 17–19.

9 Arne Naess, *Ecology, Community and Lifestyle: Outline of an Ecosophy* (Cambridge University Press, 1989), p. 29.

10 See E. O. Wilson, *Biophilia* (Cambridge, MA: Harvard University Press, 1984) and *The Biophilia Hypothesis* (Washington, DC: Island Press, 1993).

11 Cowper, *The Task, a Poem, in Six Books* (1785), pp. 247–8 [VI, 321–6]; all quotations are from this first edition, with book and line numbers supplied parenthetically.

12 For helpful annotations on this and many other parts of *The Task* I am indebted to John D. Baird and Charles Ryskamp, eds., *The Poems of William Cowper*, 3 vols. (Oxford: Clarendon Press, 1980–95).

13 William Somervil[l]e, *Field-Sports: A Poem* (1742), p. 5.

14 Abraham Tucker, *The Light of Nature Pursued*, 4 vols. (1777), II, 361 and III, 115–18.

15 The quotations are, respectively, from Wordsworth, Preface, in *Lyrical Ballads, with Other Poems*, 2nd edition, 2 vols., I, xxvi; Keats, *Lamia*, II, 231–7, in Edward Hirsch and Jim Pollock, eds., *Complete Poems and Selected Letters of John Keats* (New York: The Modern Library, 2001), p. 205; Thomson, *Spring. A Poem* (1728), p. 13 ("Philosophic Eye" later became "sage-instructed Eye" [line 210]); and Mark Akenside, *The Pleasures of Imagination* (1744), p. 51, Book II, lines 103–8. The classic study of the influence of Newton's *Opticks* (1704) on eighteenth-century poets is Marjorie Hope Nicholson, *Newton Demands the Muse* (Princeton University Press, 1946).

16 *Milton: A Poem*, dated by Blake as completed in 1804, Plate 41, in Mary Lynn Johnson and John E. Grant, eds., *Blake's Poetry and Designs* (New York: W. W. Norton, 1979), p. 304.

17 James Sambrook quotes this phrase from Bernard de Fontenelle's *The Plurality of Worlds* (trans. 1688) in his commentary on this passage (p. 370).

18 *On the Omniscience of the Supreme Being. A Poetical Essay* (1752), p. 14 [lines 168–74].

19 Smart's poem appeared in his *Ode to the Right Honourable the Earl of Northumberland … With Some Other Pieces* (1764), pp. 22–3.

20 Sallie McFague, *Life Abundant: Rethinking Theology and Economy for a Planet in Peril* (Minneapolis: Fortress Press, 2001), p. 33.

21 James M. Gustafson, *Ethics from a Theocentric Perspective*, 2 vols. (University of Chicago Press, 1981, 1984).

22 See, e.g., Murray Bookchin, *The Ecology of Freedom: The Emergence and Dissolution of Hierarchy* (Palo Alta, CA: Cheshire Books, 1982) and *The Philosophy of Social Ecology: Essays on Dialectical Naturalism* (Montreal: Black Rose Books, 1995).

23 Seward's copy of the 1785 edition of *The Task* is in the British Library, shelfmark BL C71. c. 22. The remarks are written on pp. 196–7; a note on p. 205 indicates that she was rereading the poem in 1800.

24 The OED's first definition is "The fact or condition of thriving or prospering; prosperity, success, good luck." Cowper's line is cited as an illustration for definition 3.a.: "Economical management, economy; sparing use or careful expenditure of means; frugality, saving."

25 Even Gerard Manley Hopkins's moving celebration of "wildness and wet" in the poem *Inversnaid* (1881) is about a waterfall rather than a swamp.

26 *Poetry and Place* appears in Berry's *Standing By Words* (San Francisco: North Point Press, 1983; rpt. Berkeley: Counterpoint, 2005), pp. 106–213; the quotation is from pp. 140–1.

27 Originally published in *Entries* (1997); quoted from *The Selected Poems of Wendell Berry* (Berkeley, Cal: Counterpoint, 1998), pp. 156–7.

A concluding note: then and now

1 Edward Young, *Conjectures on Original Composition* (1759), p. 13: "He that imitates the divine *Iliad*, does not imitate *Homer*; but he [does] who takes the same method, which *Homer* took, for arriving at a capacity of accomplishing a work so great." Johnson told Boswell that he "was surprised to find Young receive as novelties what he thought very common maxims." James Boswell, *Journal of a Tour to the Hebrides, with Samuel Johnson, LL. D.* (1785), p. 333.
2 Bacon writes of works meant "really to instruct and suborn action and active life, these Georgics of the mind, concerning the husbandry and tillage thereof" in Book Two of *The Advancement of Learning*; see Brian Vickers, ed., *Francis Bacon: A Critical Edition of the Major Works* (Oxford University Press, 1996), p. 245.
3 Ammons's *Essay on Poetics* appeared in *Hudson Review* 23.3 (1970), pp. 425–48, and is included in his *Collected Poems, 1951–1971* (New York: W. W. Norton, 1972); *Sphere: The Form of a Motion* (New York: W. W. Norton, 1974); Bernstein's *The Absorption of Artifice* was first published as a book (Philadelphia: Singing Horse Press, 1987) and then as part of the volume *A Poetics* (Cambridge, MA: Harvard University Press, 1992), pp. 9–89. Pinsky's *Essay on Psychiatrists* appeared first in his *Sadness and Happiness* (Princeton University Press, 1975), and is included in *The Figured Wheel: New and Collected Poems* (New York: Farrar, Strauss, and Giroux, 1996), pp. 265–80.
4 R. G. Collingwood, *Principles of Art* (Oxford: Clarendon Press, 1938), p. 336.
5 Allen Ginsberg, *Wichita Vortex Sutra* (San Francisco: Coyote, 1966), p. 9.
6 Jean-Jacques Lecercle and Denise Riley, *The Force of Language* (New York: Palgrave Macmillan, 2004), p. 21.

Further reading

1. Selected works that address all or most of the period

Backscheider, Paula R., *Eighteenth-Century Women Poets and their Poetry: Inventing Agency, Inventing Genre*. Baltimore: Johns Hopkins University Press, 2005.

Doody, Margaret Anne, *The Daring Muse: Augustan Poetry Reconsidered*. Cambridge University Press, 1985.

Fairer, David, *English Poetry of the Eighteenth Century, 1700–1789*. London and New York: Longman, 2003.

Gerrard, Christine, ed., *A Companion to Eighteenth-Century Poetry*. Malden, MA: Blackwell, 2006.

Greene, Donald, *The Age of Exuberance: Backgrounds to Eighteenth-Century English Literature*. New York: Random House, 1970; rpt. 1988.

Kaul, Suvir, *Poems of Nation, Anthems of Empire: English Verse in the Long Eighteenth Century*. Charlottesville: University of Virginia Press, 2000.

Keith, Jennifer, *Poetry and the Feminine from Behn to Cowper*. Newark: University of Delaware Press, 2005.

Porter, Roy, *English Society in the Eighteenth Century*. London; New York: Penguin Books, 1990.

Rothstein, Eric, *Restoration and Eighteenth Century Poetry, 1660–1780*. Boston: Routledge and Kegan Paul, 1981.

Sambrook, James, *The Eighteenth Century: Intellectual and Cultural Context of English Literature, 1700–89*. London; New York: Longman, 2nd edn., 1993.

Sitter, John, ed., *The Cambridge Companion to Eighteenth-Century Poetry*. Cambridge University Press, 2001.

Spacks, Patricia Meyer, *Reading Eighteenth-Century Poetry*. Chichester, UK; Malden, MA: Wiley-Blackwell, 2009.

Speck, W. A., *Society and Literature in Eighteenth-Century England, 1680–1820: Ideology, Politics, and Culture*. London; New York: Longman, 1998.

Sutherland, James, *A Preface to Eighteenth-Century Poetry*. Oxford: Clarendon Press, 1948; rpt. 1975.

Weinbrot, Howard, *Britannia's Issue: The Rise of British Literature from Dryden to Ossian*. Cambridge University Press, 1993.

2. Significant anthologies

Backscheider, Paula R., and Catherine Ingrassia, eds., *British Women Poets of the Long Eighteenth Century*. Baltimore: Johns Hopkins University Press, 2009.
Fairer, David, and Christine Gerrard, *Eighteenth-Century Poetry: An Annotated Anthology*, second edition. Malden, MA: Blackwell Publishing, 2004.
Lonsdale, Roger, *Eighteenth Century Women Poets: An Oxford Anthology*. Oxford University Press, 1989.
   The New Oxford Book of Eighteenth Century Verse. Oxford University Press, 1984.

Index

Abram, David, 200
abstraction and generalization, 154–6
Addison, Joseph, 63–4, 104, 227
Akenside, Mark, 143
  Pleasures of Imagination, 13, 143,
    206, 229, 234
  The Remonstrance of Shakespeare, 180
Alcock, Mary, 51, 223
Aleghieri, Dante, 115
Amhurst, Nicholas, 68, 223
Ammons, A.R.
  Essay on Poetics, 217, 235
  Sphere: The Form of a Motion, 1,
    217, 219, 235
Aristotle, 171
Arthos, John, 201, 233
Attridge, Derek, 223
Auden, W.H., 113, 121, 222
  Lectures on Shakespeare, 50
Austen, Jane, 146

Backsheider, Paula, x, 219
Bacon, Francis, 217
  The Advancement of Learning, 235
Baker, Henry, 167
Barash, Carole, 219
Barbauld, Anna Laetitia, 81, 220, 224,
    228
  A Summer Evening's Meditation,
    78–9
  Corsica, 78
  on Collins, 140
  *On the Expected General Rising of
    the French Nation in 1792*, 82
  The Mouse's Petition, 82

The Rights of Woman, 82
To Mr. S.T. Coleridge, 78
Washing Day, 78
Barber, Mary, 52, 223
Bate, Jonathan, 198, 233
Bate, W.J., 116, 226
Beattie, James
  Ode to Peace, 167
  The Minstrel, 88, 224
Benedict, Barbara M., 221
Beowulf, 119
Berger, Thomas, 34, 221
Berkeley, George, 169, 170, 186
Bernstein, Charles, 217, 235
Berry, Wendell, 214–15
  Entries, 235
  *In a Hotel Parking Lot, Thinking of
    Dr. Williams*, 215
  Poetry and Place, 234
Blacklock, Thomas, 202, 233
Blair, Hugh, 160, 162
  "Critical Dissertation on the poems
    of Ossian", 196
  *Lectures on Rhetoric and Belles
    Lettres*, 160–1, 230, 231
Blair, Robert, 166
  The Grave, 230
Blake, William, 60–2, 132, 234
blank verse, 74–80
Bloom, Harold, 228
book production and appearance,
    13–15
Bookchin, Murray, 211, 234
Booth, Wayne, 103
Boswell, James, 235

Boyle, Robert, 206
Boyse, Samuel, 233
Bradford, Richard, 220
Brown, John
  Essay on Satire, 167, 230
Browning, Robert, 17, 18, 220
Buell, Lawrence, 200, 233
Butler, Joseph, 171, 231
Butler, Samuel, 47–50, 56
Byron, George Gordon, Lord, 113

Carruth, Hayden, 30
Cawthorn, James, 167, 230
Chapin, Chester, 229
Charleton, Walter, 206
Chatterton, Thomas, 194, 196, 197,
  228
Chaucer, Geoffrey, 16–18, 116, 220
Chudleigh, Lady Mary, 56–8, 223
Churchill, Charles, 96, 109, 110–12
  Epistle to William Hogarth, 111–12
  Night, 111, 226
  The Apology, 18–19, 109, 110–11,
    226
  The Ghost, 167, 230
Churchland, Paul M., 172, 231
Cicero, 161
Clark, Jonathan, 229
Coleridge, Samuel Taylor, 7, 30
  Biographia Literaria, 217, 221
  Frost at Midnight, 80, 146, 224
  Kubla Khan, 139
Collingwood, R.G., 218, 235
Collins, William, 62, 86, 159, 177, 220,
  228
  Lines Addressed to James Harris, 167,
    230
  Manners. An Ode, 180
  Ode on the Poetical Character, 66,
    141, 142, 186
    as metapoetry, 139–41
  Ode to Evening, 167
  Ode to Fear, 138–9
  Ode to Liberty, 66
    visions of society in, 185–7

Ode to Pity, 138, 228
Ode to Simplicity, 139
*Ode, Written at the Beginning of the
  Year 1746*, 167
The Passions, 66
Congreve, William, 116
Conrad, Joseph, 184
Cooke, Thomas
  Hesiod's *Theogony*, 167, 230
Cowper, William, 85, 96, 167, 209, 216,
  228
  Charity, 230
  Retirement, 29, 221
  Table-Talk, 109, 112–13, 226,
    230
  The Task, 13, 79–81, 146, 178, 193,
    224, 230, 233, 234
    and questions of satire, 113
    personification in, 162, 167–8
    social ecology in, 211–14
    society in, 179
  *Vertumnus, or The Progress of the
    Spring*, 230
Crabbe, George
  The Village, 178
    society in, 192–3
Crashaw, Richard, 48, 56, 116
Creech, Thomas
  Epistles of Horace Done Into English,
    225
  Satire II.i, 98

Davie, Donald, 229, 230
Defoe, Daniel, 118
Denham, Sir John, 103
Dennis, John, 199
Derham, William, 206
Dickens, Charles, 35
Donaldson, John, 177
Donne, John, 26, 48
  Satires, 22, 23, 26
Doody, Margaret, 52, 223
Dryden, John, 86, 95, 116, 132, 202,
  227
  Absalom and Achitophel, 93, 114

Dryden, John (*cont.*)
    and innovations in versification,
        17–18
    and poetic representation, 141–3
    and translation theory, 98
    "Discourse concerning the Original
        and Progress of Satire", 95
    Epistles of Ovid, 225
    Georgic III, 233
    MacFlecknoe, 17, 93, 220
    Of Dramatic Poesy, 220, 225
    "The Author's Apology for Heroic
        Poetry", 131, 228
Duff, William
    An Essay on Original Genius, 139,
        228
Dyer, John
    Grongar Hill, 59, 61–2, 63, 67, 223
    The Country Walk, 58, 60–1
    The Fleece, 13

Eagleton, Terry
    How to Read a Poem, 34, 221
ecology, 3, 198–9, 203–6
ecotheology, 209–10
Ehrenpreis, Irwin, 226
Eliot, George, 75, 224
Eliot, T.S., 35, 87
Elliot, Robert C., 222
Ellman, Mary, 230
Emerson, Ralph Waldo, 222
Empson, William, 191, 232
epic, 119
Erasmus, 126
Erskine-Hall, Howard, 229

Fairchild, B. H., 223
Fanshawe, Sir Richard, 87
Ferguson, Moira, 219
Finch, Anne, 228, 231
    A Nocturnal Reverie, 30–1, 135, 221
        nature in, 209
    and poetic vocation, 133–5
    Ardelia to Melancholy, 135
    Love, Death, and Reputation, 176

    Petition for an Absolute Retreat,
        59–60, 61–2, 63, 135
    Reputation, 167
    Sir Plausible, 47, 222
    The Bird, 56, 58, 223
    The Hurricane, 176, 209
    The Spleen, 134, 176
    The Tree, 56, 223
    To the Nightingale, 134
Fish, Stanley, 102, 226
Fodor, Jerry A., 170, 230
de Fontenelle, Bernard le Bouvier,
        234
Frost, Robert, 16, 220

Gally, Henry
    *Theophrastus, Moral Characters,
        with notes and a critical essay
        on Characteristic Writings*,
        225
Gay, John, 2
Glover, Richard
    *London: or, The Progress of
        Commerce*, 178, 184, 185
Goldsmith, Oliver, 82, 193, 232
    "A City Night-Piece", 179, 196
    The Beauties of English Poesy, 224
    The Deserted Village, 179, 189–91
    The Traveller, 178
Goodman, Kevis, 229
Grainger, James, 166, 230
Grant, John E., 234
Gray, Thomas, 62, 86, 159, 193, 229
    *Designs by Mr. R. Bentley for Six
        Poems by Mr. T. Gray*, 225
    *Elegy Written in a Country
        Churchyard*, 82–4, 158, 224
        melancholy and poetry in, 133
        personification in, 163, 164, 167
        society in, 191–2
    *Ode on a Distant Prospect of Eton
        College*, 166
    Ode on the Death of a Favorite Cat,
        89
    Ode to Adversity, 160

On the Progress of Poesy, 229
  and poetic ambition, 141–3
Sonnet on the Death of Richard West,
  7–8, 155, 158
The Bard, 141
Griffin, Dustin, 224
Grossman, Allen, 219
Guerinot, J.V., 125, 227
Guillory, John, 232
Gustafson, James, 234
Guthrie, William, 225

Hall, Donald
  Claims for Poetry, 221
Hallows, Daniel, 19, 220
Harris, James
  *Hermes: or, a Philosophical Inquiry
    concerning Language and
    Universal Grammar*, 164–6,
    230
Hazlitt, William, 103
heroic couplet, 16–33
  and mock-epic, 26–7
  and parallelism/opposition, 27–9
  and the verse paragraph, 29–33
  as innovation, 18–20
Herrick, Robert, 48, 56
Hervey, Lord, 104
Hogarth, William
  Harlot's Progress, 50
  Rake's Progress, 50
  Satan, Sin, and Death, 165
Home, Henry (Lord Kames), 160, 161,
  162, 220, 230
Homer, 118, 123
  Iliad, 119
Hopkins, Gerard Manley, 234
Horace, 63, 86, 94
  and eighteenth-century translations,
    95
  and "Horatian" formal verse satire,
    95–8
  and the "Horatian" speaker,
    107
  Ars Poetica, 34, 44

Satire II.i, 100
Satire X.i, 11
Howard, Henry (Earl of Surrey), 154,
  229
Hughes, John, 202, 233
Hume, David, 169–70
  *Treatise concerning Human
    Understanding*, 115, 226
  Treatise on Human Nature, 170
Hutcheson, Francis, 143

imagery
  and psychology, 152–4
Ingrassia, Catherine, 219

Jackson, H.J., 221
Johnson, Mark, 231
Johnson, Mary Lynn, 234
Johnson, Samuel, 77, 96, 156, 216
  and sophistication, 197
  "Life of Cowley", 222
  "Life of Gray", 232
  Lives of the Poets, 225, 227
  London, 93, 184, 226
    as Juvenalian satire, 107–8
  on Thomas Gray, 191
  Prologue Spoken by Mr. Garrick, 167,
    224
  Rasselas, 156
  Vanity of Human Wishes, 18, 29, 31,
    93, 94, 156, 158, 229
    as failed satire, 107–9
Jones, Mary, 110
  Epistle to Lady Bowyer, 109–10
  *Of Desire. An Epistle to the
    Honorable Miss Lovelace*, 109
Jones, Vivien, 223
Jonson, Ben, 48, 56, 86
Juvenal, 94
  and eighteenth-century translations,
    95
  and "Juvenalian" poetry, 95–6
  Satire III, 107
  Satire X, 96, 107, 108
  Satires, 95

Kaminski, Thomas, 229
Kaul, Suvir, 232
Keats, John, 86, 166, 198, 222
    Lamia, 205, 234
    Ode on a Grecian Urn, 169
    Ode to a Nightingale, 114
    To Autumn, 166
Keenleyside, Heather, 232
Keil, F., 231
Keith, Jennifer, 219
King, William. *see* Swift, Jonathan,
        Verses on the Death of Dr. Swift
Knox, Vicesimus, 197, 233
Kroeber, Karl, 233

Lakoff, George, 171, 231
Leapor, Mary
    Crumble-Hall, 109
    Epistle of Deborah Dough, 53, 223
    Epistle to Artemesia. On Fame, 97,
        109–10, 225
    Man the Monarch, 221
    versification of, 31–3
    The Head-Ach. To Aurelia, 52–3, 223
Lecercle, Jean Jacques, 235
Lewis, C.S., 119
Lichtheim, Miriam, 226
Locke, John, 169
    *Essay Concerning Human
        Understanding*, 175
Lucretius, 34

Mack, Maynard, 104, 221, 232
Macpherson, James, 197
    Ossian poems, 194, 232
    primitivism in, 195–6
Mallett, David, 85–6
Mandeville, Bernard
    The Fable of the Bees, 178, 180, 200
Marvell, Andrew, 48
    *A Dialogue between the Soul and
        Body*, 56
    and meditative tetrameter, 56
    Bermudas, 56
    The Garden, 56

*The Nymph Complaining for the
    Death of her Faun*, 56
The Unfortunate Lover, 56
To His Coy Mistress, 56
Upon Appleton House, 56
Masters, Mary, 167
McCauley, Robert N., 172, 231
McFague, Sallie, 234
Mervis, Carolyn B., 230
metapoetry, 3, 12, 114, 115
    and poetic vocation, 139
Mickle, William James, 89, 225
Mill, John Stuart, 9, 12, 219
Milton, John, 48, 63, 115, 141
    and influence on Pope, 123
    Il Penseroso, 62, 134
    L'Allegro, 62, 133
    Of Education, 198
    Paradise Lost, 12, 26, 119, 140, 155,
        165, 179
        and poetic vision, 129
        and Pope, 123
        and Pope's *Dunciad*, 126
Montagu, Lady Mary Wortley, 99, 104,
    117
Morris, David B., 222

Naess, Arne, 233
Nagel, Thomas, 227
Nason, Richard, 227
Neisser, Ulric, 171
Nicholson, Marjorie Hope,
    234

Odyssey, 119
Osborn, James M., 224

Parnell, Thomas, 2, 133
    *An Essay on the Different Stiles of
        Poetry*, 135, 228
    and poetic vocation, 135–6
    Donne's *Satire III*, 24–6, 221
    Hymn to Contentment, 66, 223,
        228
        poetic vocation in, 136

Night-Piece on Death, 56, 58, 223
Piety: or, The Vision, 228
   and poetic vocation, 136
The Happy Man, 56
The Soul in Sorrow, 56
The Way to Happiness, 56
pentameter, 10, 13, 16–17, 29, 37, 49, 53
   versus tetrameter, 50–2
Persius, 94
personification, 3
   and cognition, 169
   and cultural determinism, 175–7
   and gender, 164–9
   and imagism, 151–2
   and society in poetry, 181
   and theories of agency/causation, 170–7
   eighteenth-century definitions of, 159–63
   modern attitudes regarding, 159, 169
   modern rejection of, 159
Philips, John
   Cyder, 76
   The Splendid Shilling, 76, 224
Phillips, Ambrose
   A Winter Piece, 209
physicotheology, 206–10
Pindar, 63, 86, 142
Pinsky, Robert, 217, 235
Plath, Sylvia, 1, 16, 219
Pope, Alexander, 2, 9, 13, 52, 93, 94, 109, 111, 137, 198, 224
   An Essay on Man, 141
   and poetic progress, 216
   and Spenser, 87
   Correspondence, 225
   Dunciad, 94, 95, 106, 145, 184, 217, 227
      as metapoetry, 128
      Dulness in, 187–8
   Elegy to the Memory of an Unfortunate Lady, 117, 227
   Eloisa to Abelard, 227

   and printing conventions, 15
   literary history in, 116–17
   personification in, 167
Epilogue to the Satires, 112
   and efficacy of satire, 113
   Vice in, 189
Epistle to a Lady, 105, 109, 181
Epistle to Bathurst, 130, 228
   corruption in, 188–9
   society in, 181
Epistle to Burlington, 109
   nature and progress in, 214
Epistle to Cobham, 181, 228
   as metapoetry, 130–1
   conversation in, 9–11
Epistle to Dr. Arbuthnot, 98, 99, 109, 112, 129, 221
   as formal verse satire, 100–1, 104–7
Epistles to Several Persons, 96, 113
Essay on Criticism, 19, 28, 30, 33, 124, 127–8, 135, 220, 221, 222
   and literary history, 116
   as metapoetry, 118–19
   multiplicity of voice in, 34–45
   print features of the first edition, 35–6
   truth and prophetic voice in, 44–5
Essay on Man, 17, 28, 31, 114, 118, 129, 156, 178, 211, 227, 228
   as metapoetry, 129–30
   ecological consciousness in, 210
   nature and progress in, 214
   nature in, 199
   people in, 202
   poet and society in, 193–4
Homer's *Iliad*, 26–7, 221
Imitations of Horace, 114
   Epistle I.vii, 53, 223
   Satire II.i, 98–100
   Satire II.i, 181
   Satire II.i., 225
nature and progress, 214–15
on Milton, 75, 81
Pastorals, 35

Prologue to Sophonisba, 167
Satire II.i, 220
The Alley, 87
The Fourth Satire of Dr. Donne, 22–3
The Messiah, 128
The Pastorals, 116, 227
The Rape of the Lock, 95, 126, 128,
    227
  and mortality, 118
  as metapoetry, 118–24
  as mock-epic, 26–8
  personification in, 176
The Second Satire of Dr. Donne, 20–2
The Temple of Fame, 116, 128, 227
*To Mr. Jervas, with Fresnoy's Art of
    Painting*, 227
Windsor-Forest, 35, 119, 128, 178,
    227, 229
  visions of society in, 187–8
Priestley, Joseph, 160, 162
Prior, Matthew, 47
  Alma, or The Progress of the Mind,
    49–50, 222
pseudo-doggerel, 46

quatrains, 63, 81–6
  heroic, 82–4
  long meter, 85
  short meter, 85–6
Quintilian, 94, 225

Ray, John, 206
Reid, Thomas, 169
Riley, Denise, 218, 235
de la Rochefoucauld, Duc François
  Maximes, 101, 226
Rogers, Pat, 222
Rosch, Eleanor, 230
Rosenheim Jr., Edward W., 93, 225
Rousseau, G.S., 222
Rousseau, Jean-Jacques, 114

San Juan, Jr., E., 222
satire
  and formal verse satire, 100

definition of, 93–4
genre and paragenre, 94–5
Savage, Richard, 229
Seward, Anna, 234
Shakespeare, William, 141
  Antony and Cleopatra, 160
  Julius Caesar, 161
  The Merchant of Venice, 161
Shelley, Percy Bysshe, 86, 198
  Defense of Poetry, 156
  Mont-Blanc, 169
Shenstone, William
  *The School-Mistress. A Poem. In
    Imitation of Spencer's Stile*,
    81–6, 224
Sidney, Philip
  Defence of Poesie, 106
Sitter, John
  Arguments of Augustan Wit, 229
  *The Cambridge Companion to
    Eighteenth-Century Poetry*, 221
  The Poetry of Pope's 'Dunciad', 227
Slepian, Barry, 102, 226
Smart, Christopher, 13, 64, 228, 229
  *A Morning Piece, or An Hymn for
    the Hay-Makers*
    personification in, 173–4
  Jubilate Agno, 7, 143, 219
  *On the Omniscience of the Supreme
    Being*, 201, 208
  Song to David, 88, 224, 231
    and poetic vocation, 136
    as metapoetry, 144, 147
    nature in, 208
    personification in, 177
  The Hop-Garden, 76, 224
  The Sweets of Evening, 209, 234
Smith, Adam, 180
  agency and the invisible hand, 175
  Theory of Moral Sentiments, 220
Smollett, Tobias
  Humphrey Clinker, 75
society, 3
  and social theory in poetry, 178
Somerville, William

Field-Sports: A Poem, 234
Spence, Joseph
    *Observations, Anecdotes, and
        Characters of Books and Men*,
        224, 227, 228
Spenser, Edmund, 115, 141
    Mutability Cantos, 166
    The Faerie Queen, 87, 119, 137, 140
Spenserian stanza, 81, 87–8
Stein, Gertrude, 115, 226
Sterne, Laurence, 111
Stevens, Wallace, 140
    Notes toward a Supreme Fiction,
        114
    Sunday Morning, 118
    "The Noble Reader and the Sound
        of Words", 2, 219
Stevenson, William, 167
Swift, Jonathan, 2, 13, 47, 52–6, 111,
    216
    A Tale of a Tub, 126
    and the tetrameter couplet, 46
    Battle of the Books, 113
    Cadenus and Vanessa, 52
        versification of, 70–3
    Gulliver's Travels, 156
    Horatian satires, 100
    Journal of a Modern Lady, 48–9
    *On the Death of a Late Famous
        General*, 46
        versification of, 69
    Phyllis, or The Progress of Love, 46,
        50, 222
    Stella poems, 52
    Stella's Birth-Day, 55–6
    The Furniture of a Woman's Mind,
        51
    The Legion Club, 46
    The Progress of Marriage, 50
    The Progress of Poetry, 50
    To Stella, Visiting me in my Sickness,
        54
    *To Stella. Written on the Day of her
        Birth, but not the Subject, when
        I was sick in Bed*, 54–5, 223

Verses on the Death of Dr. Swift,
    46, 67, 70, 98, 100–4, 229
    publication issues, 102

Terence, 210
tetrameter, 13, 46–73
    and ballad/popular song, 50, 85
    and burlesque, 47–8
    and non-satiric poetry, 48
    and parody, 51
    and satire, 73
    and the familiar mode, 52–6
    and the ode, 62–7
Theophrastus, 225
Thomson, James, 81, 167, 198, 209, 230
    attitudes toward nature, 201
    Castle of Indolence, 88, 178, 193
        poet and society in, 194–5
    Liberty, 178
        nationalism in, 184–5
    *On the Omniscience of the Supreme
        Being: A Poetical Essay*, 234
    Spring: A Poem, 234
    The Seasons, 12, 78, 167, 209, 228,
        229
        nature in, 201
        people in, 202
        personification in, 161, 167
        physicotheology and ecology in,
        208
        withdrawal and poetic
        vocation in, 137
Thoreau, Henry, 214
Tollet, Elizabeth
    On a Death's Head, 56
    *On the Prospect from Westminster
        Bridge, March, 1750*
        visions of society in, 181–4
    Psalm CX, 56
    Sacred Ode, 64
    The Winter Song, 56
    Written in a Book of Novels, 50, 222
Toulmin, Stephen, 172–3, 231
Tucker, Abraham
    The Light of Nature Pursued, 234

Turner, Mark, 171, 231
Twain, Mark, 219
typographical convention, 13–14

Virgil
    Aeneid, 119
        and Pope, 126
    Georgics, 34, 76, 200
voice
    and dialogism, 9, 12
    and textual performance, 8–13

Wall, Cynthia, 227
Waller, Edmund, 18, 48
Warton, Joseph, 143
    Essay on the Genius and Writings of
        Pope, 232
    Ode to Evening, 84
    The Enthusiast: or, The Lover of
        Nature. A Poem 138, 228
Warton, Thomas
    Ode Written at Vale-Abbey in
        Cheshire, 195, 232
    The Pleasures of Melancholy, 87,
        137–8, 228
Watts, Isaac
    Few Happy Matches, 89, 225
    Horae Lyricae, 76, 224
    Psalm 90, 85
    The Day of Judgment, An ode, 89

Williams, Raymond, 179, 231
Wilmot, John (Earl of Rochester)
    A Ramble in St. James's Park, 51
Wilson, E.O., 233
Wilson, R., 231
Wordsworth, William, 158, 198, 209
    and rural vs. urban, 197
    attitudes toward nature, 201
    Composed upon Westminster Bridge,
        September 3, 1802
        visions of society in, 181–3
    Descriptive Sketches
        people in, 202
    "Intimations Ode", 86
    Lyrical Ballads (1800), 7–8, 219, 229,
        233, 234
        on personification, 157
    The Prelude, 114, 233
    The Prelude (1799)
        nature in, 199–200

Yeats, William Butler, 12, 113
    Byzantium poems, 114, 139
Young, Edward, 80, 111, 216, 224
    Conjectures on Original
        Composition, 81, 224, 235
    Love of Fame. The Universal Passion.
        In Seven Characteristical
        Satires, 96–7
    Night-Thoughts, 12, 75, 78–9, 224

Cambridge Introductions to …

AUTHORS

Margaret Atwood Heidi Macpherson

Jane Austen Janet Todd

Samuel Beckett Ronan McDonald

Walter Benjamin David Ferris

Chekhov James N. Loehlin

J. M. Coetzee Dominic Head

Samuel Taylor Coleridge John Worthen

Joseph Conrad John Peters

Jacques Derrida Leslie Hill

Charles Dickens Jon Mee

Emily Dickinson Wendy Martin

George Eliot Nancy Henry

T. S. Eliot John Xiros Cooper

William Faulkner Theresa M. Towner

F. Scott Fitzgerald Kirk Curnutt

Michel Foucault Lisa Downing

Robert Frost Robert Faggen

Nathaniel Hawthorne Leland S. Person

Zora Neale Hurston Lovalerie King

James Joyce Eric Bulson

Thomas Mann Todd Kontje

Herman Melville Kevin J. Hayes

Milton Stephen B. Dobranski

Sylvia Plath Jo Gill

Edgar Allan Poe Benjamin F. Fisher

Ezra Pound Ira Nadel

Marcel Proust Adam Watt

Jean Rhys Elaine Savory

Edward Said Conor McCarthy

Shakespeare Emma Smith

Shakespeare's Comedies Penny Gay

Shakespeare's History Plays Warren Chernaik

Shakespeare's Poetry Michael Schoenfeldt

Shakespeare's Tragedies Janette Dillon

Harriet Beecher Stowe Sarah Robbins

Mark Twain Peter Messent

Edith Wharton Pamela Knights

Walt Whitman M. Jimmie Killingsworth

Virginia Woolf Jane Goldman

William Wordsworth Emma Mason

W. B. Yeats David Holdeman

TOPICS

American Literary Realism Phillip Barrish

The American Short Story Martin Scofield

Anglo-Saxon Literature Hugh Magennis

Comedy Eric Weitz

Creative Writing David Morley

Early English Theatre Janette Dillon

Eighteenth-Century Poetry John Sitter

English Theatre, 1660–1900 Peter Thomson

Francophone Literature Patrick Corcoran

Literature and the Environment Timothy Clark

Modern British Theatre Simon Shepherd

Modern Irish Poetry Justin Quinn

Modernism Pericles Lewis

Modernist Poetry Peter Howarth

Narrative (second edition) H. Porter Abbott

The Nineteenth-Century American Novel Gregg Crane

The Novel Marina MacKay

Old Norse Sagas Margaret Clunies Ross

Postcolonial Literatures C. L. Innes

Postmodern Fiction Bran Nicol

Russian Literature Caryl Emerson

Scenography Joslin McKinney and Philip Butterworth

The Short Story in English Adrian Hunter

Theatre Historiography Thomas Postlewait

Theatre Studies Christopher B. Balme

Tragedy Jennifer Wallace

Victorian Poetry Linda K. Hughes